W9-CJR-109

MAFIOSA™

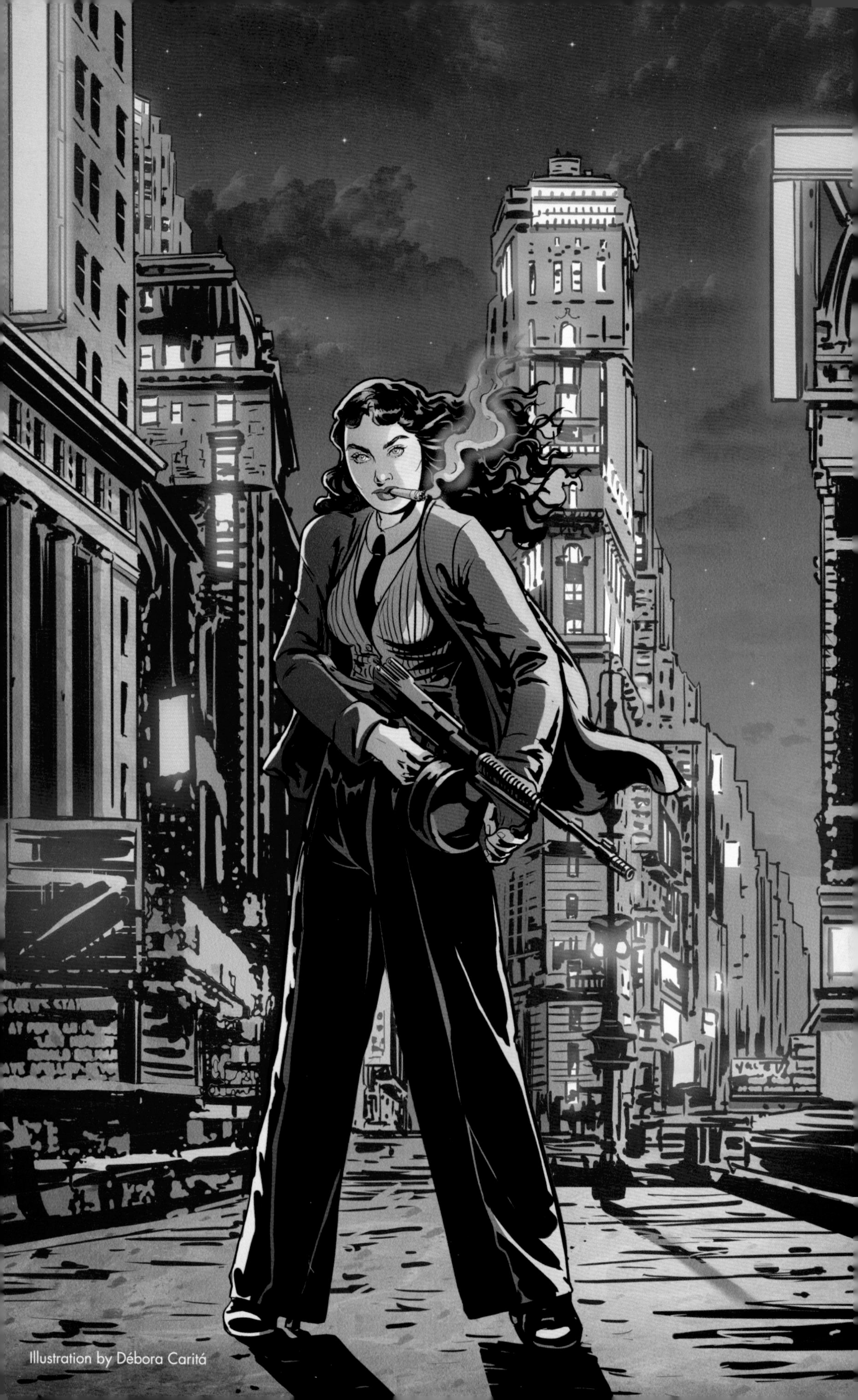

Illustration by Débora Caritá

MAFIOSA

SCRIPT
SUNSHINE BARBITO

ART
ALESSIA ALFANO
DÉBORA CARITÁ

COLORS
RONDA PATTISON
MARIACRISTINA FEDERICO

LETTERING
CLEM ROBINS

COVER ART
JENNY FRISON

FROM AN ORIGINAL STORY BY
THOMAS BROOKE

DARK HORSE BOOKS

PRESIDENT AND PUBLISHER
MIKE RICHARDSON

COLLECTION EDITOR
FREDDYE MILLER

COLLECTION ASSOCIATE EDITOR
JUDY KHUU

COLLECTION ASSISTANT EDITOR
ROSE WEITZ

DESIGNER
RICK DeLUCCO

DIGITAL ART TECHNICIAN
ALLYSON HALLER

SPECIAL THANKS TO **JEREMY ATKINS AT RAINWERKS, TO DAVID CAMPITI AT GLASS HOUSE GRAPHICS, AND TO SALVATORE DI MARCO AT GRAFIMATED CARTOON.**

MAFIOSA

Text and illustrations of Mafiosa™ © 2019, 2021 Rainwerks LLC. Dark Horse Books® and the Dark Horse logo are registered trademarks of Dark Horse Comics LLC. All rights reserved. No portion of this publication may be reproduced or transmitted, in any form or by any means, without the express written permission of Dark Horse Comics LLC. Names, characters, places, and incidents featured in this publication either are the product of the author's imagination or are used fictitiously. Any resemblance to actual persons (living or dead), events, institutions, or locales, without satiric intent, is coincidental.

Along with previously unpublished materials, this volume collects the Mafiosa special edition, originally published in September 2019 by Rainwerks LLC.

Published by Dark Horse Books
A division of Dark Horse Comics LLC
10956 SE Main Street
Milwaukie, OR 97222

DarkHorse.com

To find a comics shop in your area, visit comicshoplocator.com

Library of Congress Cataloging-in-Publication Data

Names: Barbito, Sunshine, writer. | Alfano, Alessia, artist. | Carita,
   Debora, artist. | Pattison, Ronda, colourist. | Federico, Mariacristina,
   colourist. | Robins, Clem, 1955- letterer. | Frison, Jenny, cover
   artist.
Title: Mafiosa / writer, Sunshine Barbito ; artist, Alessia Alfano, Débora
   Caritá ; colors, Ronda Pattison, Mariacristina Federico ; letters, Clem
   Robins ; cover art, Jenny Frison.
Description: Milwaukie, OR : Dark Horse Books, 2021.
Identifiers: LCCN 2021015125 (print) | LCCN 2021015126 (ebook) | ISBN
   9781506721545 (trade paperback) | ISBN 9781506721552 (ebook other)
Subjects: LCSH: Sicilian Americans–New York (State)–New York–Comic
   books, strips, etc. | Mafia–New York (State)–New York–Comic books,
   strips, etc. | Graphic novels.
Classification: LCC PN6727.B3436 M34 2021 (print) | LCC PN6727.B3436
   (ebook) | DDC 741.5/973–dc23
LC record available at https://lccn.loc.gov/2021015125
LC ebook record available at https://lccn.loc.gov/2021015126

First Edition: October 2021
Ebook ISBN 978-1-50672-155-2
Trade Paperback ISBN 978-1-50672-154-5

10 9 8 7 6 5 4 3 2 1
Printed in China

Mike Richardson President and Publisher **Neil Hankerson** Executive Vice President **Tom Weddle** Chief Financial Officer **Dale LaFountain** Chief Information Officer **Tim Wiesch** Vice President of Licensing **Matt Parkinson** Vice President of Marketing **Vanessa Todd-Holmes** Vice President of Production and Scheduling **Mark Bernardi** Vice President of Book Trade and Digital Sales **Ken Lizzi** General Counsel **Dave Marshall** Editor in Chief **Davey Estrada** Editorial Director **Chris Warner** Senior Books Editor **Cary Grazzini** Director of Specialty Projects **Lia Ribacchi** Art Director **Matt Dryer** Director of Digital Art and Prepress **Michael Gombos** Senior Director of Licensed Publications **Kari Yadro** Director of Custom Programs **Kari Torson** Director of International Licensing **Sean Brice** Director of Trade Sales **Randy Lahrman** Director of Product Sales

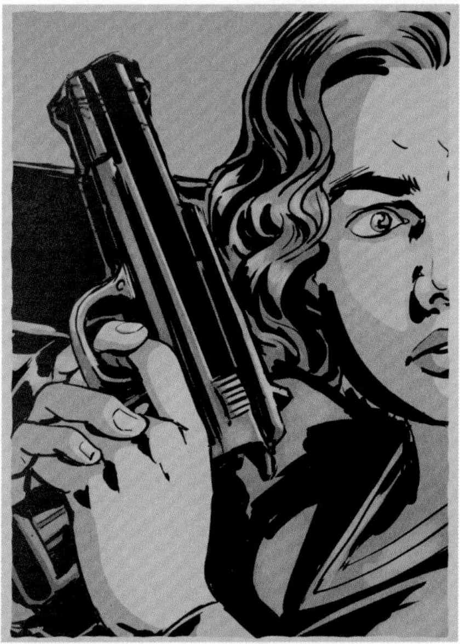

CHAPTER
ONE

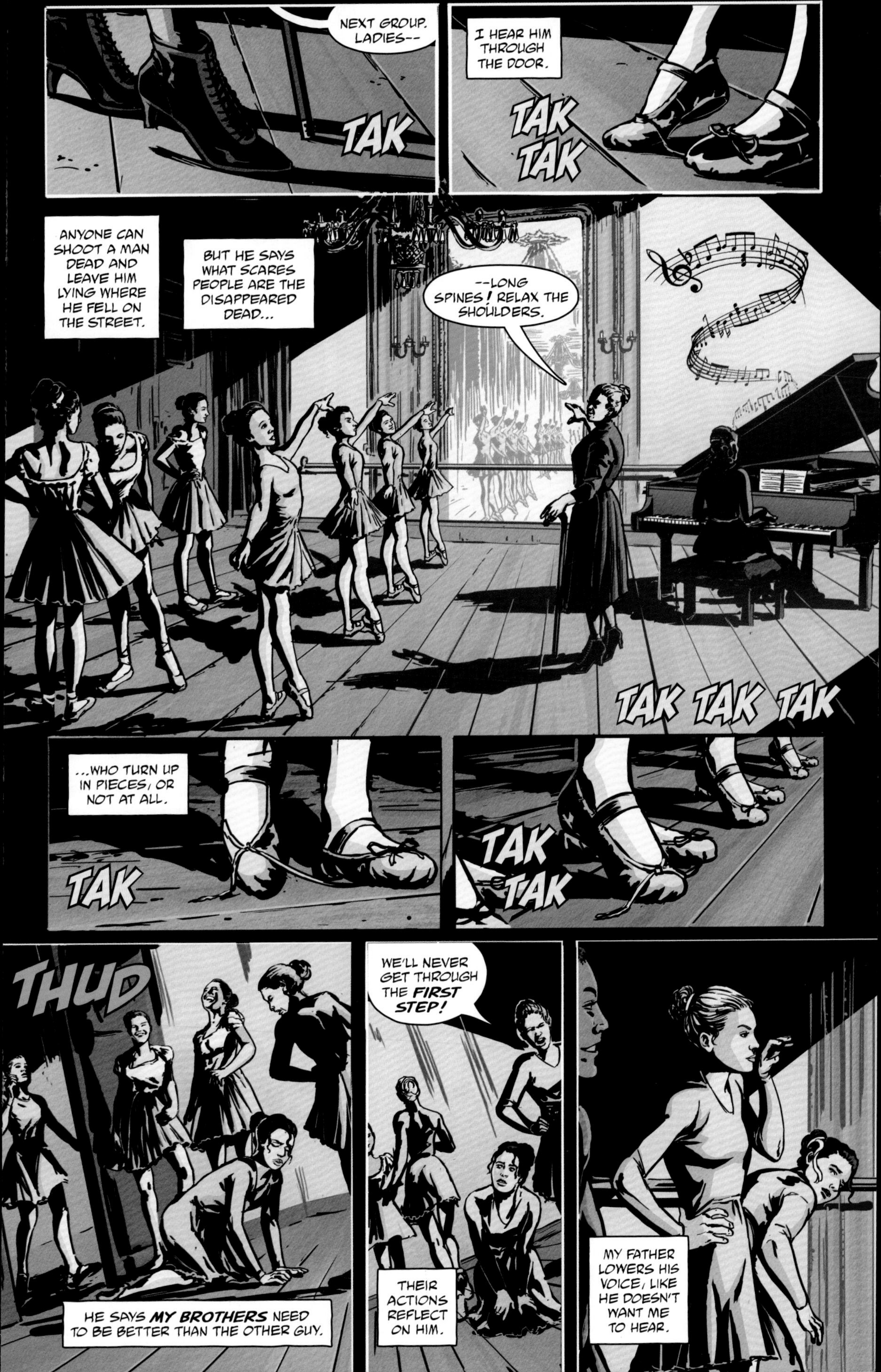
NEXT GROUP. LADIES--
TAK
I HEAR HIM THROUGH THE DOOR.
TAK TAK
ANYONE CAN SHOOT A MAN DEAD AND LEAVE HIM LYING WHERE HE FELL ON THE STREET.
BUT HE SAYS WHAT SCARES PEOPLE ARE THE DISAPPEARED DEAD...
--LONG SPINES! RELAX THE SHOULDERS.
TAK TAK TAK
...WHO TURN UP IN PIECES, OR NOT AT ALL.
TAK
TAK TAK
THUD
HE SAYS MY BROTHERS NEED TO BE BETTER THAN THE OTHER GUY.
WE'LL NEVER GET THROUGH THE FIRST STEP!
THEIR ACTIONS REFLECT ON HIM.
MY FATHER LOWERS HIS VOICE, LIKE HE DOESN'T WANT ME TO HEAR.

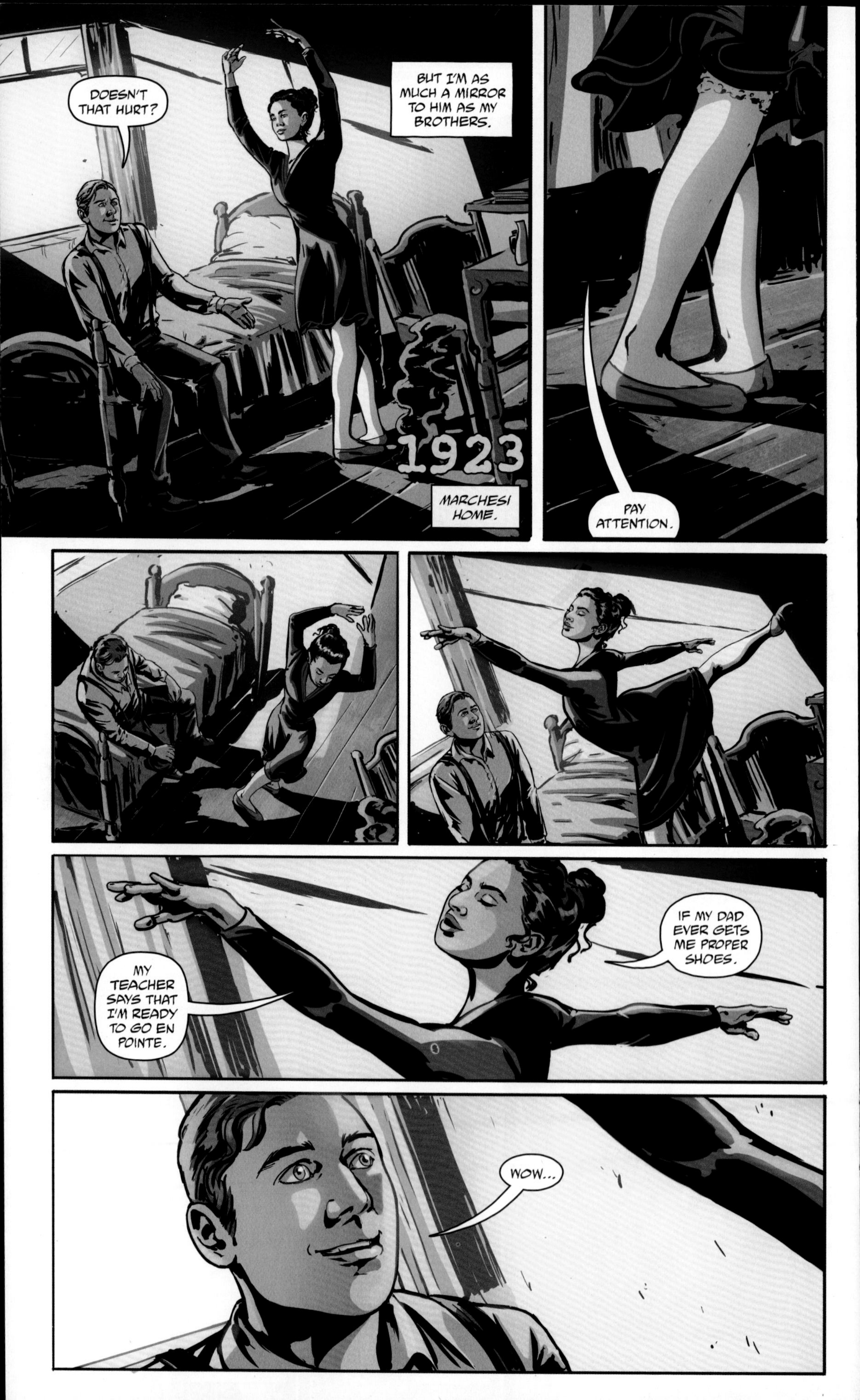
DOESN'T THAT HURT?
BUT I'M AS MUCH A MIRROR TO HIM AS MY BROTHERS.
1923
MARCHESI HOME.
PAY ATTENTION.
MY TEACHER SAYS THAT I'M READY TO GO EN POINTE.
IF MY DAD EVER GETS ME PROPER SHOES.
WOW...

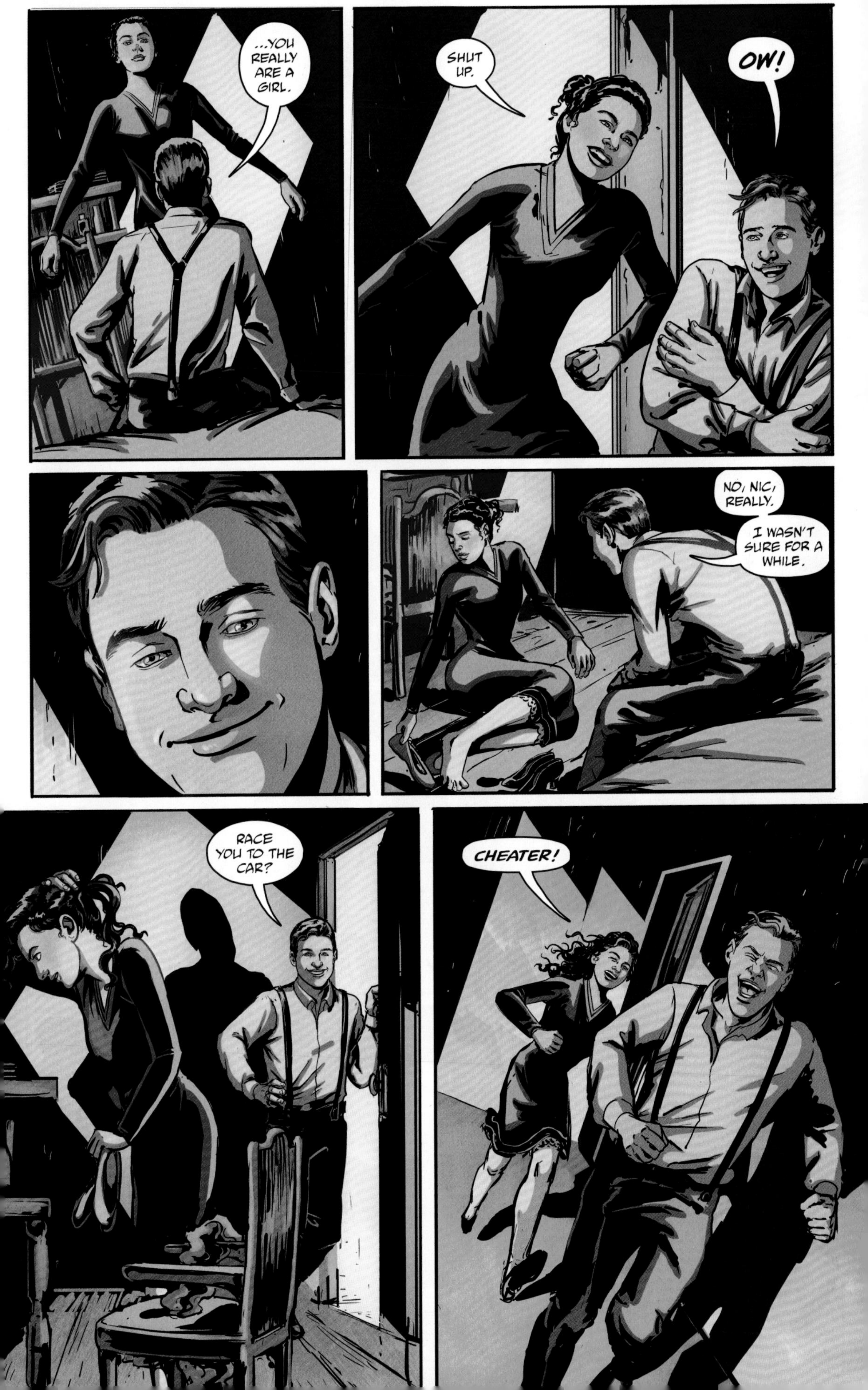
...YOU REALLY ARE A GIRL.
SHUT UP.
OW!
NO, NIC, REALLY.
I WASN'T SURE FOR A WHILE.
RACE YOU TO THE CAR?
CHEATER!

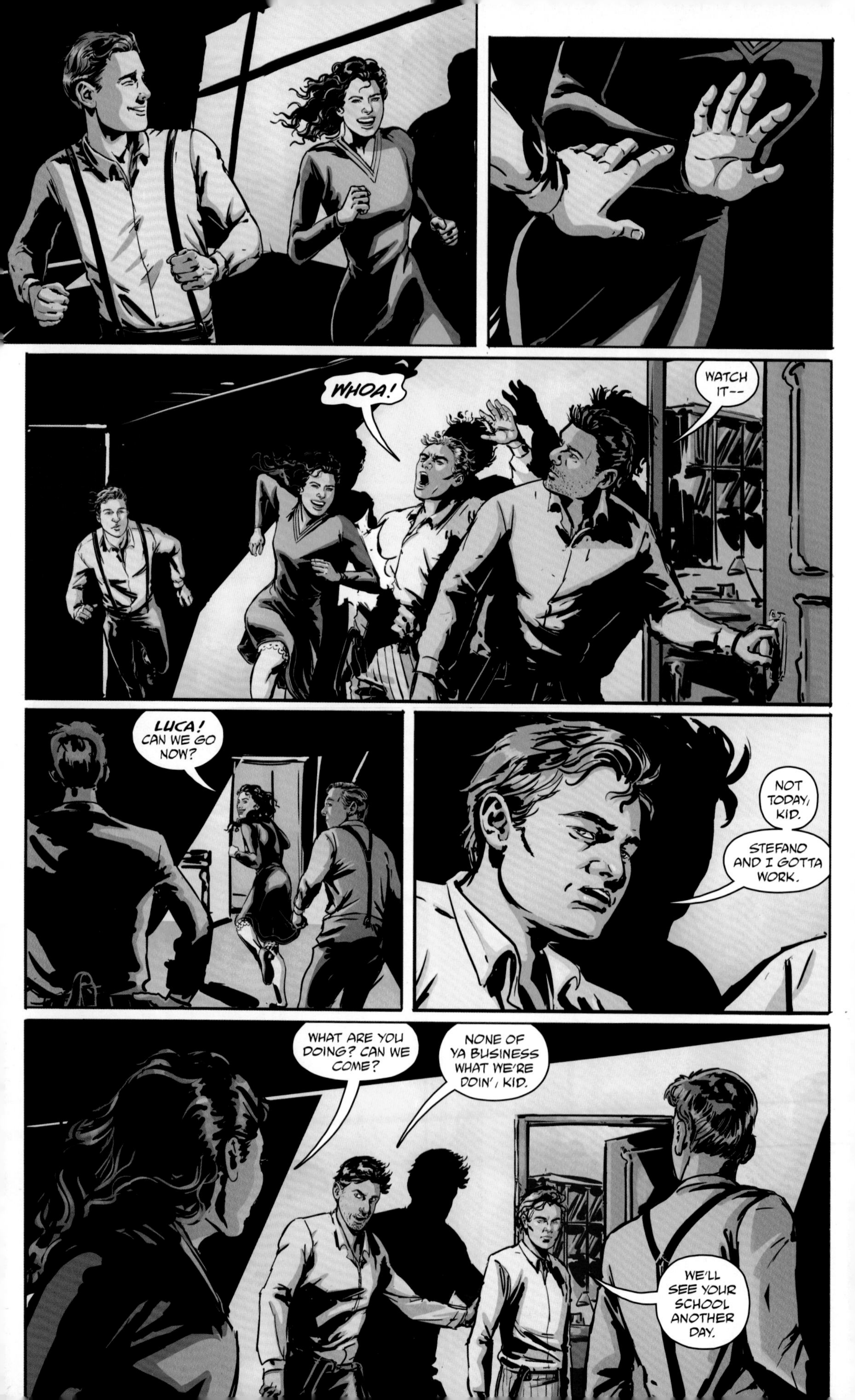
WHOA!
WATCH IT--
LUCA! CAN WE GO NOW?
NOT TODAY, KID.
STEFANO AND I GOTTA WORK.
WHAT ARE YOU DOING? CAN WE COME?
NONE OF YA BUSINESS WHAT WE'RE DOIN', KID.
WE'LL SEE YOUR SCHOOL ANOTHER DAY.

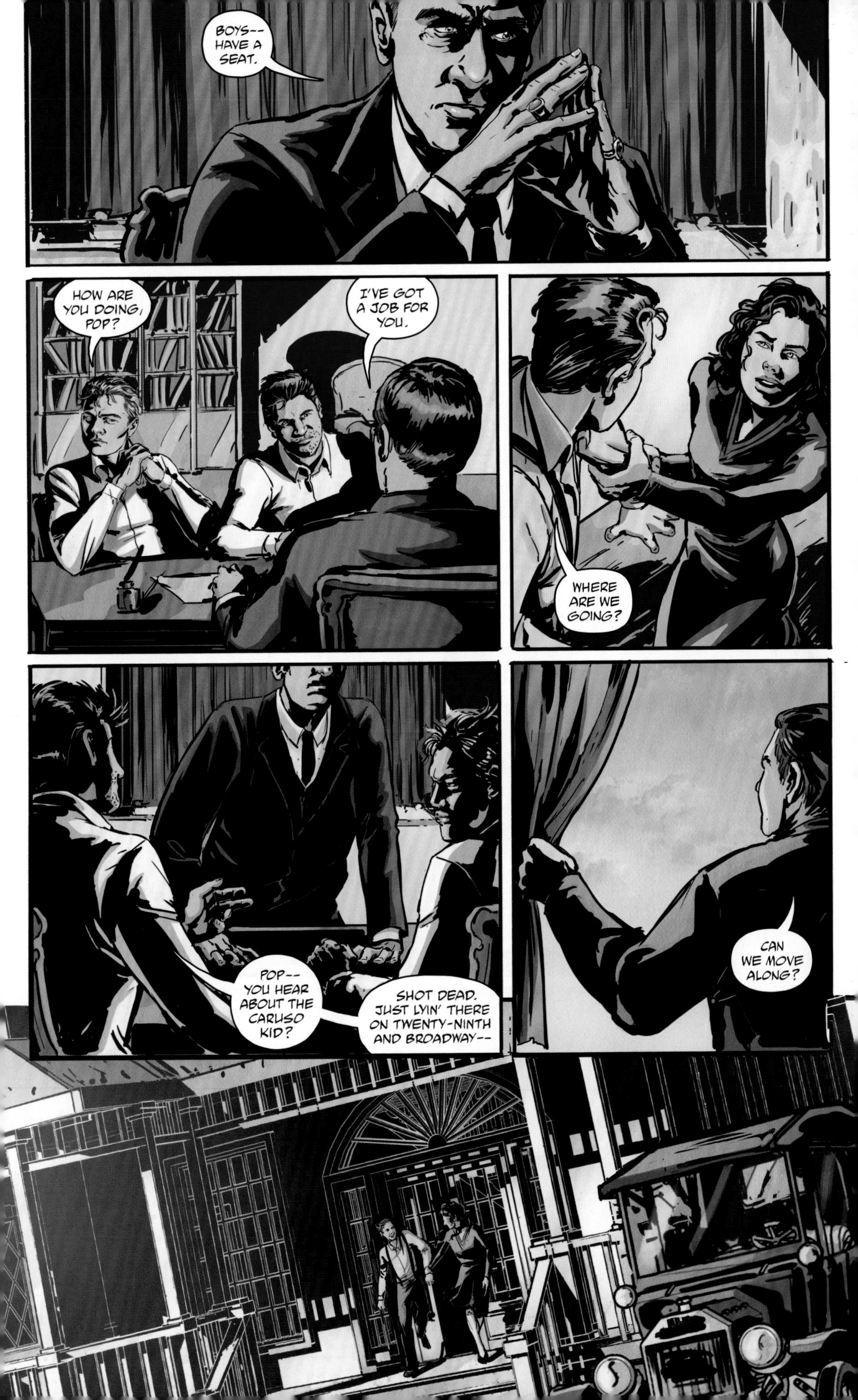
BOYS--
HAVE A
SEAT.
HOW ARE
YOU DOING,
POP?
I'VE GOT
A JOB FOR
YOU.
WHERE
ARE WE
GOING?
POP--
YOU HEAR
ABOUT THE
CARUSO
KID?
SHOT DEAD.
JUST LYIN' THERE
ON TWENTY-NINTH
AND BROADWAY--
CAN
WE MOVE
ALONG?

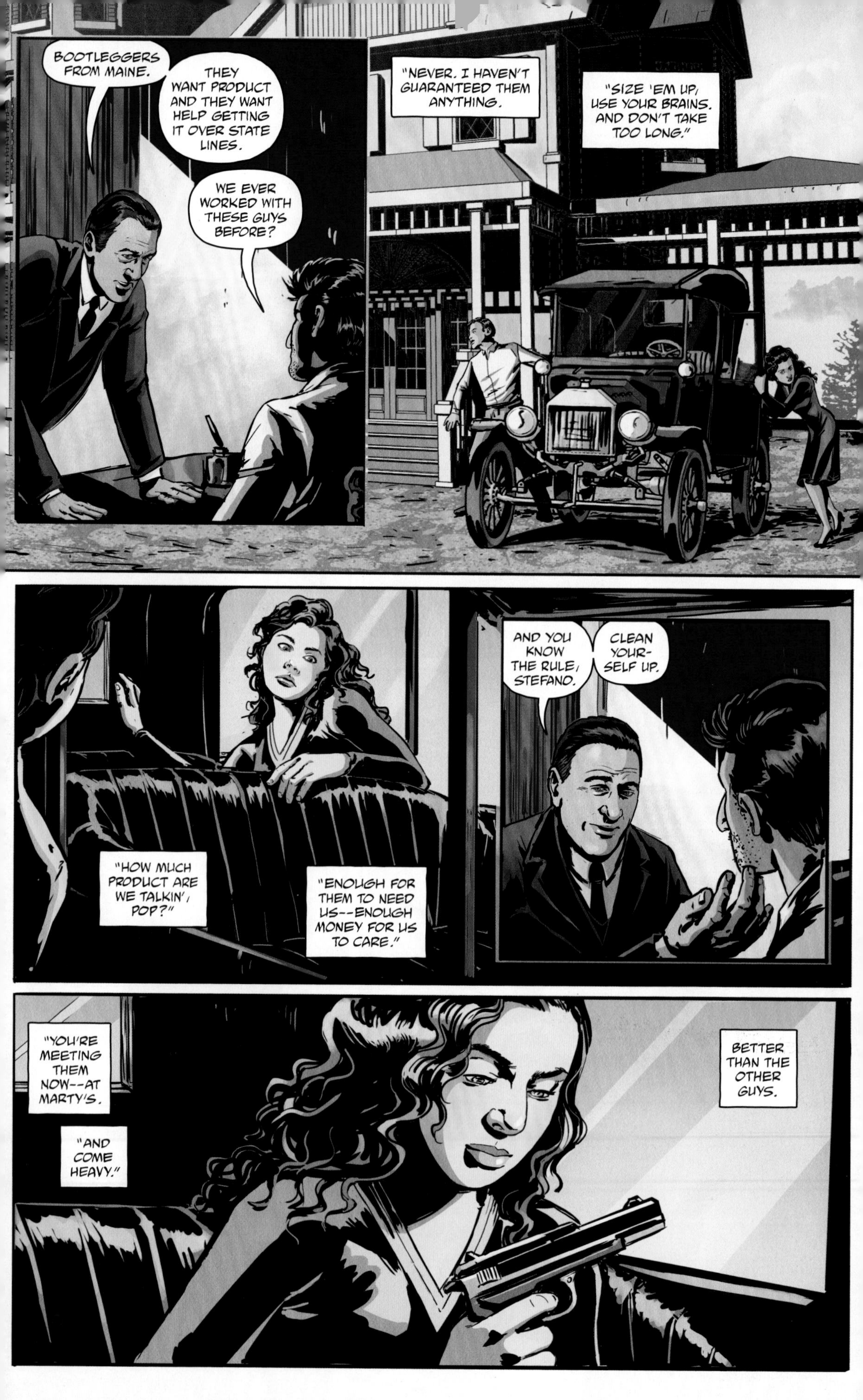
BOOTLEGGERS FROM MAINE.
THEY WANT PRODUCT AND THEY WANT HELP GETTING IT OVER STATE LINES.
WE EVER WORKED WITH THESE GUYS BEFORE?
"NEVER. I HAVEN'T GUARANTEED THEM ANYTHING.
"SIZE 'EM UP, USE YOUR BRAINS. AND DON'T TAKE TOO LONG."
"HOW MUCH PRODUCT ARE WE TALKIN', POP?"
"ENOUGH FOR THEM TO NEED US--ENOUGH MONEY FOR US TO CARE."
AND YOU KNOW THE RULE, STEFANO.
CLEAN YOURSELF UP.
"YOU'RE MEETING THEM NOW--AT MARTY'S.
"AND COME HEAVY."
BETTER THAN THE OTHER GUYS.

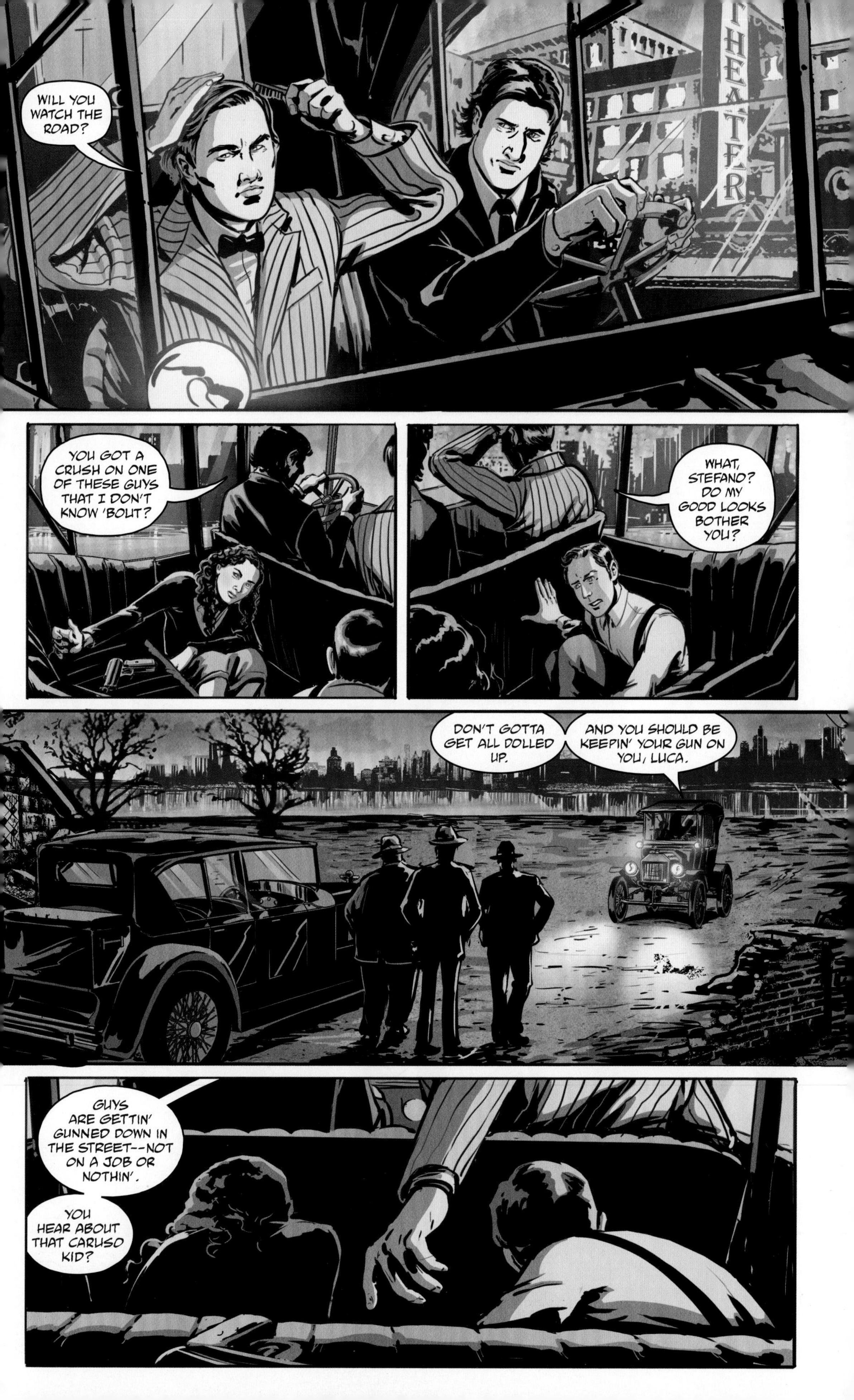
WILL YOU WATCH THE ROAD?
YOU GOT A CRUSH ON ONE OF THESE GUYS THAT I DON'T KNOW 'BOUT?
WHAT, STEFANO? DO MY GOOD LOOKS BOTHER YOU?
DON'T GOTTA GET ALL DOLLED UP.
AND YOU SHOULD BE KEEPIN' YOUR GUN ON YOU, LUCA.
GUYS ARE GETTIN' GUNNED DOWN IN THE STREET--NOT ON A JOB OR NOTHIN'.
YOU HEAR ABOUT THAT CARUSO KID?

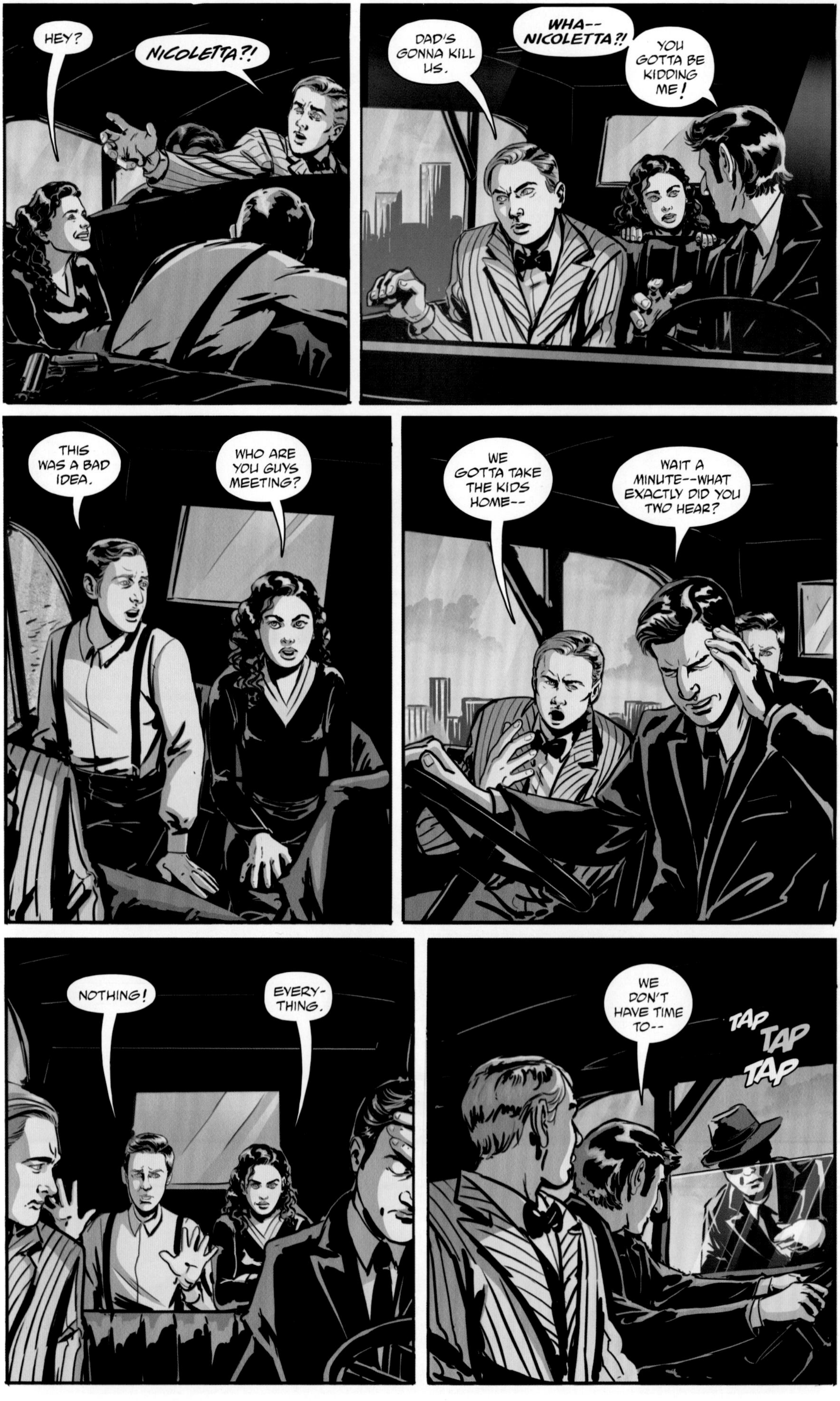
HEY?
NICOLETTA?!
DAD'S GONNA KILL US.
WHA-- NICOLETTA?!
YOU GOTTA BE KIDDING ME!
THIS WAS A BAD IDEA.
WHO ARE YOU GUYS MEETING?
WE GOTTA TAKE THE KIDS HOME--
WAIT A MINUTE--WHAT EXACTLY DID YOU TWO HEAR?
NOTHING!
EVERY-THING.
WE DON'T HAVE TIME TO--
TAP TAP TAP

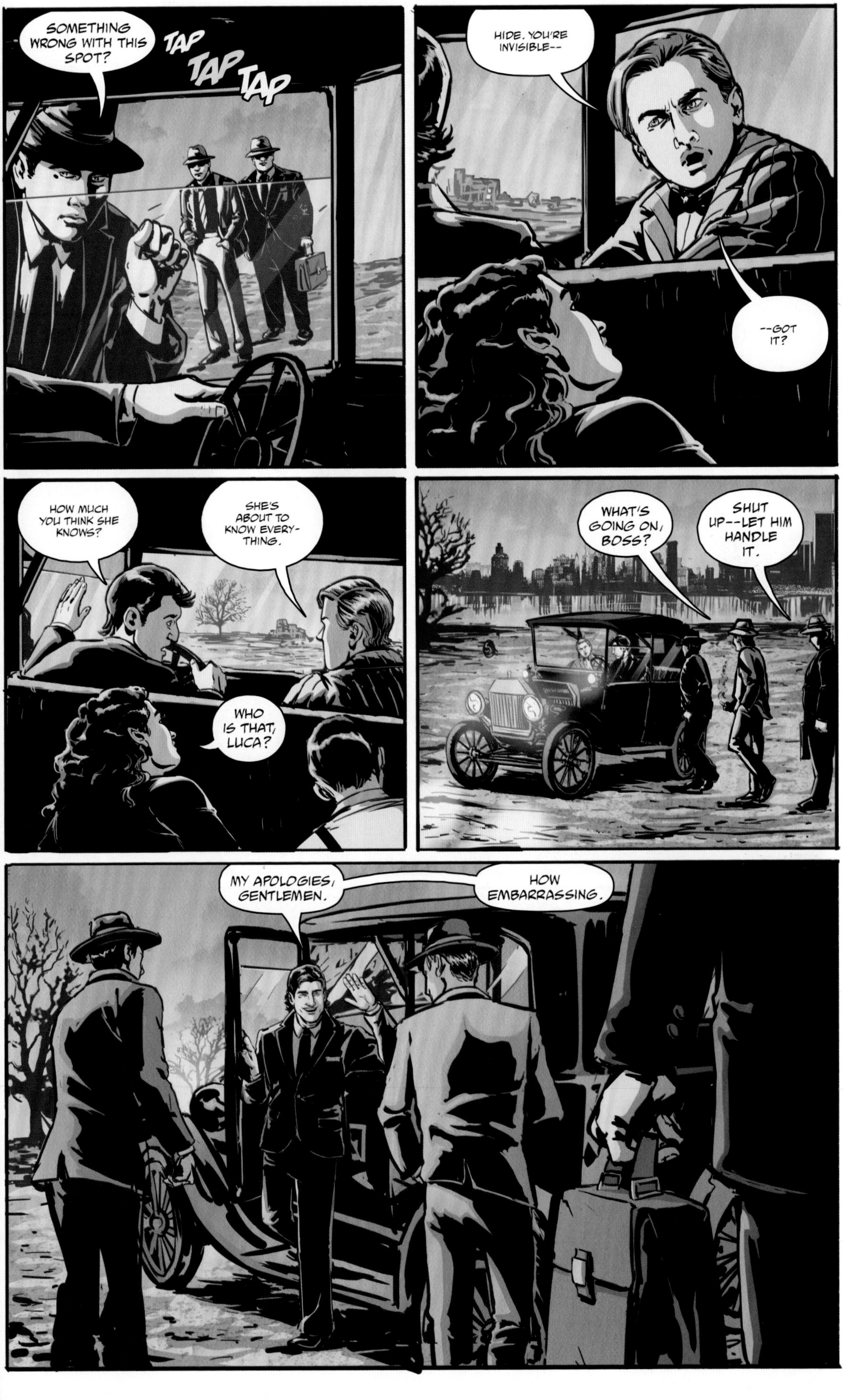
SOMETHING WRONG WITH THIS SPOT?
TAP TAP TAP
HIDE. YOU'RE INVISIBLE--
--GOT IT?
HOW MUCH YOU THINK SHE KNOWS?
SHE'S ABOUT TO KNOW EVERY-THING.
WHO IS THAT, LUCA?
WHAT'S GOING ON, BOSS?
SHUT UP--LET HIM HANDLE IT.
MY APOLOGIES, GENTLEMEN.
HOW EMBARRASSING.

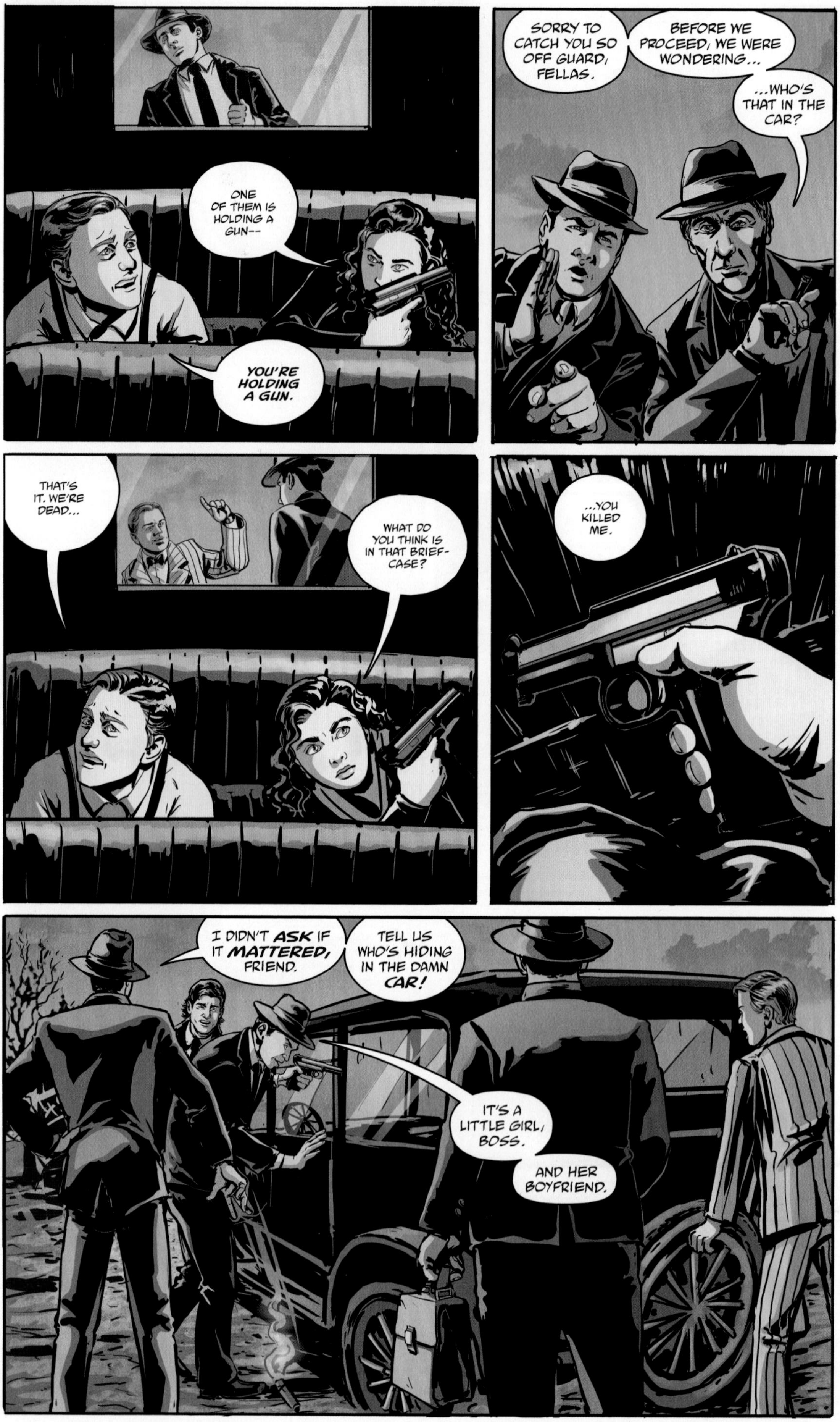
ONE OF THEM IS HOLDING A GUN--
YOU'RE HOLDING A GUN.
SORRY TO CATCH YOU SO OFF GUARD, FELLAS.
BEFORE WE PROCEED, WE WERE WONDERING...
...WHO'S THAT IN THE CAR?
THAT'S IT. WE'RE DEAD...
WHAT DO YOU THINK IS IN THAT BRIEF-CASE?
...YOU KILLED ME.
I DIDN'T ASK IF IT MATTERED, FRIEND.
TELL US WHO'S HIDING IN THE DAMN CAR!
IT'S A LITTLE GIRL, BOSS.
AND HER BOYFRIEND.

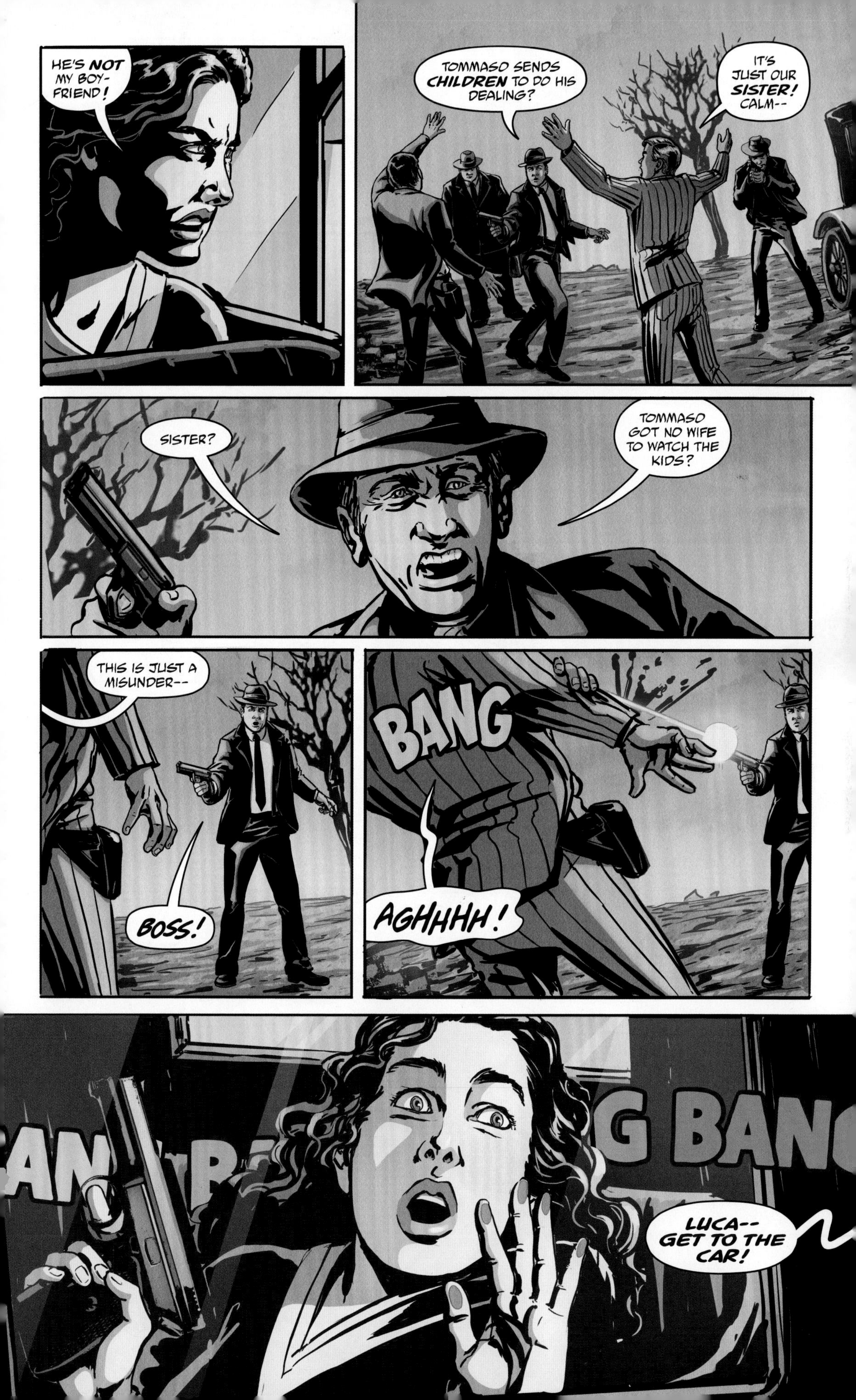
HE'S NOT MY BOY-FRIEND!
TOMMASO SENDS CHILDREN TO DO HIS DEALING?
IT'S JUST OUR SISTER! CALM--
SISTER?
TOMMASO GOT NO WIFE TO WATCH THE KIDS?
THIS IS JUST A MISUNDER--
BOSS!
BANG
AGHHHH!
G BANG
LUCA-- GET TO THE CAR!

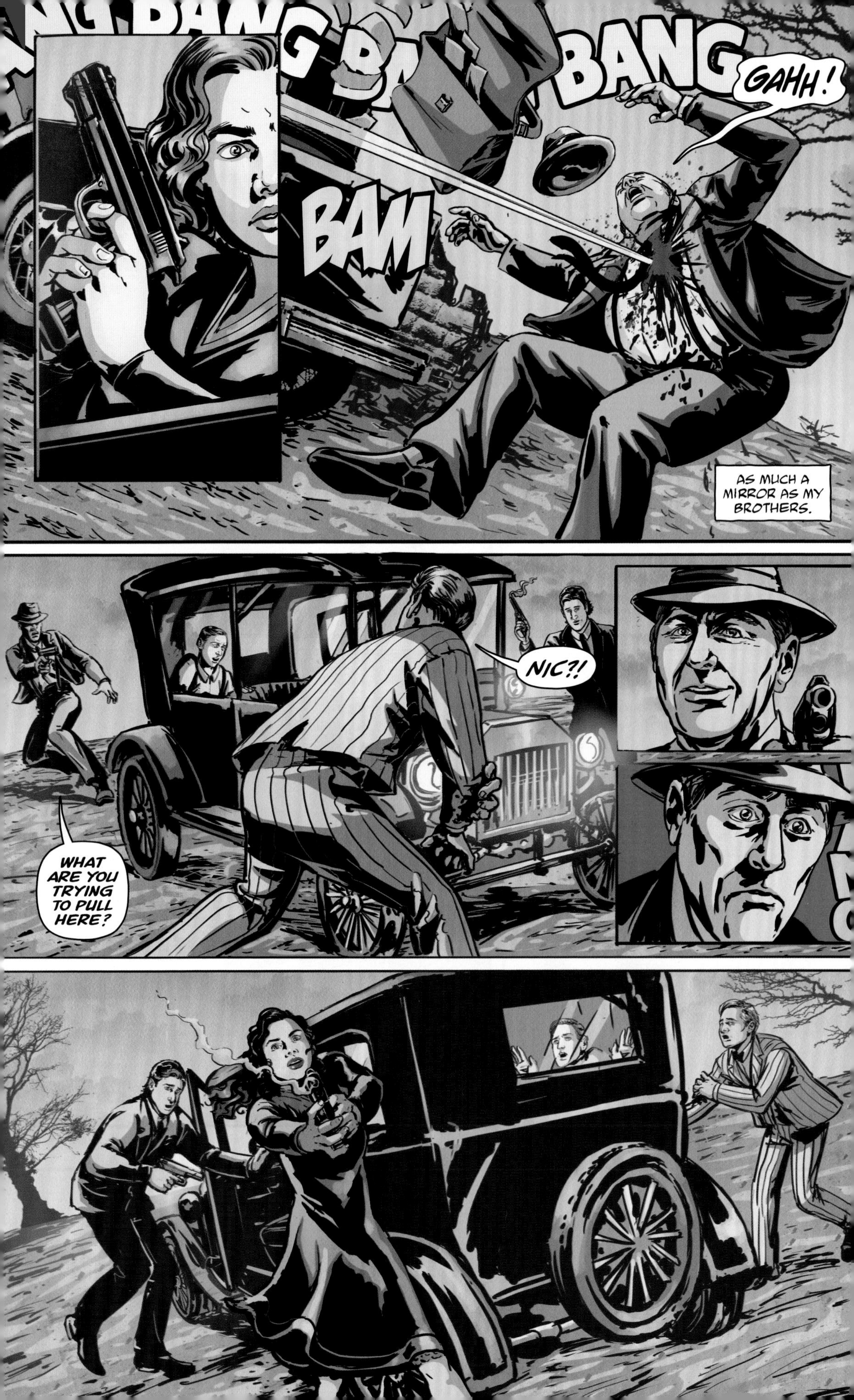
BANG
BANG
GAHH!
BAM
AS MUCH A MIRROR AS MY BROTHERS.
NIC?!
WHAT ARE YOU TRYING TO PULL HERE?

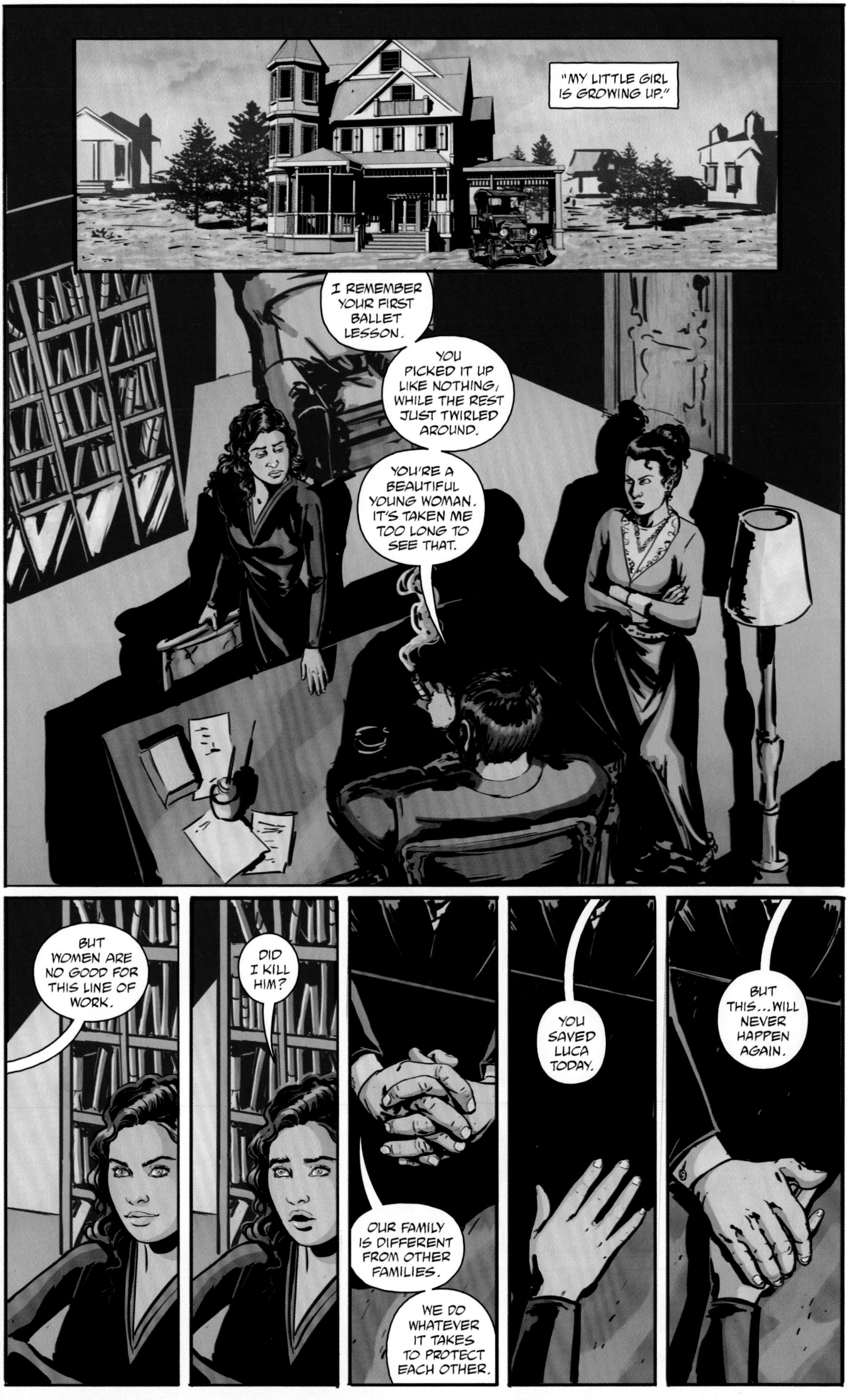
"MY LITTLE GIRL IS GROWING UP."
I REMEMBER YOUR FIRST BALLET LESSON.
YOU PICKED IT UP LIKE NOTHING, WHILE THE REST JUST TWIRLED AROUND.
YOU'RE A BEAUTIFUL YOUNG WOMAN. IT'S TAKEN ME TOO LONG TO SEE THAT.
BUT WOMEN ARE NO GOOD FOR THIS LINE OF WORK.
DID I KILL HIM?
OUR FAMILY IS DIFFERENT FROM OTHER FAMILIES.
WE DO WHATEVER IT TAKES TO PROTECT EACH OTHER.
YOU SAVED LUCA TODAY.
BUT THIS...WILL NEVER HAPPEN AGAIN.

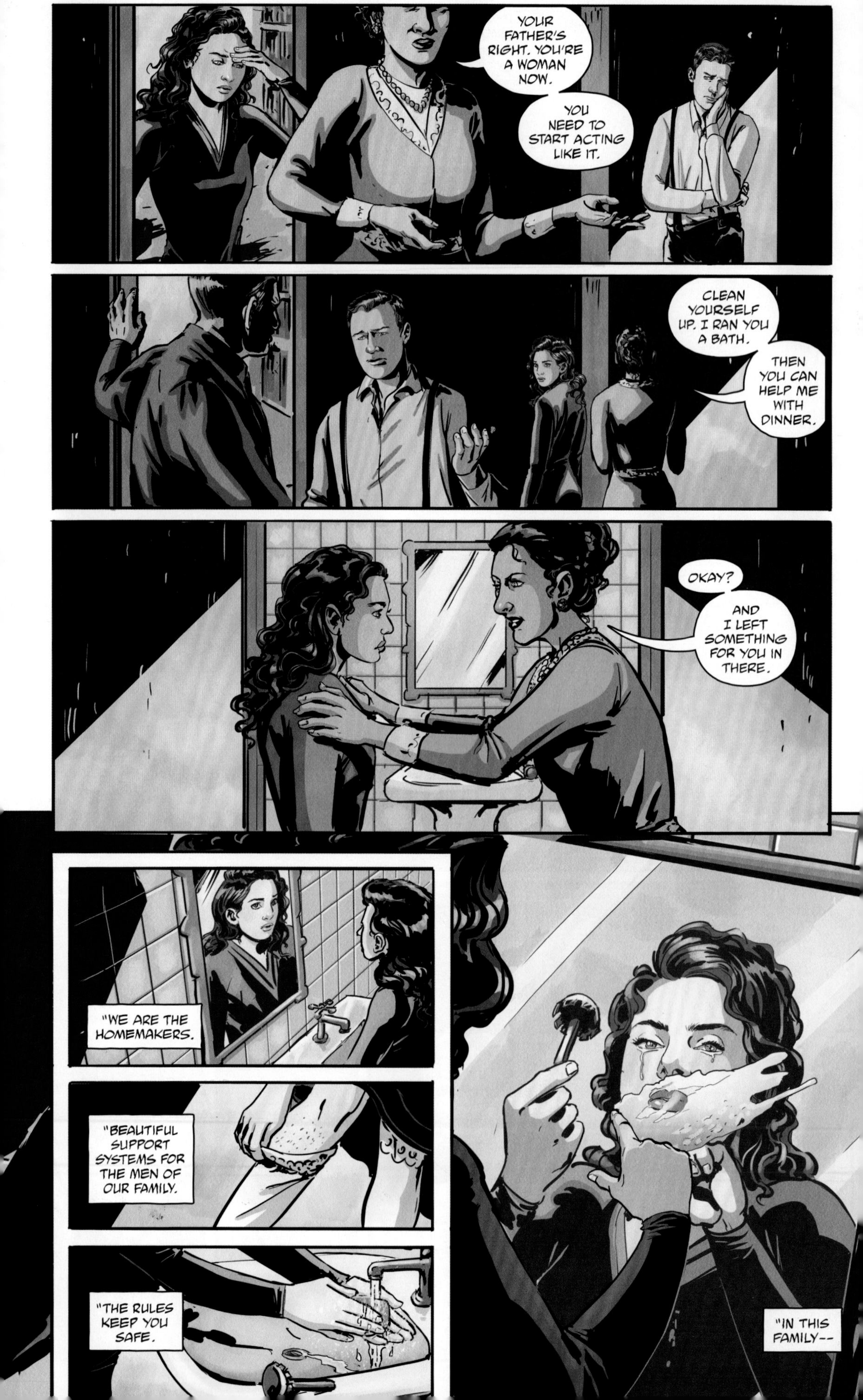
YOUR FATHER'S RIGHT. YOU'RE A WOMAN NOW.
YOU NEED TO START ACTING LIKE IT.
CLEAN YOURSELF UP. I RAN YOU A BATH.
THEN YOU CAN HELP ME WITH DINNER.
OKAY?
AND I LEFT SOMETHING FOR YOU IN THERE.
"WE ARE THE HOMEMAKERS.
"BEAUTIFUL SUPPORT SYSTEMS FOR THE MEN OF OUR FAMILY.
"THE RULES KEEP YOU SAFE.
"IN THIS FAMILY--

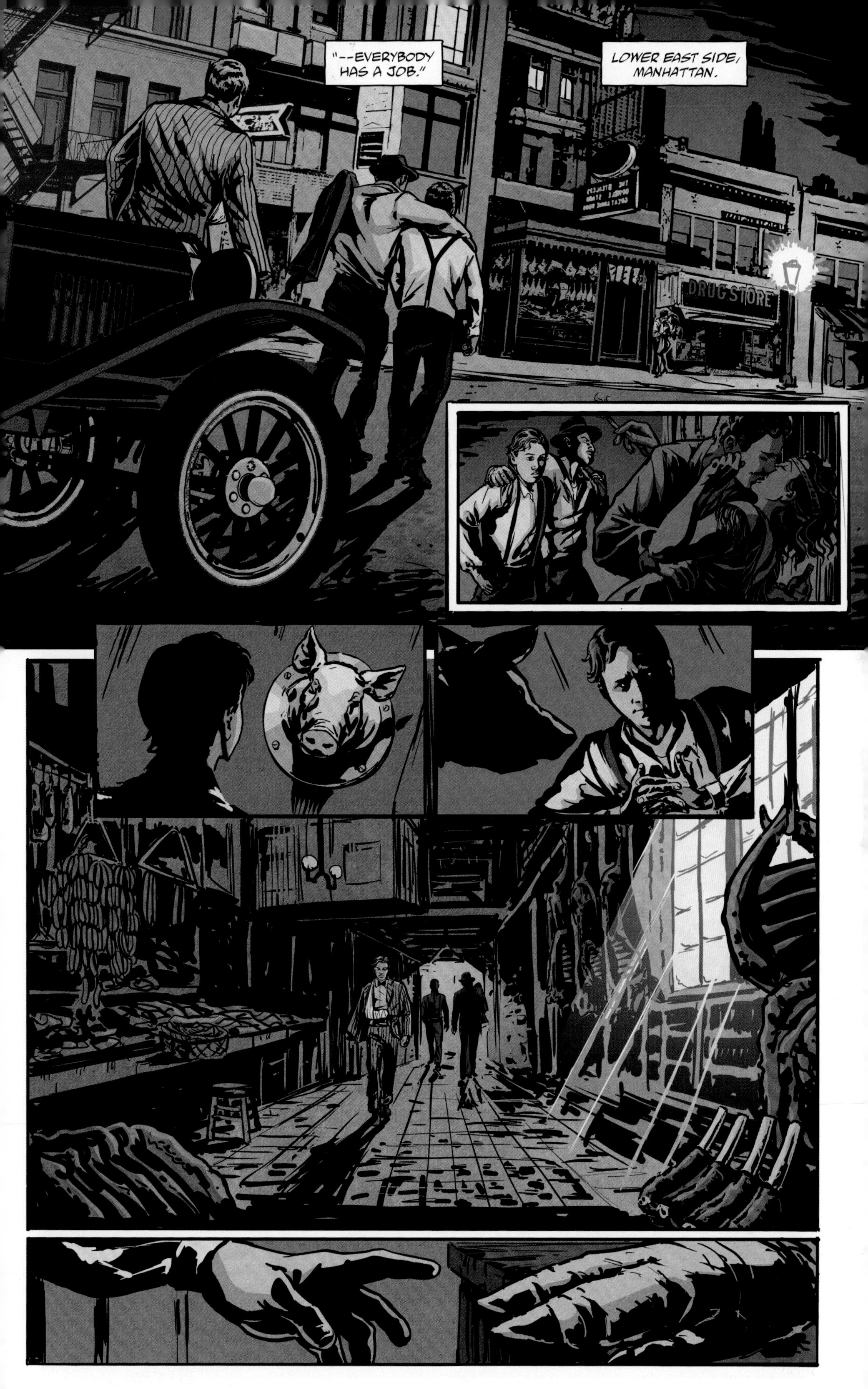
"--EVERYBODY HAS A JOB."
LOWER EAST SIDE, MANHATTAN.
DRUG STORE

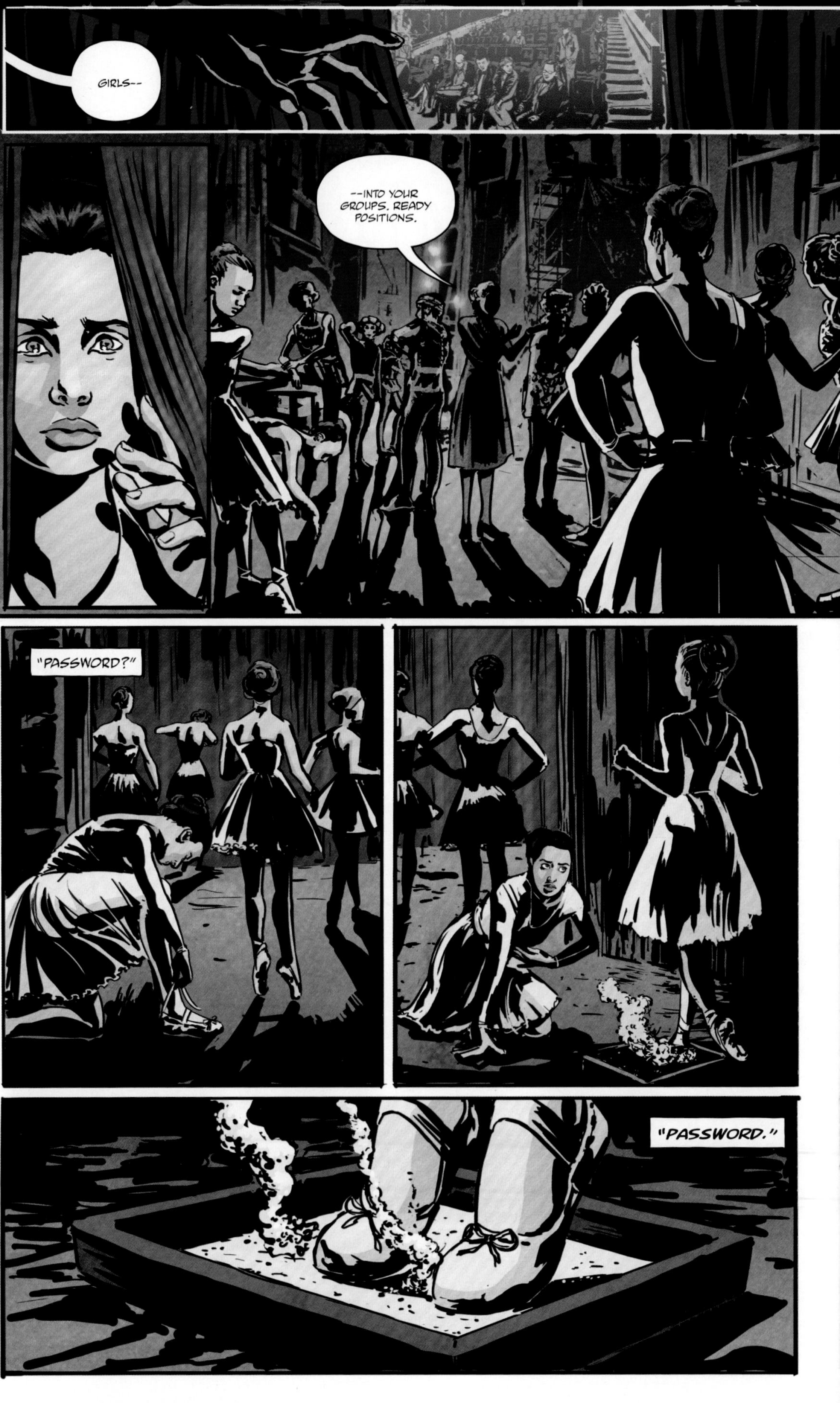
GIRLS--
--INTO YOUR GROUPS. READY POSITIONS.
"PASSWORD?"
"PASSWORD."

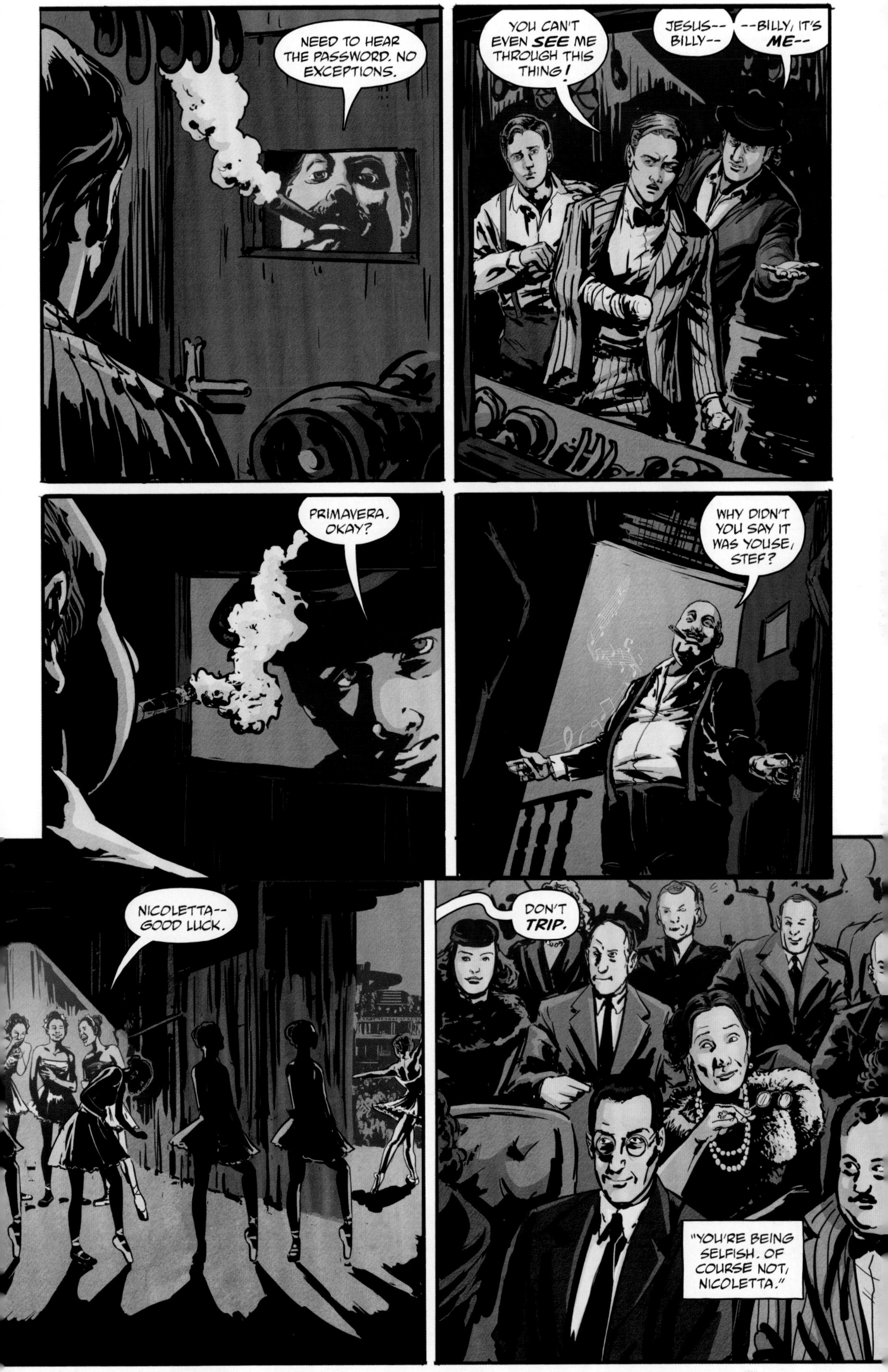
NEED TO HEAR THE PASSWORD. NO EXCEPTIONS.
YOU CAN'T EVEN SEE ME THROUGH THIS THING!
JESUS-- BILLY--
--BILLY, IT'S ME--
PRIMAVERA. OKAY?
WHY DIDN'T YOU SAY IT WAS YOUSE, STEF?
NICOLETTA-- GOOD LUCK.
DON'T TRIP.
"YOU'RE BEING SELFISH. OF COURSE NOT, NICOLETTA."

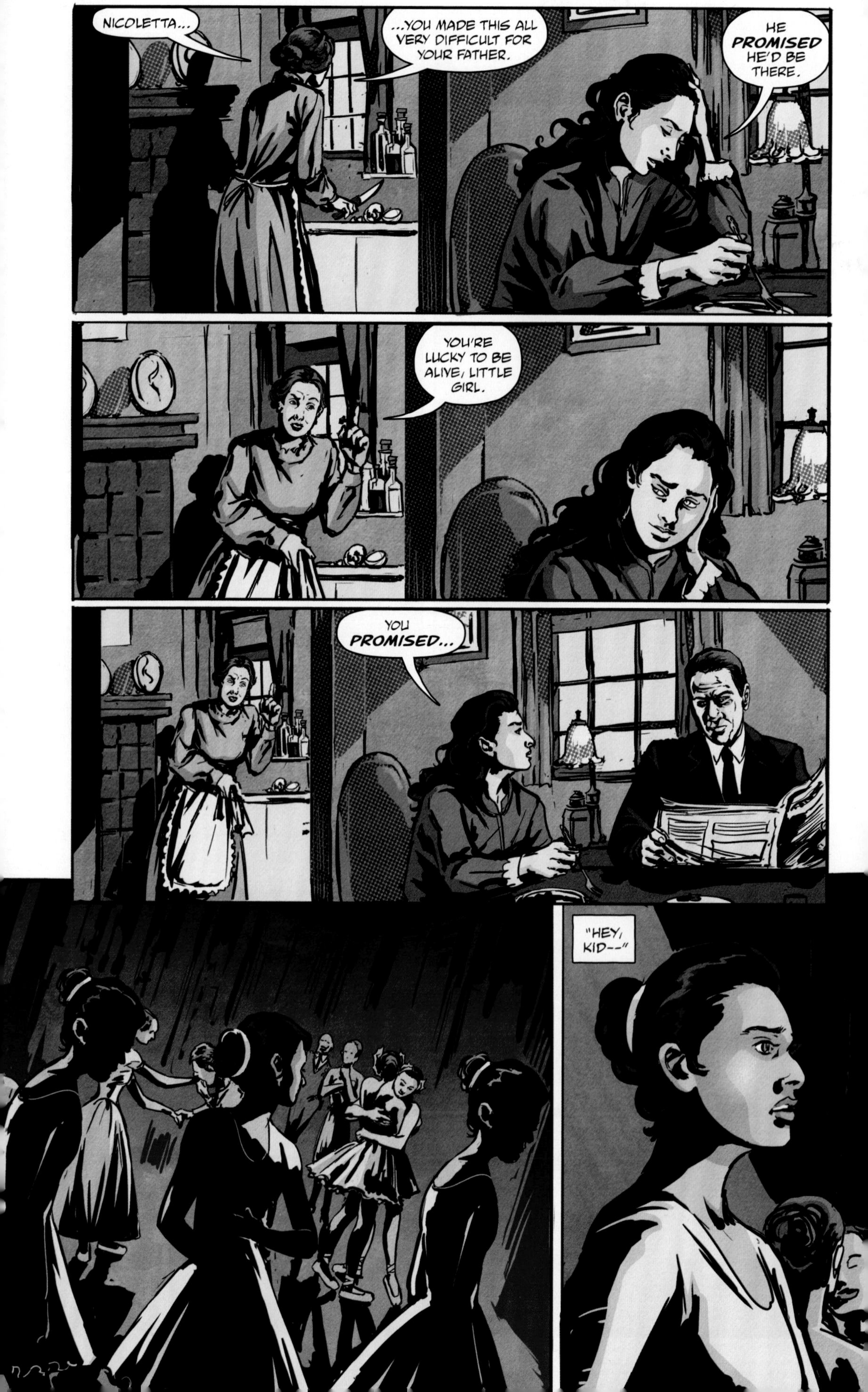
NICOLETTA...
...YOU MADE THIS ALL VERY DIFFICULT FOR YOUR FATHER.
HE PROMISED HE'D BE THERE.
YOU'RE LUCKY TO BE ALIVE, LITTLE GIRL.
YOU PROMISED...
"HEY, KID--"

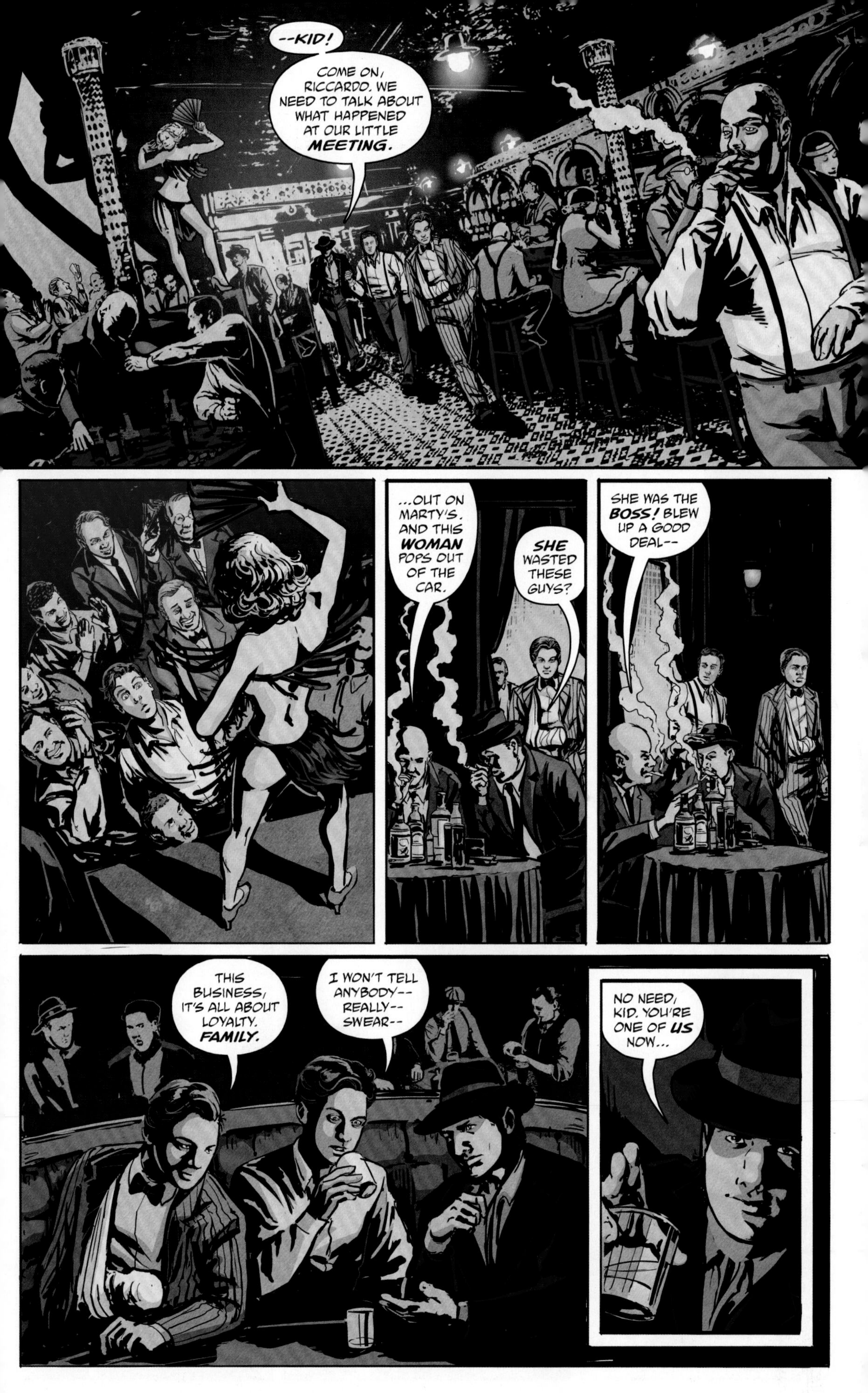
--KID!
COME ON, RICCARDO. WE NEED TO TALK ABOUT WHAT HAPPENED AT OUR LITTLE MEETING.
...OUT ON MARTY'S, AND THIS WOMAN POPS OUT OF THE CAR.
SHE WASTED THESE GUYS?
SHE WAS THE BOSS! BLEW UP A GOOD DEAL--
THIS BUSINESS, IT'S ALL ABOUT LOYALTY. FAMILY.
I WON'T TELL ANYBODY-- REALLY-- SWEAR--
NO NEED, KID. YOU'RE ONE OF US NOW...

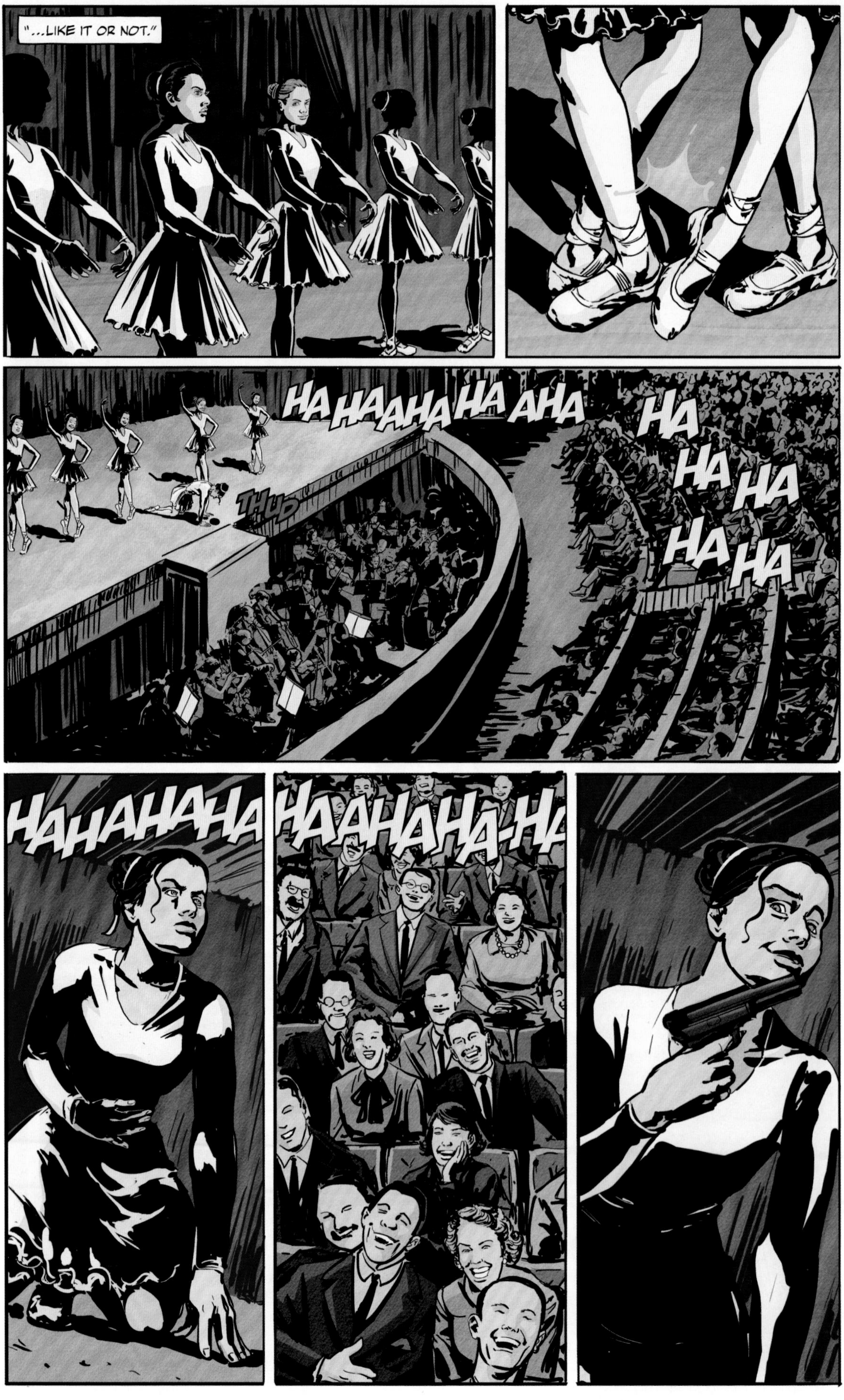
"...LIKE IT OR NOT."
HA HA AHA HA AHA
THUD
HA HA HA HA HA
HAHAHAHA
HAAHAHAHA-HA

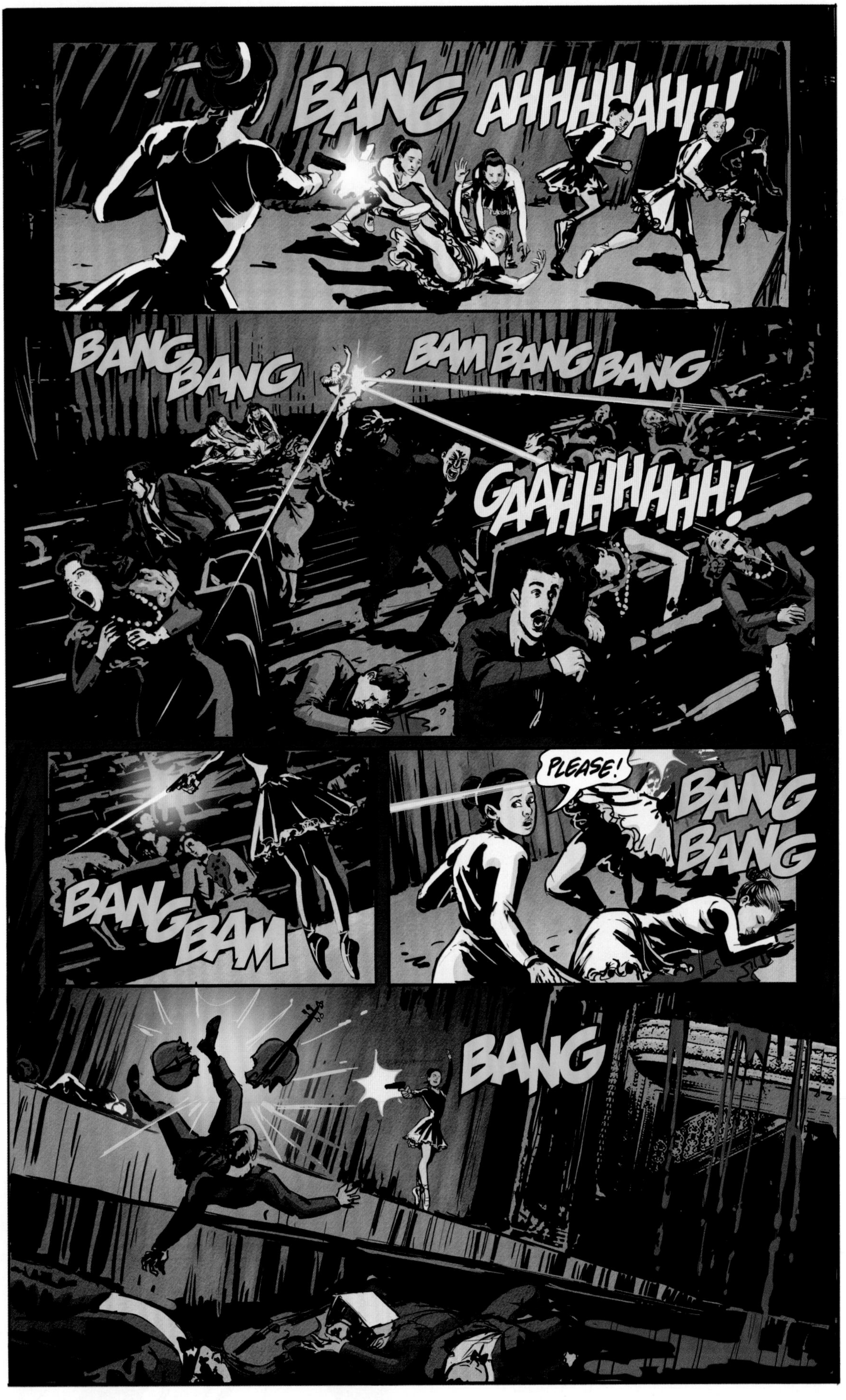
BANG
AHHHHAH!!
BANG BANG
BAM BANG BANG
GAAHHHHHH!
BANG BAM
PLEASE!
BANG BANG
BANG

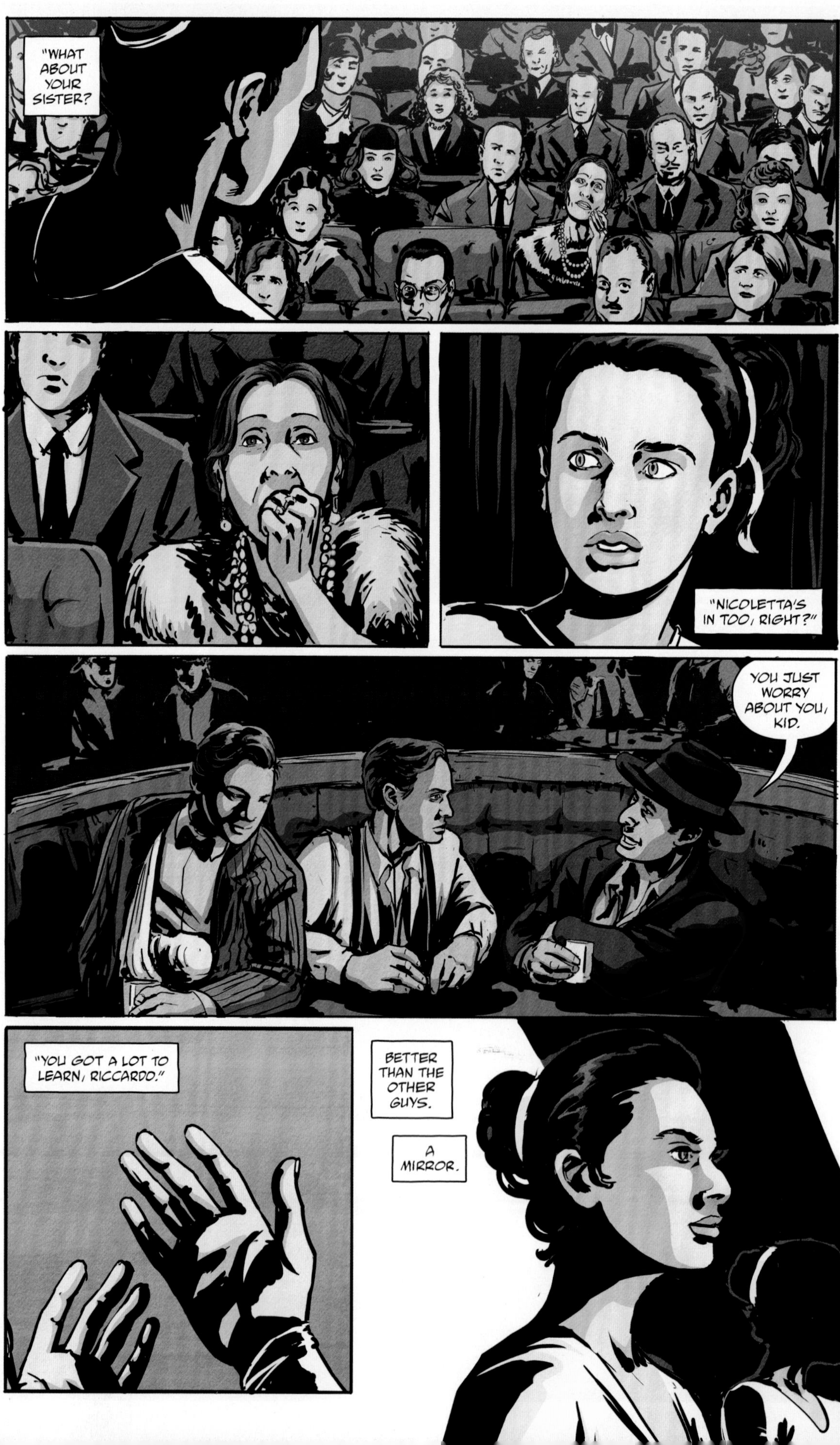
"WHAT ABOUT YOUR SISTER?
"NICOLETTA'S IN TOO, RIGHT?"
YOU JUST WORRY ABOUT YOU, KID.
"YOU GOT A LOT TO LEARN, RICCARDO."
BETTER THAN THE OTHER GUYS.
A MIRROR.

CHAPTER
TWO

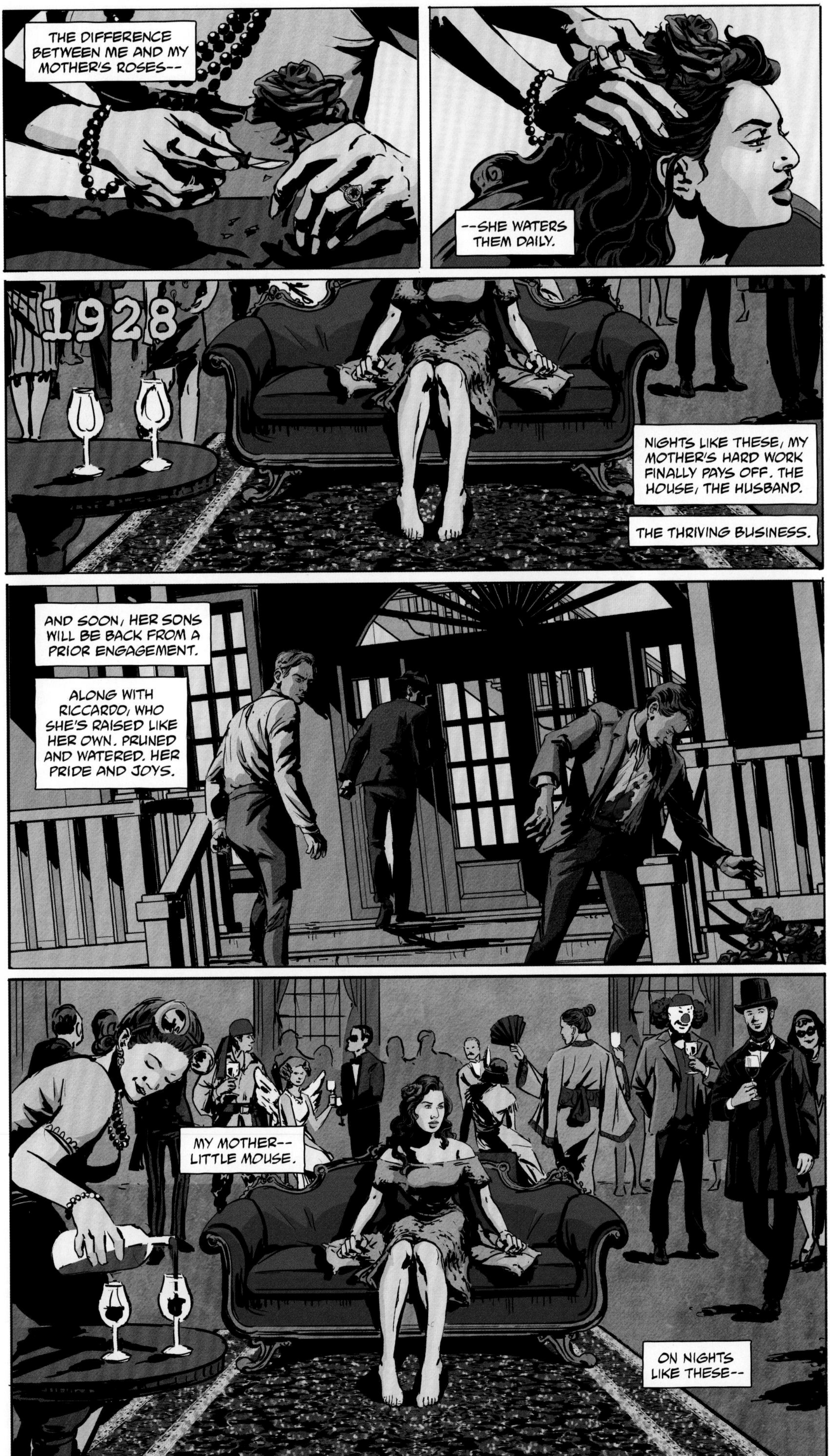
THE DIFFERENCE BETWEEN ME AND MY MOTHER'S ROSES--
--SHE WATERS THEM DAILY.
1928
NIGHTS LIKE THESE, MY MOTHER'S HARD WORK FINALLY PAYS OFF. THE HOUSE, THE HUSBAND.
THE THRIVING BUSINESS.
AND SOON, HER SONS WILL BE BACK FROM A PRIOR ENGAGEMENT.
ALONG WITH RICCARDO, WHO SHE'S RAISED LIKE HER OWN. PRUNED AND WATERED. HER PRIDE AND JOYS.
MY MOTHER-- LITTLE MOUSE.
ON NIGHTS LIKE THESE--

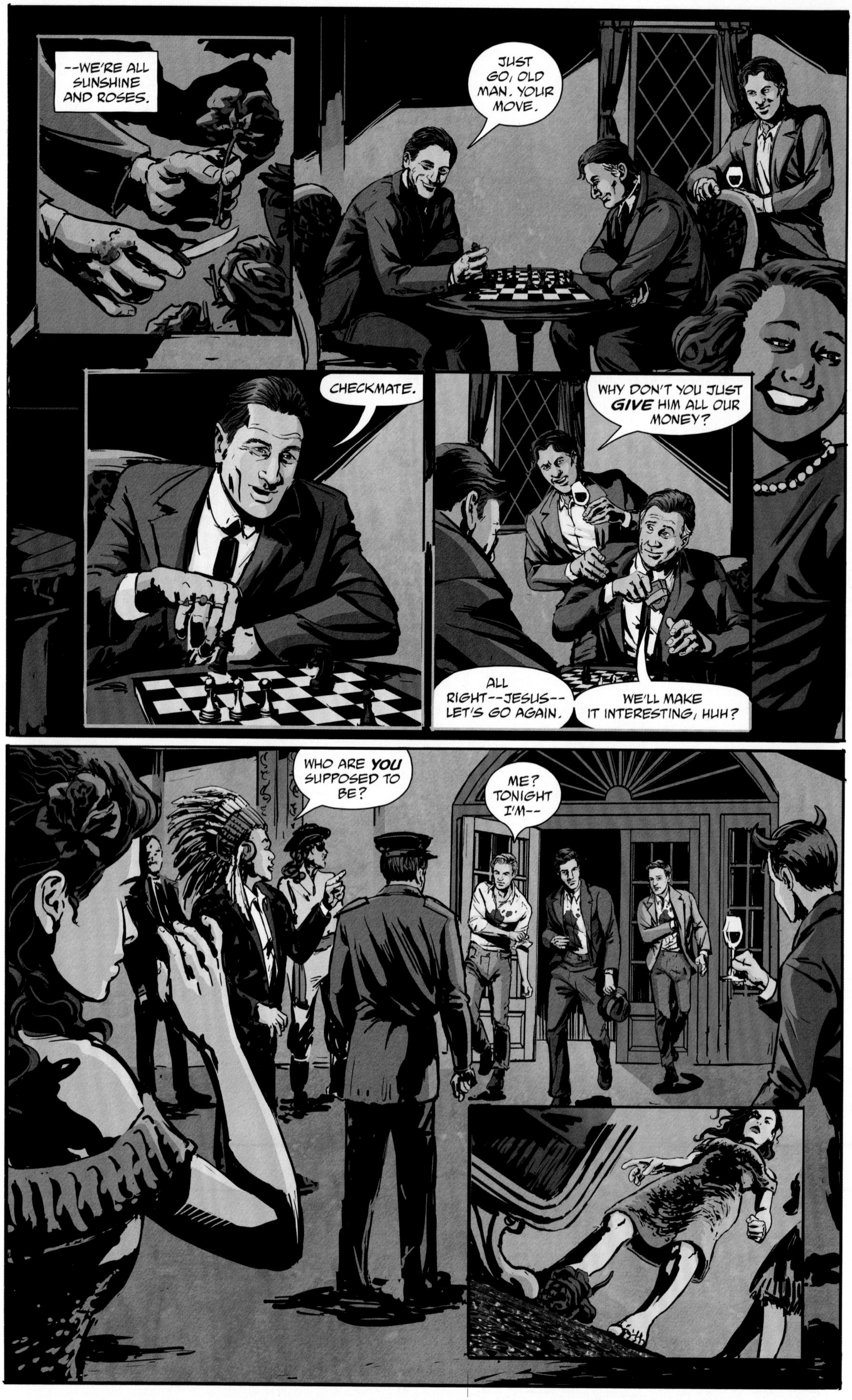
--WE'RE ALL SUNSHINE AND ROSES.
JUST GO, OLD MAN. YOUR MOVE.
CHECKMATE.
WHY DON'T YOU JUST GIVE HIM ALL OUR MONEY?
ALL RIGHT--JESUS--LET'S GO AGAIN.
WE'LL MAKE IT INTERESTING, HUH?
WHO ARE YOU SUPPOSED TO BE?
ME? TONIGHT I'M--

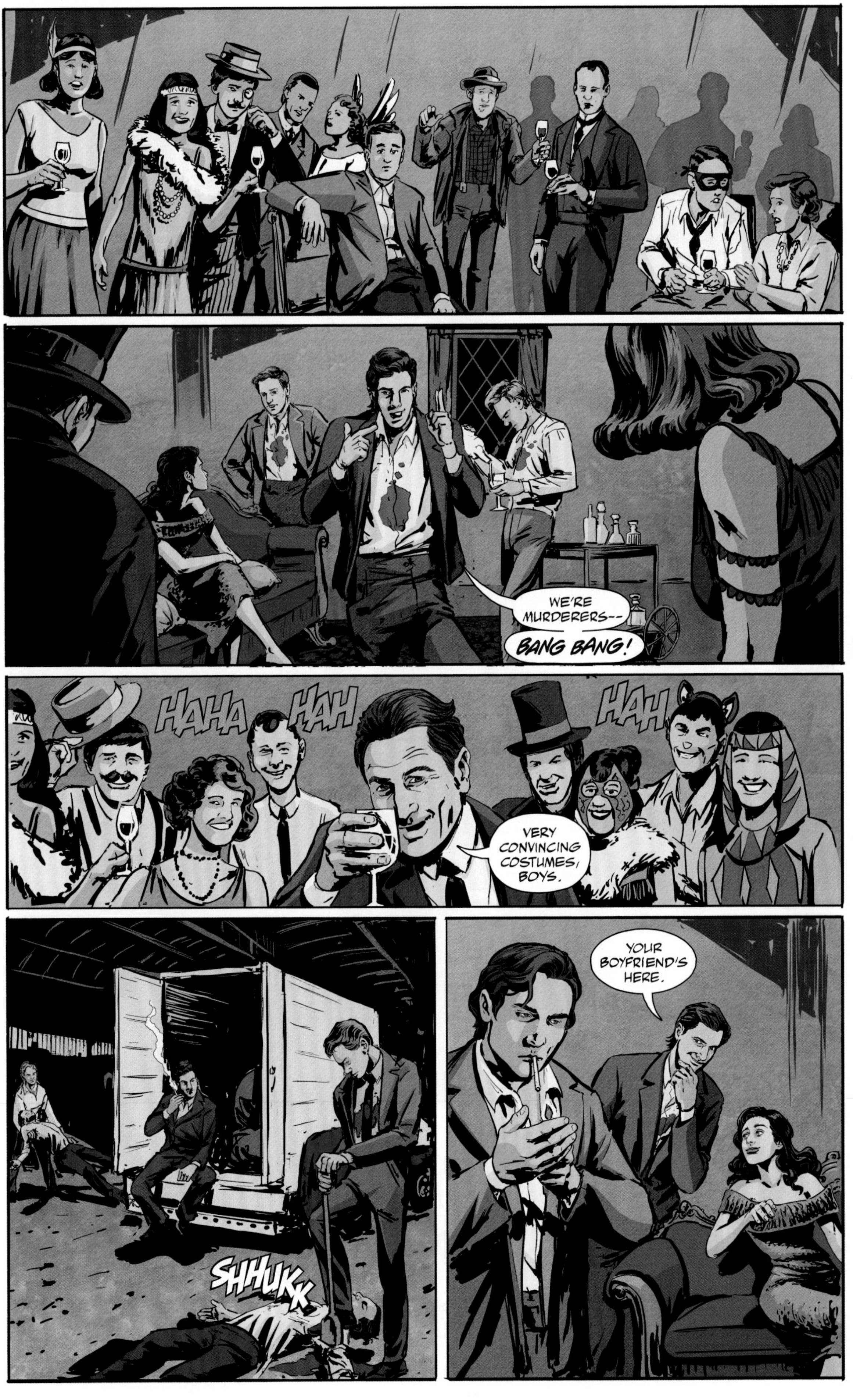
WE'RE MURDERERS--
BANG BANG!
HAHA HAH
HAH
VERY CONVINCING COSTUMES, BOYS.
SHHUKK
YOUR BOYFRIEND'S HERE.

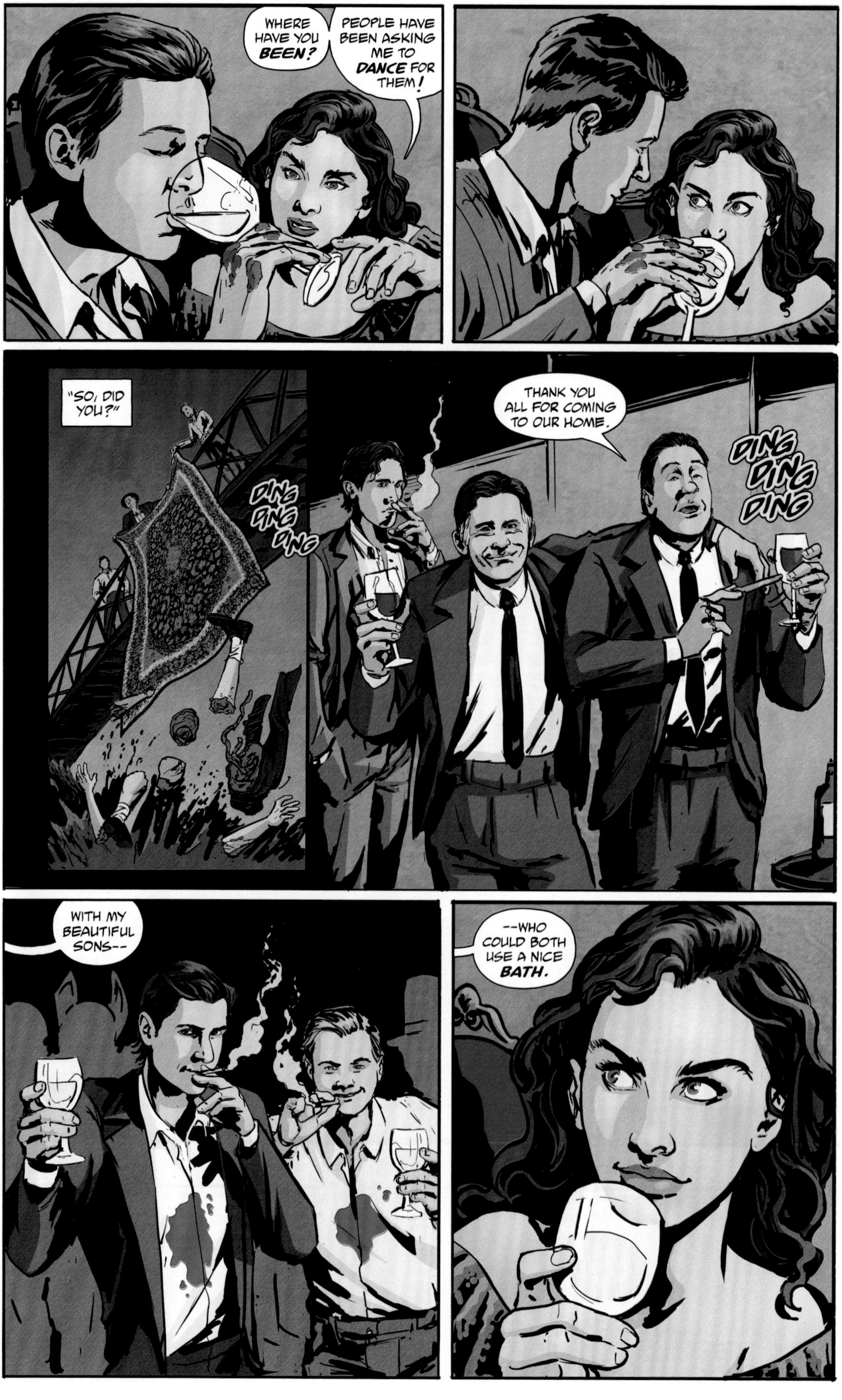
WHERE HAVE YOU BEEN?
PEOPLE HAVE BEEN ASKING ME TO DANCE FOR THEM!
"SO, DID YOU?"
DING DING DING
THANK YOU ALL FOR COMING TO OUR HOME.
DING DING DING
WITH MY BEAUTIFUL SONS--
--WHO COULD BOTH USE A NICE BATH.

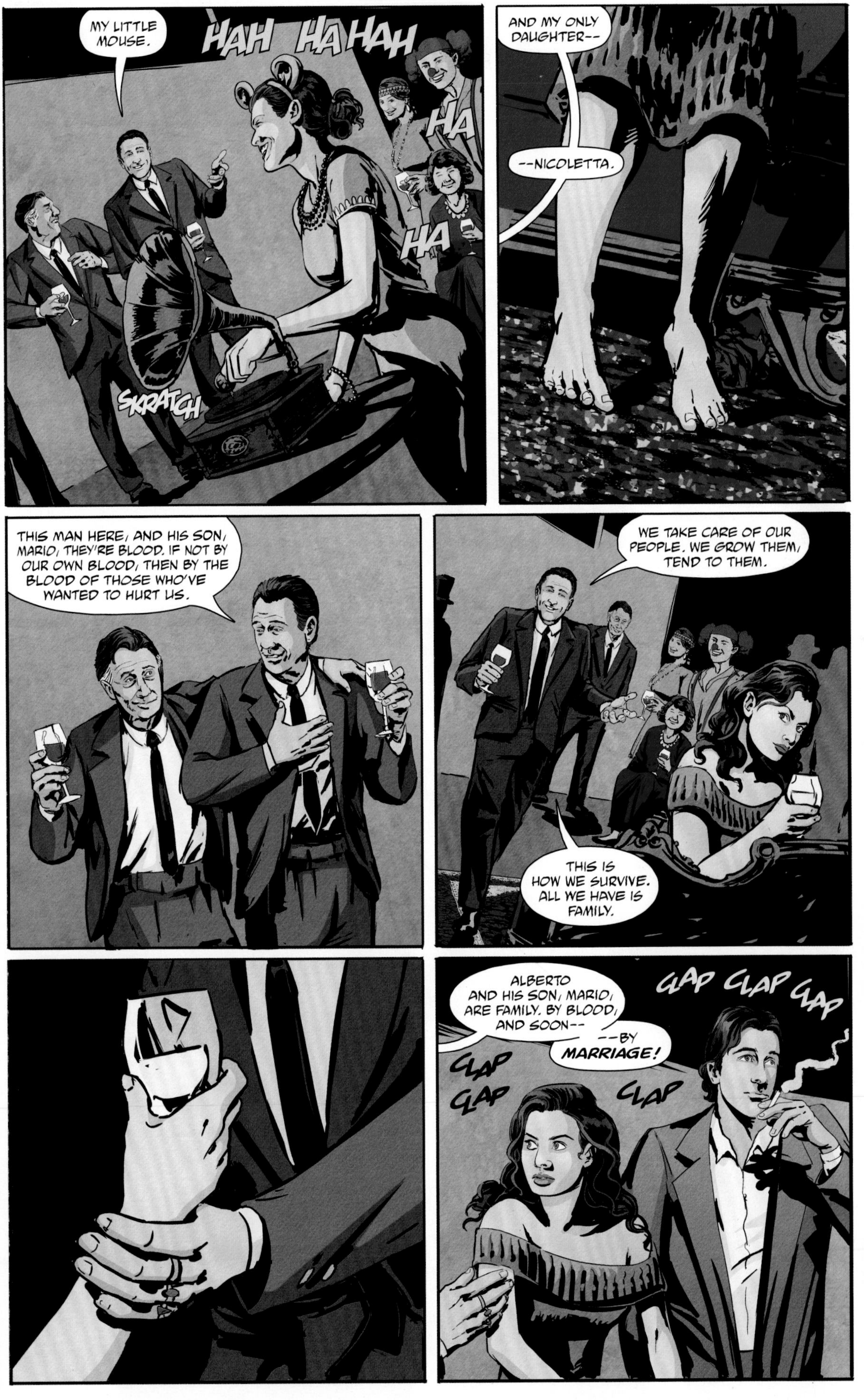
MY LITTLE MOUSE.
HAH HA HAH
HA
HA
SKRATCH
AND MY ONLY DAUGHTER--
--NICOLETTA.
THIS MAN HERE, AND HIS SON, MARIO, THEY'RE BLOOD. IF NOT BY OUR OWN BLOOD, THEN BY THE BLOOD OF THOSE WHO'VE WANTED TO HURT US.
WE TAKE CARE OF OUR PEOPLE. WE GROW THEM, TEND TO THEM.
THIS IS HOW WE SURVIVE. ALL WE HAVE IS FAMILY.
ALBERTO AND HIS SON, MARIO, ARE FAMILY. BY BLOOD, AND SOON--
--BY MARRIAGE!
CLAP CLAP CLAP
CLAP
CLAP
CLAP

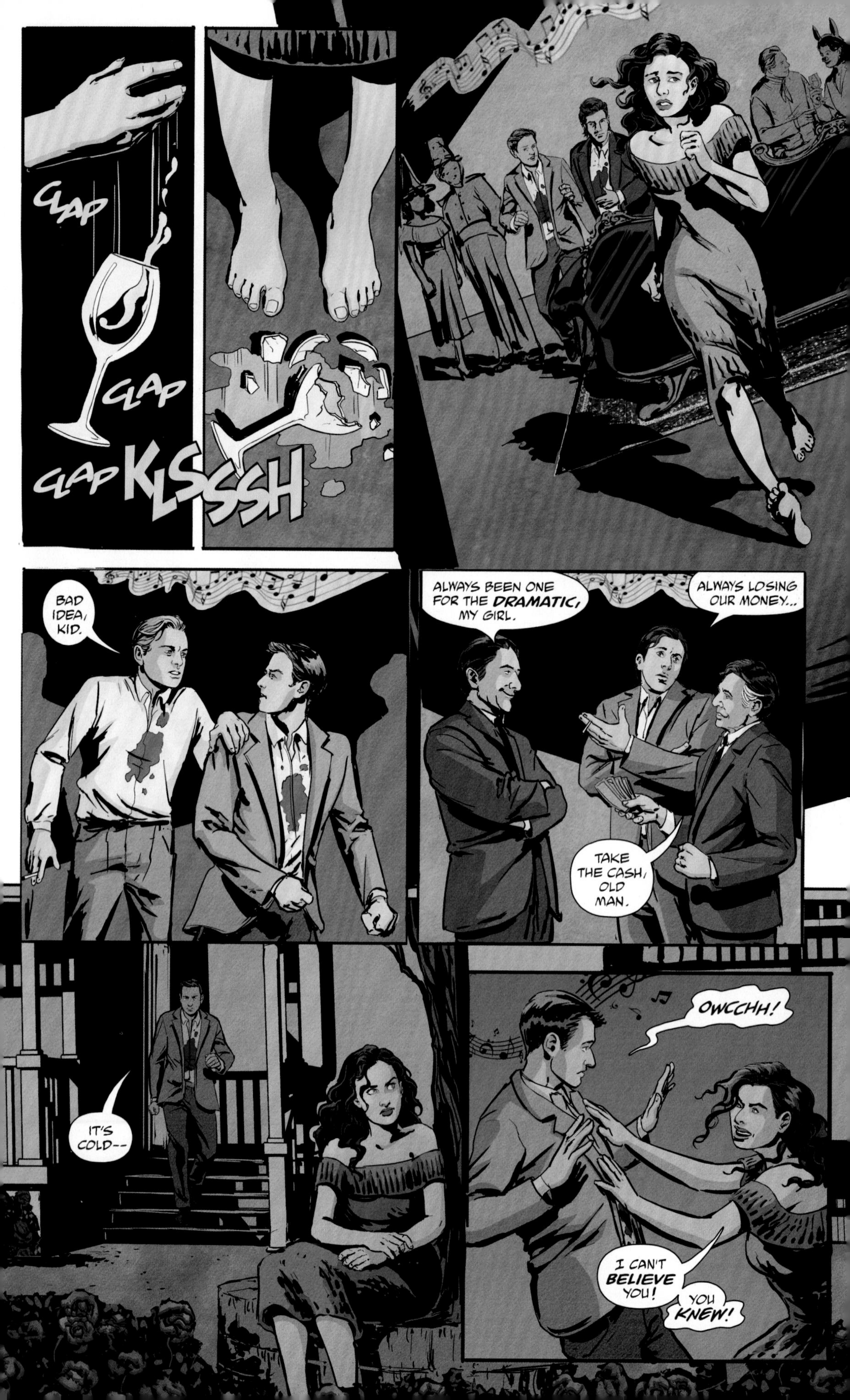
CLAP
CLAP
CLAP
KLSSSSH
BAD IDEA, KID.
ALWAYS BEEN ONE FOR THE **DRAMATIC,** MY GIRL.
ALWAYS LOSING OUR MONEY...
TAKE THE CASH, OLD MAN.
IT'S COLD--
OWCCHH!
I CAN'T **BELIEVE** YOU!
YOU **KNEW!**

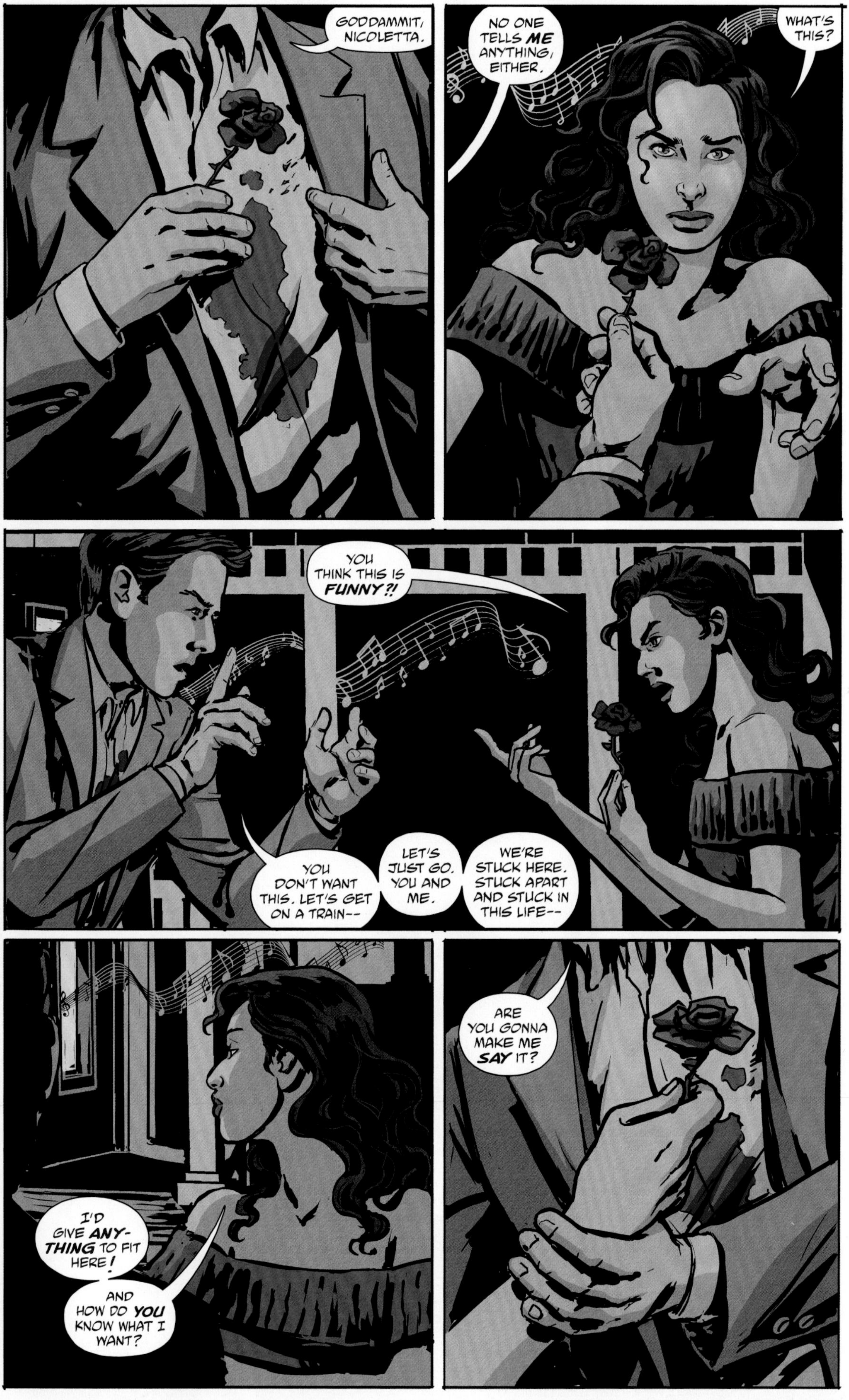
GODDAMMIT, NICOLETTA.
NO ONE TELLS ME ANYTHING, EITHER.
WHAT'S THIS?
YOU THINK THIS IS FUNNY?!
YOU DON'T WANT THIS. LET'S GET ON A TRAIN--
LET'S JUST GO. YOU AND ME.
WE'RE STUCK HERE. STUCK APART AND STUCK IN THIS LIFE--
I'D GIVE ANY-THING TO FIT HERE!
AND HOW DO YOU KNOW WHAT I WANT?
ARE YOU GONNA MAKE ME SAY IT?

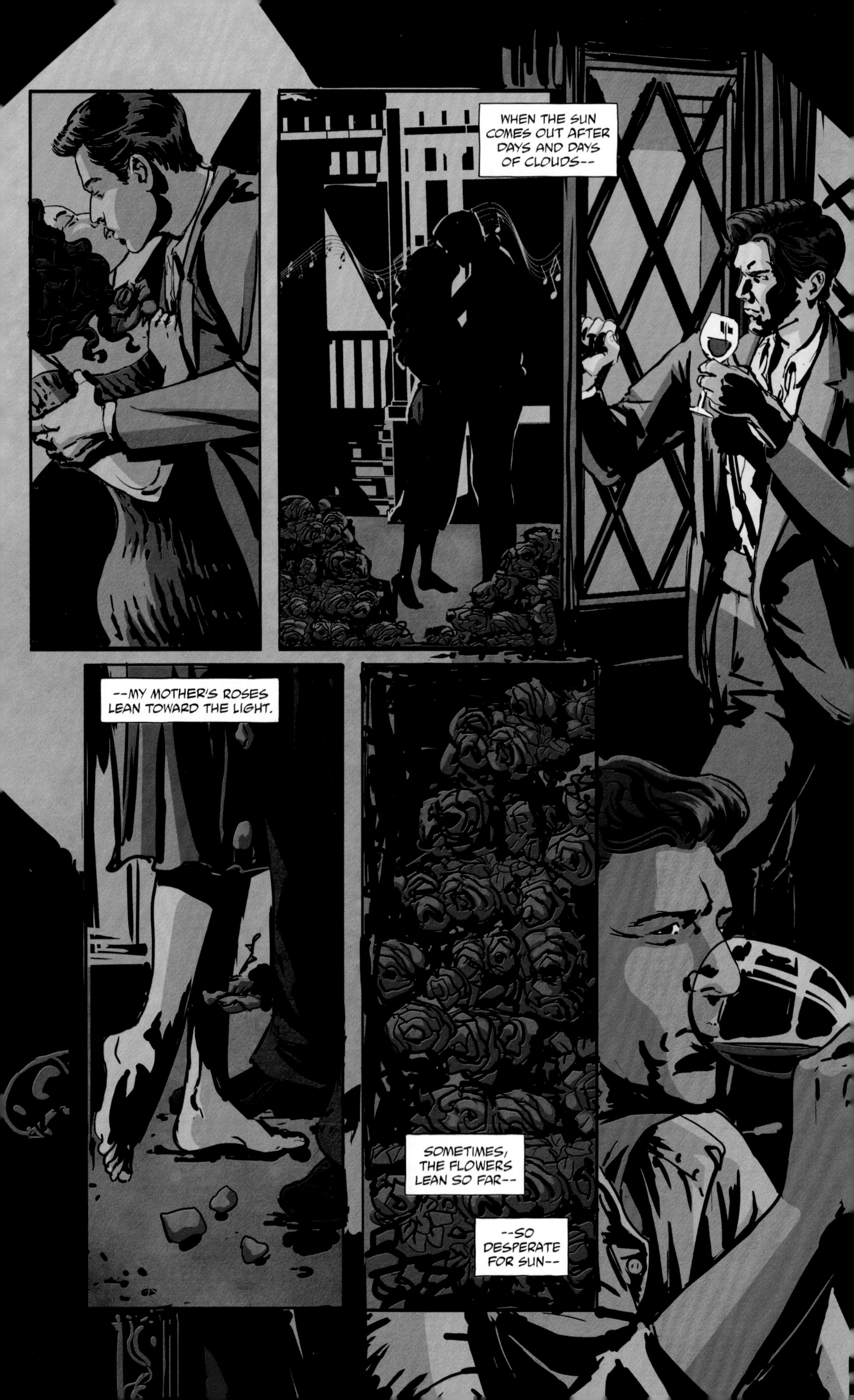
WHEN THE SUN COMES OUT AFTER DAYS AND DAYS OF CLOUDS--
--MY MOTHER'S ROSES LEAN TOWARD THE LIGHT.
SOMETIMES, THE FLOWERS LEAN SO FAR--
--SO DESPERATE FOR SUN--

--THEIR STEMS BEND, AND BREAK.

AH--

GET BACK TO THE PARTY, KID.

NIC? WHAT DO YOU SAY?

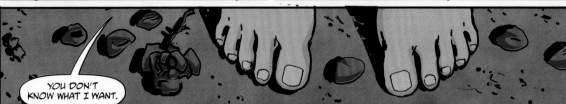

YOU DON'T KNOW WHAT I WANT.

YOU WILL NOT SPEAK TO HIM.

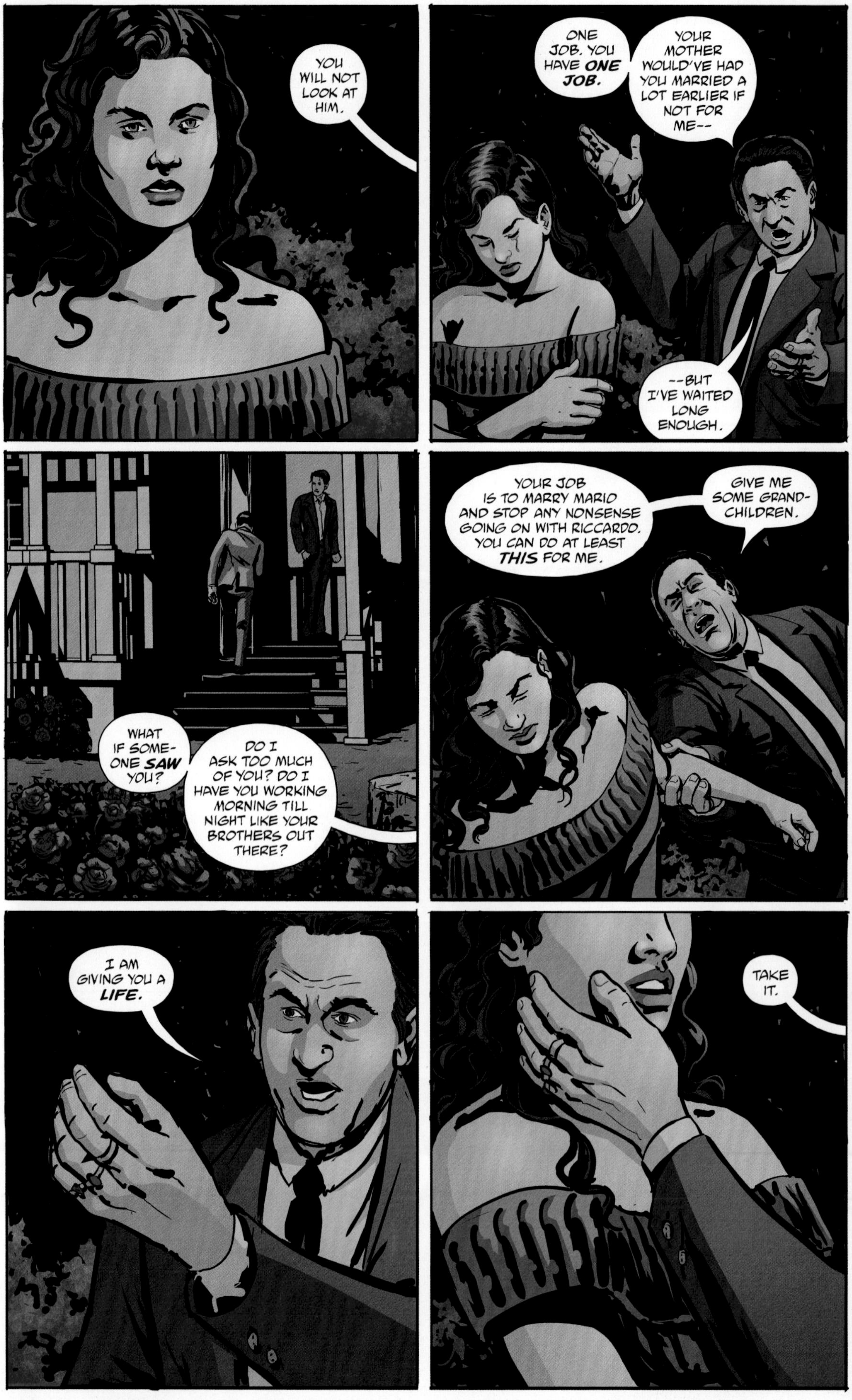
YOU WILL NOT LOOK AT HIM.
ONE JOB. YOU HAVE ONE JOB.
YOUR MOTHER WOULD'VE HAD YOU MARRIED A LOT EARLIER IF NOT FOR ME--
--BUT I'VE WAITED LONG ENOUGH.
WHAT IF SOME-ONE SAW YOU?
DO I ASK TOO MUCH OF YOU? DO I HAVE YOU WORKING MORNING TILL NIGHT LIKE YOUR BROTHERS OUT THERE?
YOUR JOB IS TO MARRY MARIO AND STOP ANY NONSENSE GOING ON WITH RICCARDO. YOU CAN DO AT LEAST THIS FOR ME.
GIVE ME SOME GRAND-CHILDREN.
I AM GIVING YOU A LIFE.
TAKE IT.

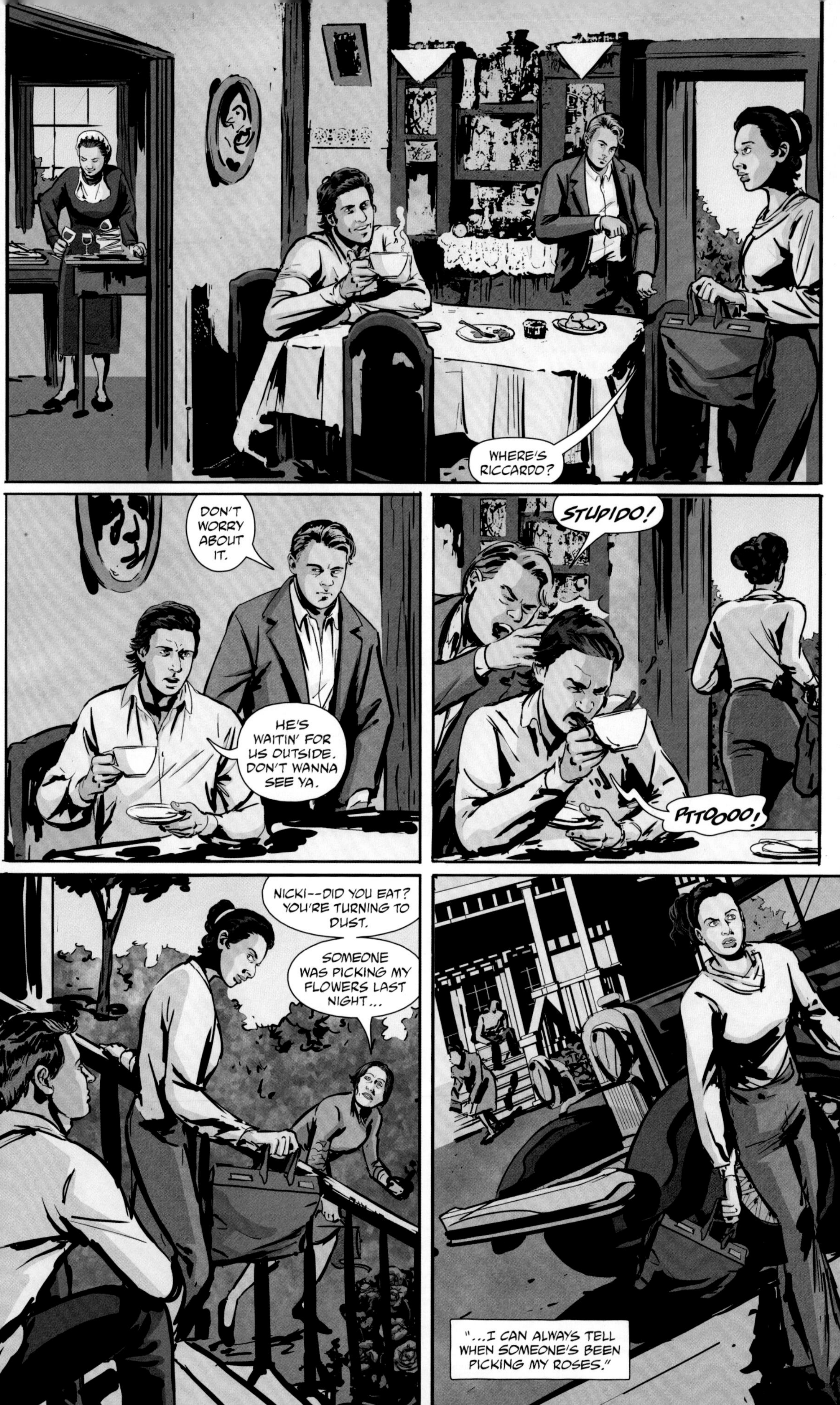
WHERE'S RICCARDO?
DON'T WORRY ABOUT IT.
HE'S WAITIN' FOR US OUTSIDE. DON'T WANNA SEE YA.
STUPIDO!
PTTOOOO!
NICKI--DID YOU EAT? YOU'RE TURNING TO DUST.
SOMEONE WAS PICKING MY FLOWERS LAST NIGHT...
"...I CAN ALWAYS TELL WHEN SOMEONE'S BEEN PICKING MY ROSES."

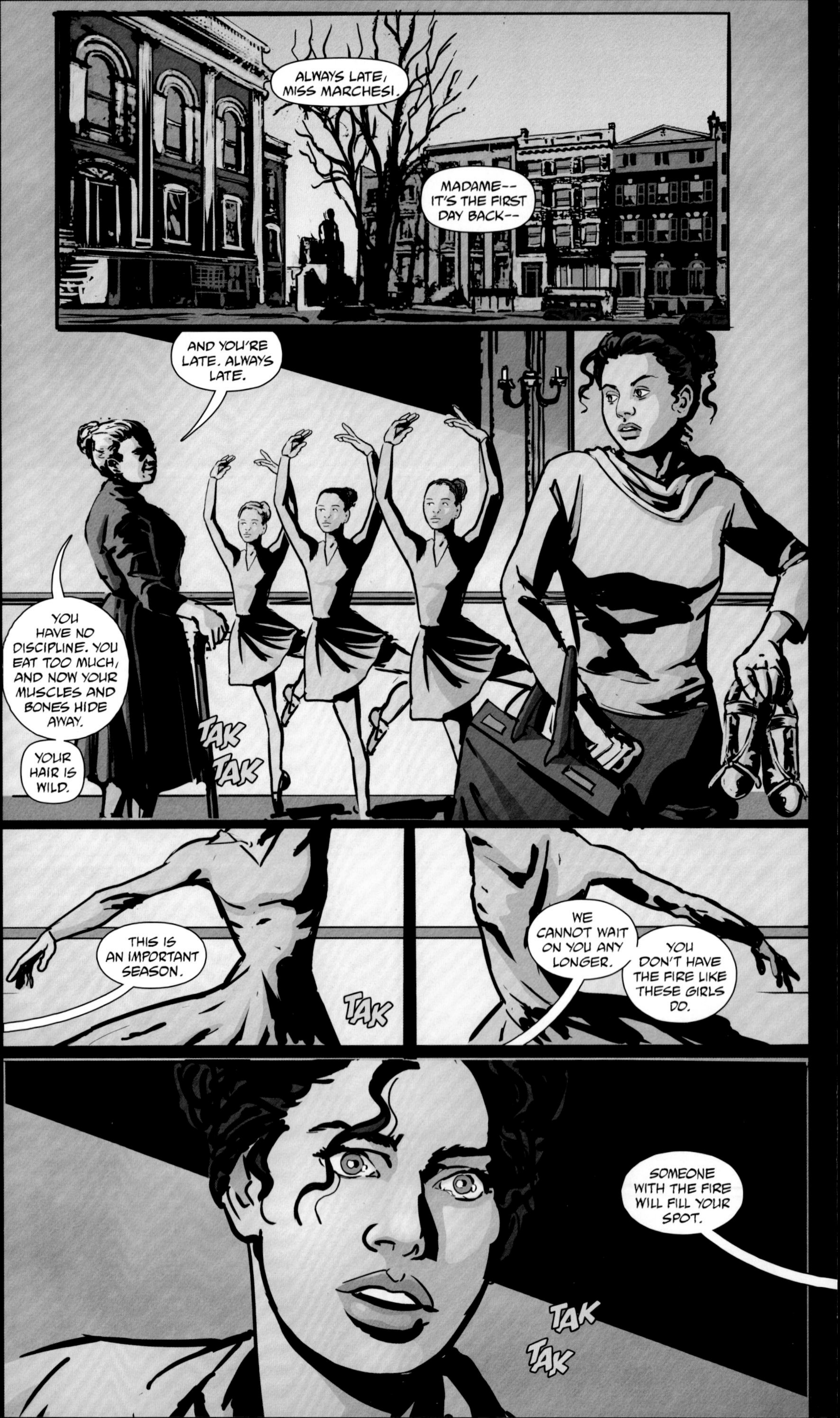
ALWAYS LATE, MISS MARCHESI.
MADAME-- IT'S THE FIRST DAY BACK--
AND YOU'RE LATE. ALWAYS LATE.
YOU HAVE NO DISCIPLINE. YOU EAT TOO MUCH, AND NOW YOUR MUSCLES AND BONES HIDE AWAY.
YOUR HAIR IS WILD.
TAK
TAK
THIS IS AN IMPORTANT SEASON.
TAK
WE CANNOT WAIT ON YOU ANY LONGER.
YOU DON'T HAVE THE FIRE LIKE THESE GIRLS DO.
SOMEONE WITH THE FIRE WILL FILL YOUR SPOT.
TAK
TAK

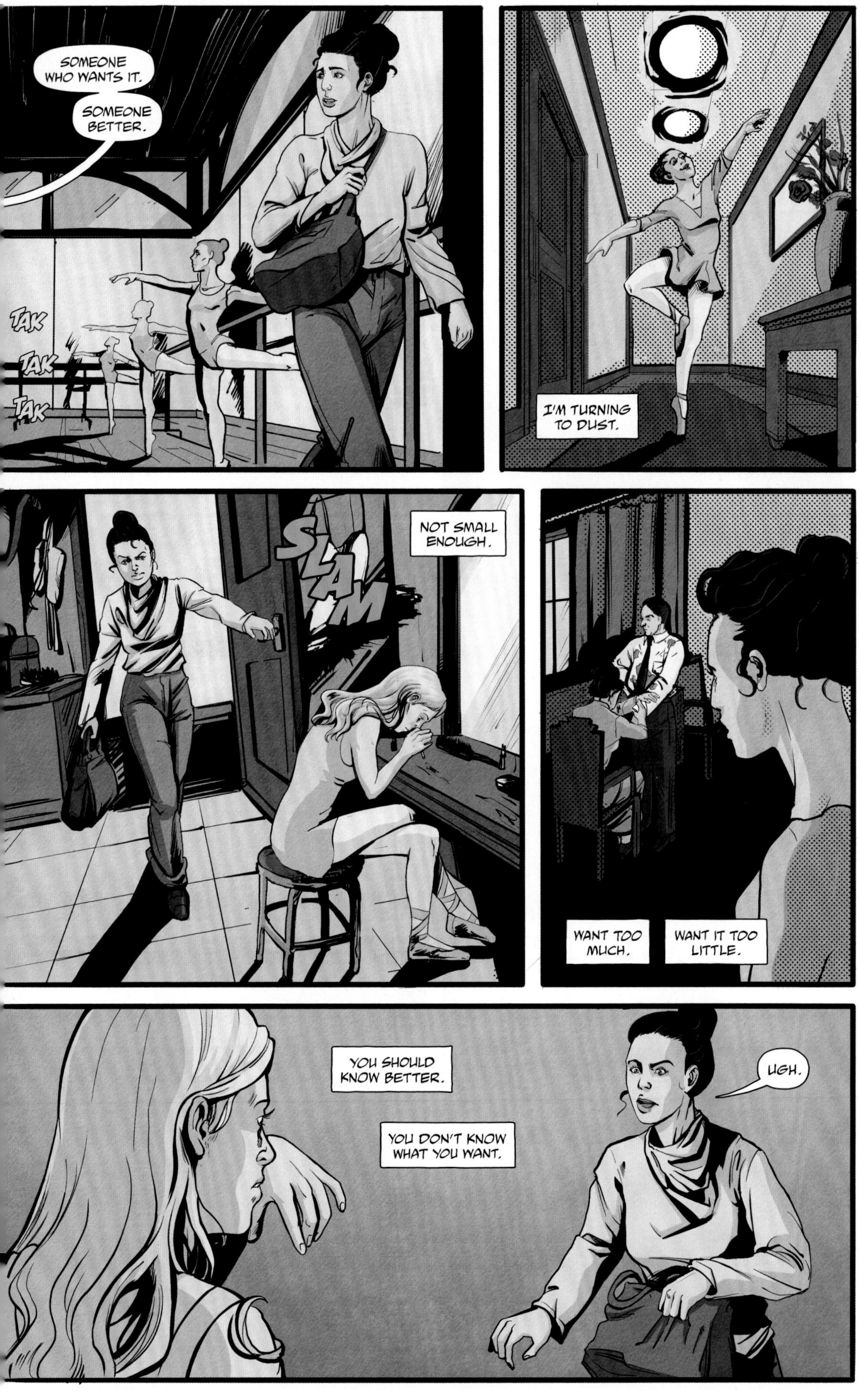
SOMEONE WHO WANTS IT.
SOMEONE BETTER.
TAK
TAK
TAK
I'M TURNING TO DUST.
SLAM
NOT SMALL ENOUGH.
WANT TOO MUCH.
WANT IT TOO LITTLE.
YOU SHOULD KNOW BETTER.
YOU DON'T KNOW WHAT YOU WANT.
UGH.

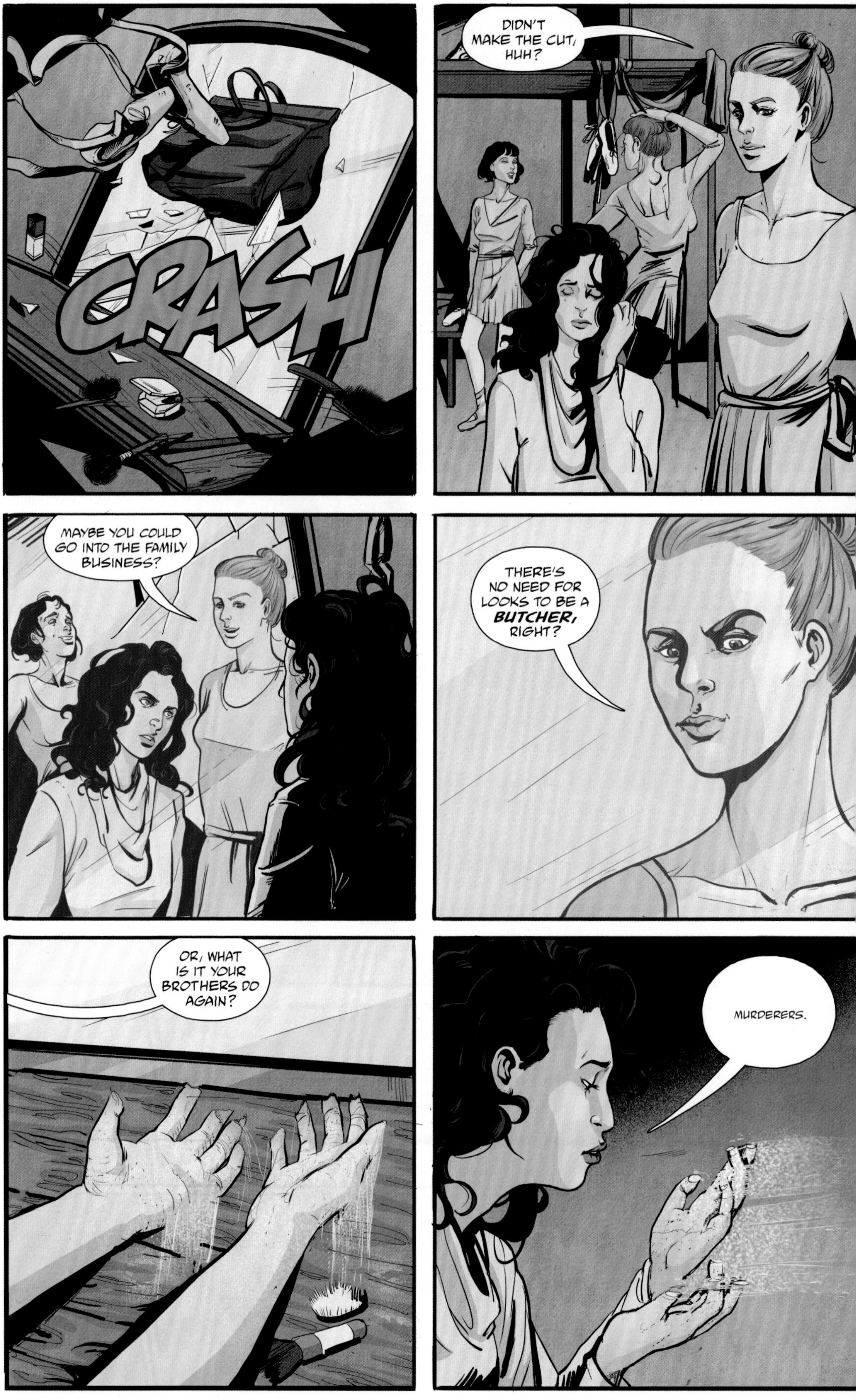
CRASH
DIDN'T MAKE THE CUT, HUH?
MAYBE YOU COULD GO INTO THE FAMILY BUSINESS?
THERE'S NO NEED FOR LOOKS TO BE A **BUTCHER,** RIGHT?
OR, WHAT IS IT YOUR BROTHERS DO AGAIN?
MURDERERS.

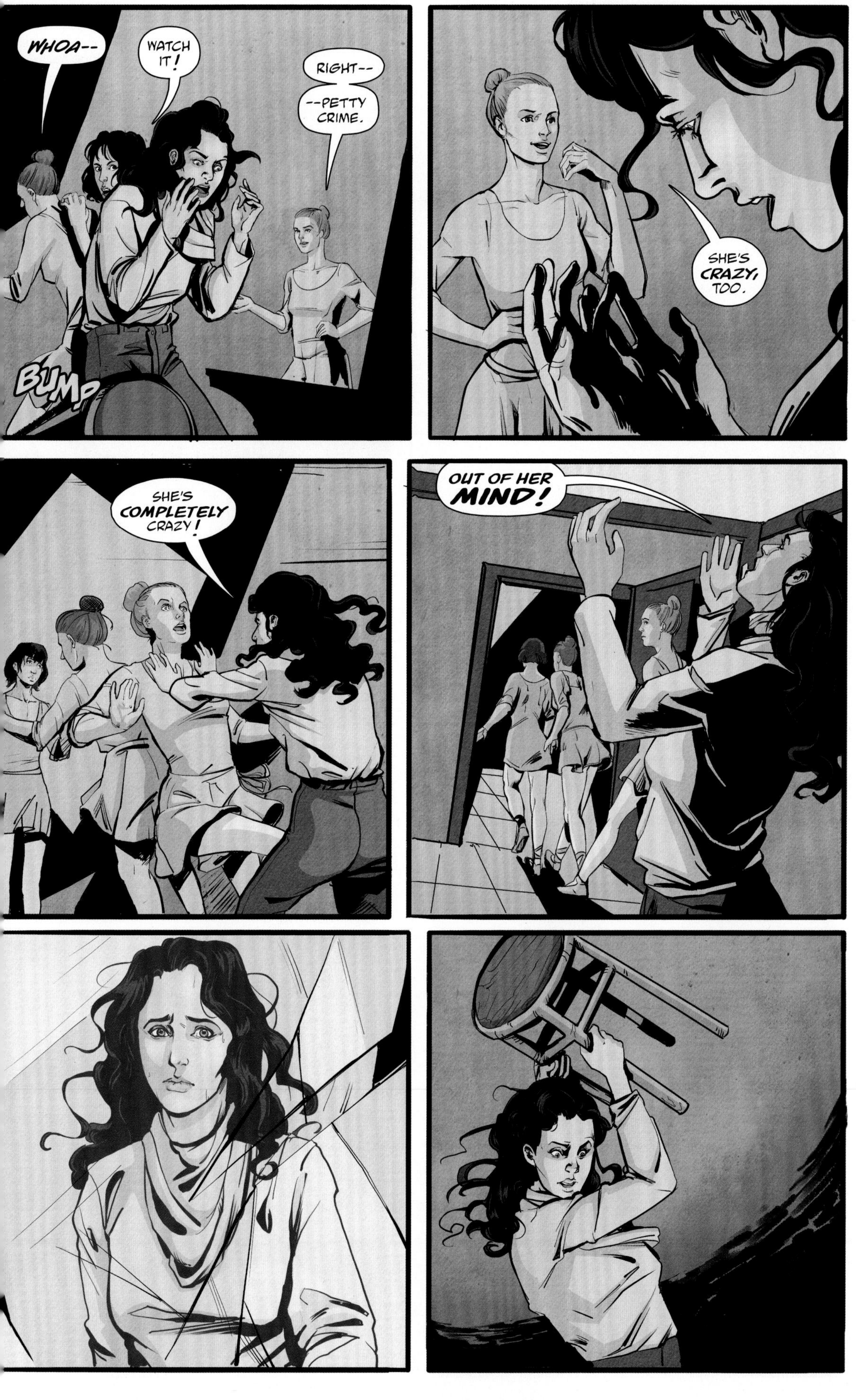
WHOA--
WATCH IT!
RIGHT--
--PETTY CRIME.
BUMP
SHE'S CRAZY, TOO.
SHE'S COMPLETELY CRAZY!
OUT OF HER MIND!

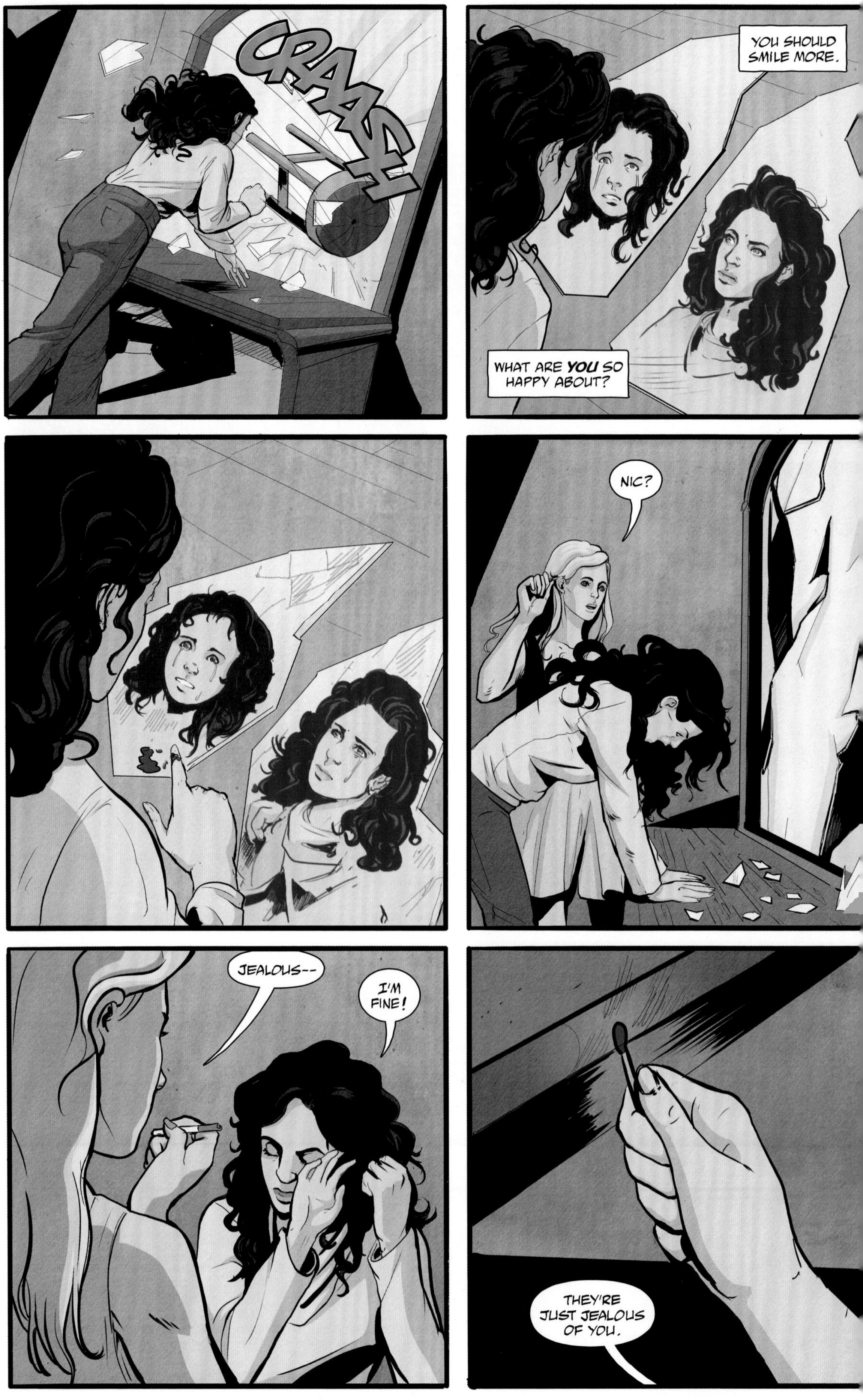
CRAASH
YOU SHOULD SMILE MORE.
WHAT ARE **YOU** SO HAPPY ABOUT?
NIC?
JEALOUS--
I'M FINE!
THEY'RE JUST JEALOUS OF YOU.

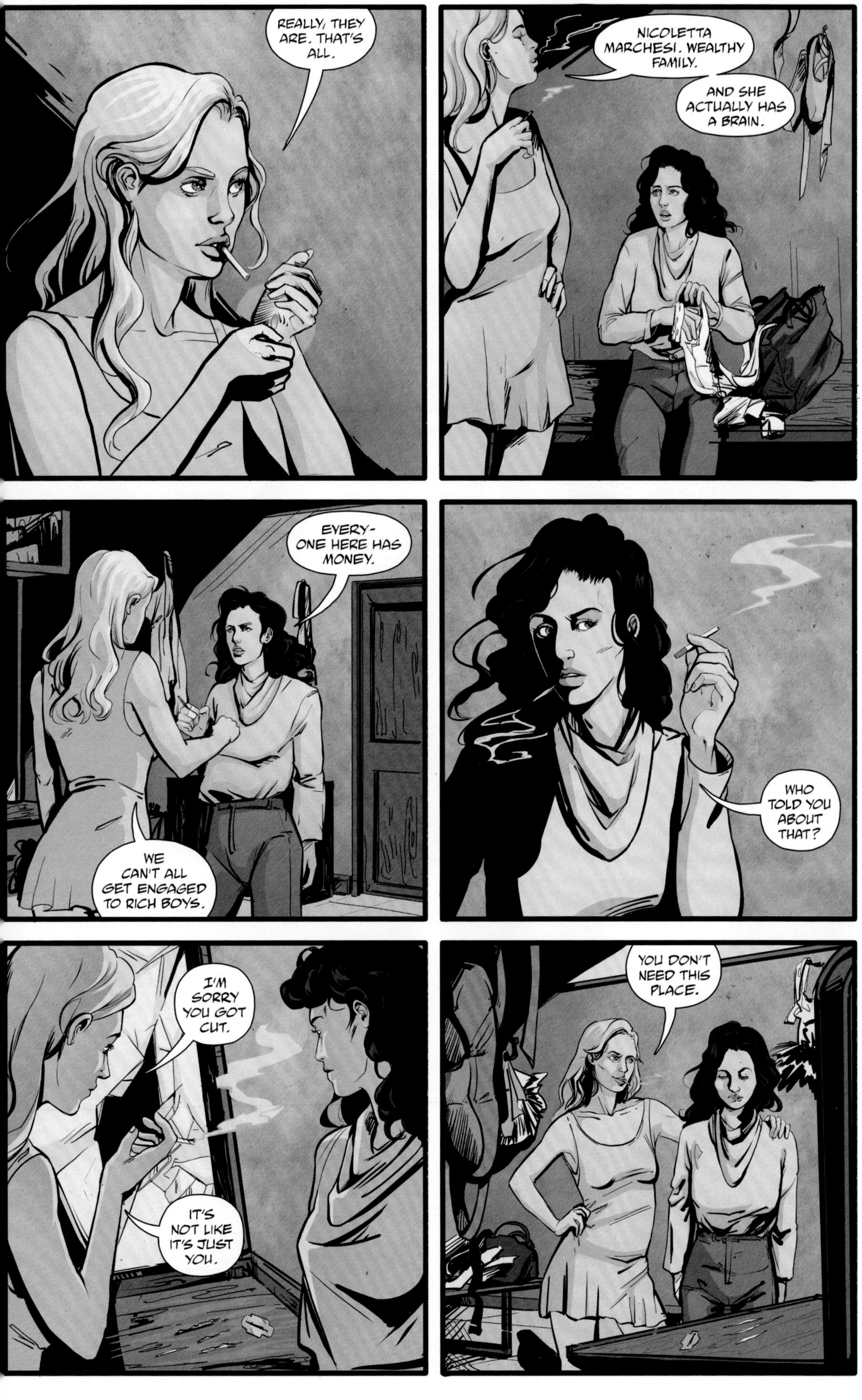
REALLY, THEY ARE. THAT'S ALL.
NICOLETTA MARCHESI. WEALTHY FAMILY.
AND SHE ACTUALLY HAS A BRAIN.
EVERY-ONE HERE HAS MONEY.
WE CAN'T ALL GET ENGAGED TO RICH BOYS.
WHO TOLD YOU ABOUT THAT?
I'M SORRY YOU GOT CUT.
IT'S NOT LIKE IT'S JUST YOU.
YOU DON'T NEED THIS PLACE.

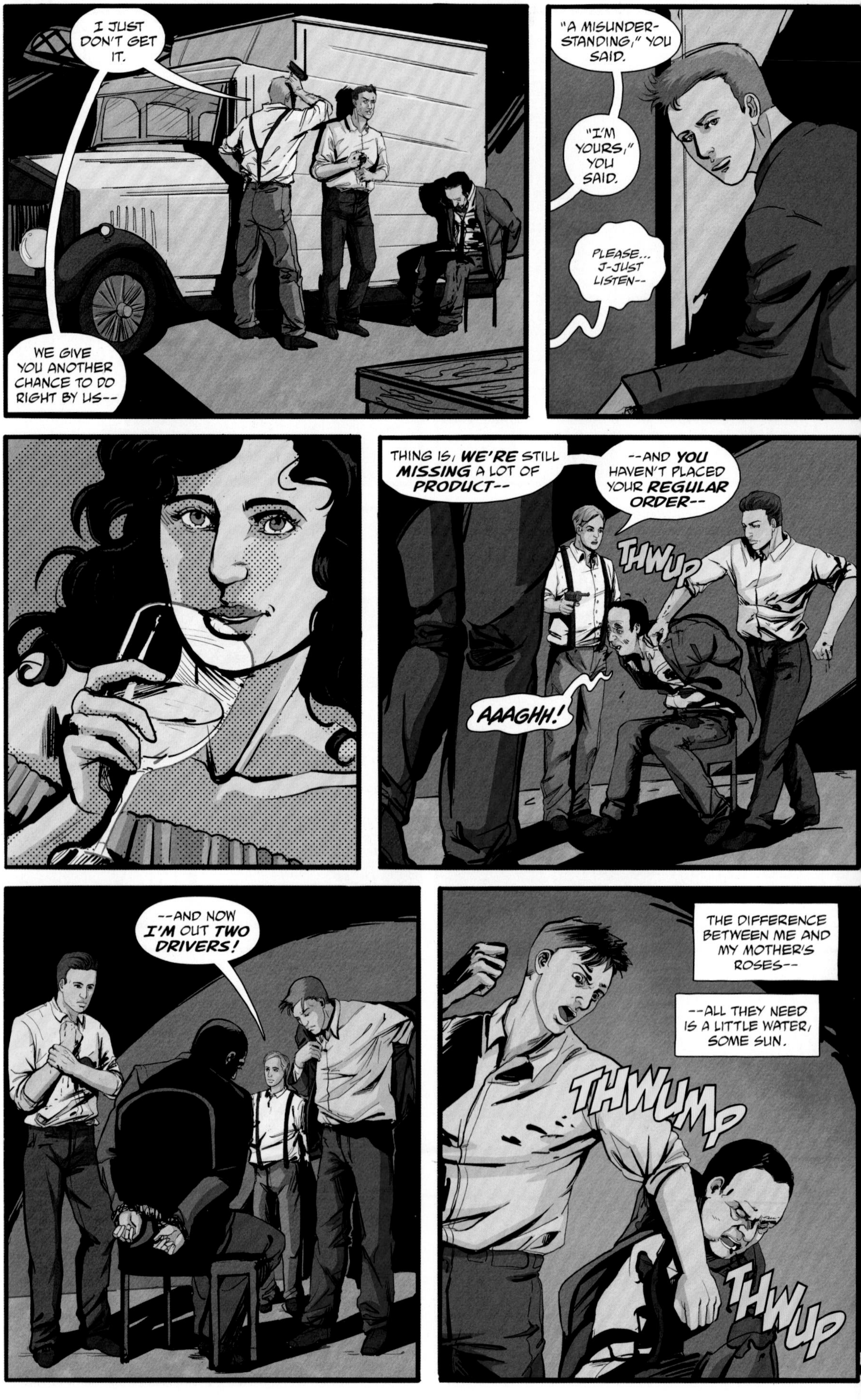
I JUST DON'T GET IT.
WE GIVE YOU ANOTHER CHANCE TO DO RIGHT BY US--
"A MISUNDER-STANDING," YOU SAID.
"I'M YOURS," YOU SAID.
PLEASE... J-JUST LISTEN--
THING IS, WE'RE STILL MISSING A LOT OF PRODUCT--
--AND YOU HAVEN'T PLACED YOUR REGULAR ORDER--
THWUP
AAAGHH!
--AND NOW I'M OUT TWO DRIVERS!
THE DIFFERENCE BETWEEN ME AND MY MOTHER'S ROSES--
--ALL THEY NEED IS A LITTLE WATER, SOME SUN.
THWUMP
THWUP

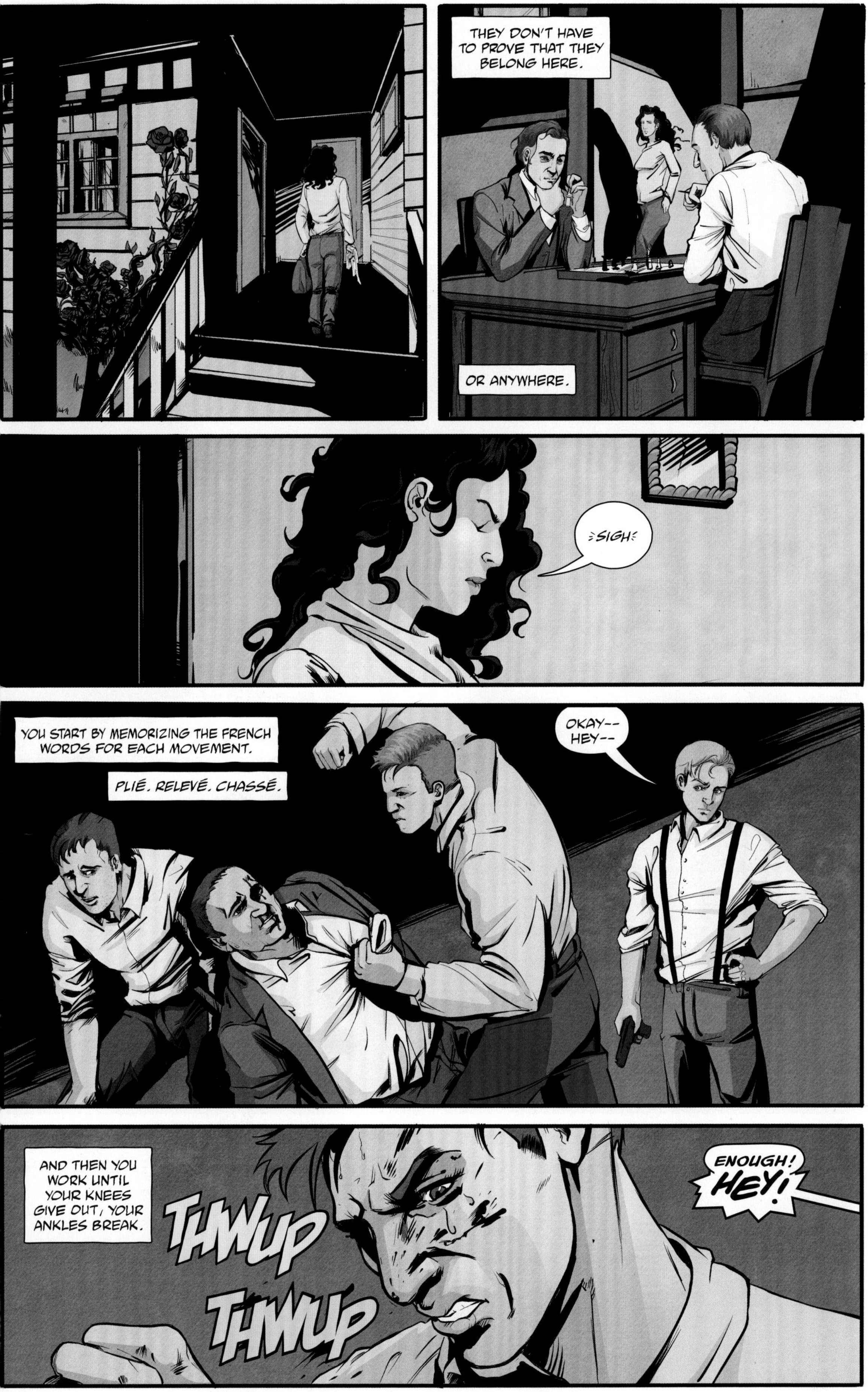
THEY DON'T HAVE TO PROVE THAT THEY BELONG HERE.
OR ANYWHERE.
SIGH
YOU START BY MEMORIZING THE FRENCH WORDS FOR EACH MOVEMENT.
PLIÉ. RELEVÉ. CHASSÉ.
OKAY-- HEY--
AND THEN YOU WORK UNTIL YOUR KNEES GIVE OUT, YOUR ANKLES BREAK.
THWUP
THWUP
ENOUGH! HEY!

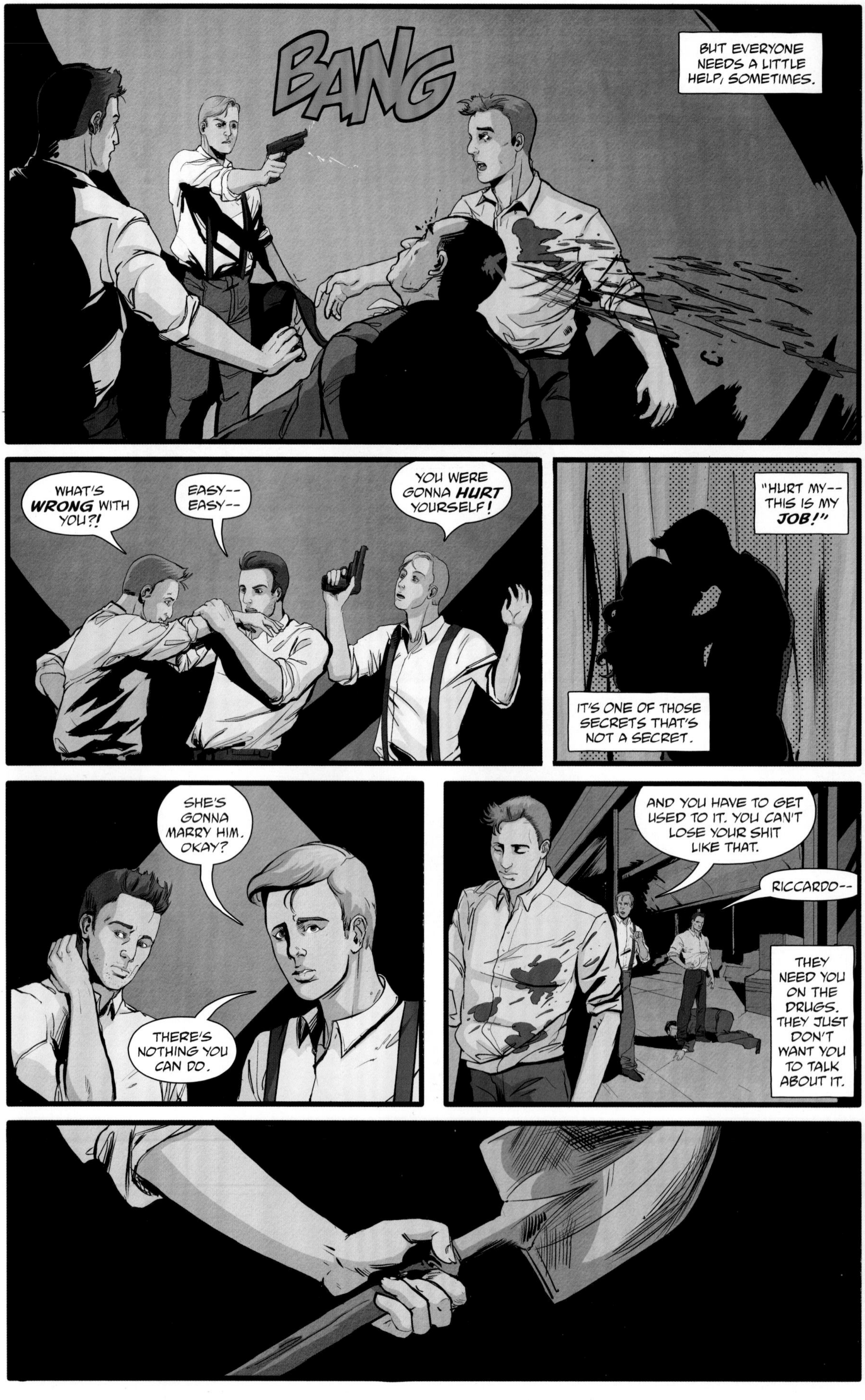
BANG
BUT EVERYONE NEEDS A LITTLE HELP, SOMETIMES.
WHAT'S **WRONG** WITH YOU?!
EASY-- EASY--
YOU WERE GONNA **HURT** YOURSELF!
"HURT MY-- THIS IS MY **JOB!**"
IT'S ONE OF THOSE SECRETS THAT'S NOT A SECRET.
SHE'S GONNA MARRY HIM. OKAY?
THERE'S NOTHING YOU CAN DO.
AND YOU HAVE TO GET USED TO IT. YOU CAN'T LOSE YOUR SHIT LIKE THAT.
RICCARDO--
THEY NEED YOU ON THE DRUGS. THEY JUST DON'T WANT YOU TO TALK ABOUT IT.

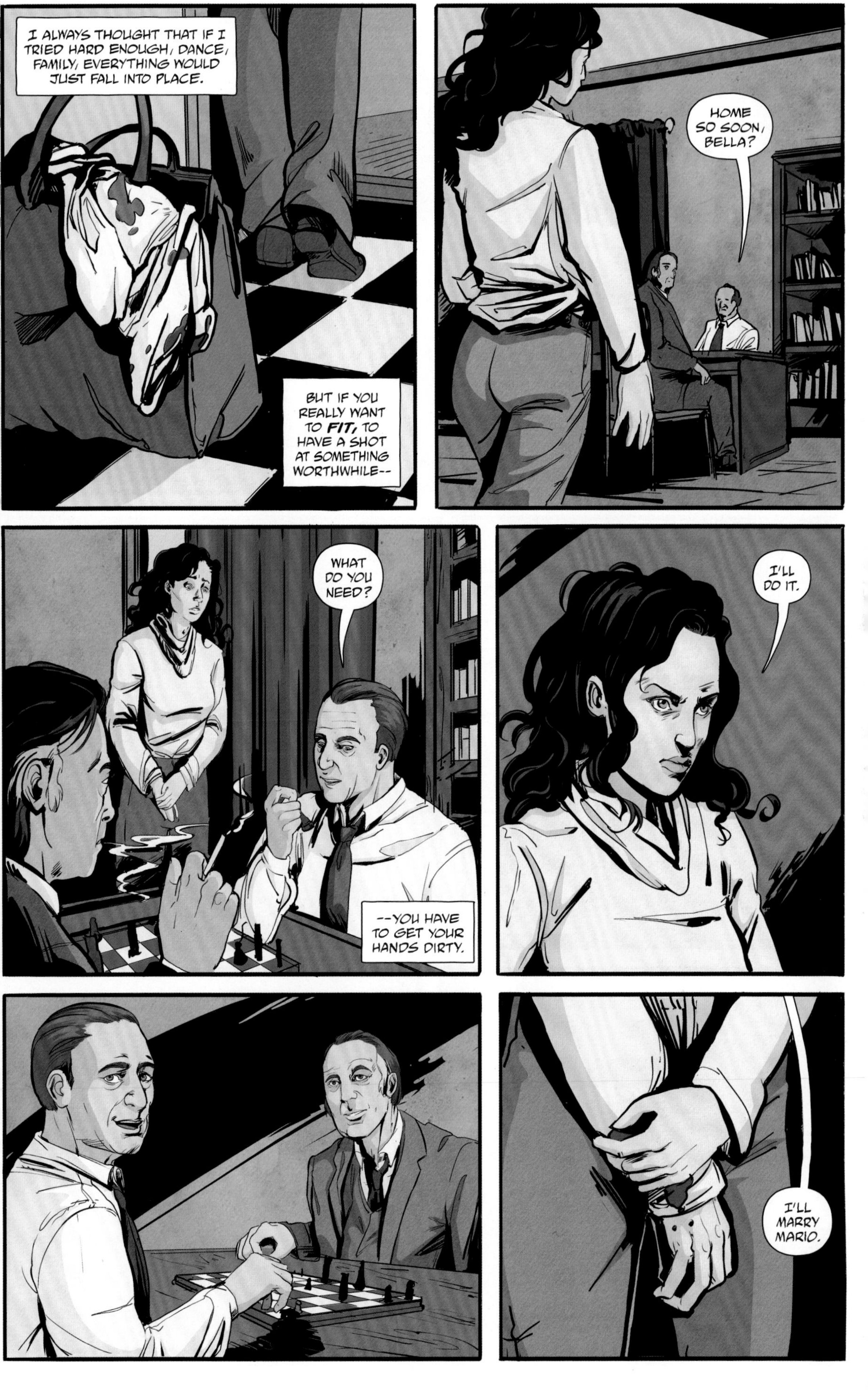
I ALWAYS THOUGHT THAT IF I TRIED HARD ENOUGH, DANCE, FAMILY, EVERYTHING WOULD JUST FALL INTO PLACE.
BUT IF YOU REALLY WANT TO FIT, TO HAVE A SHOT AT SOMETHING WORTHWHILE--
HOME SO SOON, BELLA?
WHAT DO YOU NEED?
--YOU HAVE TO GET YOUR HANDS DIRTY.
I'LL DO IT.
I'LL MARRY MARIO.

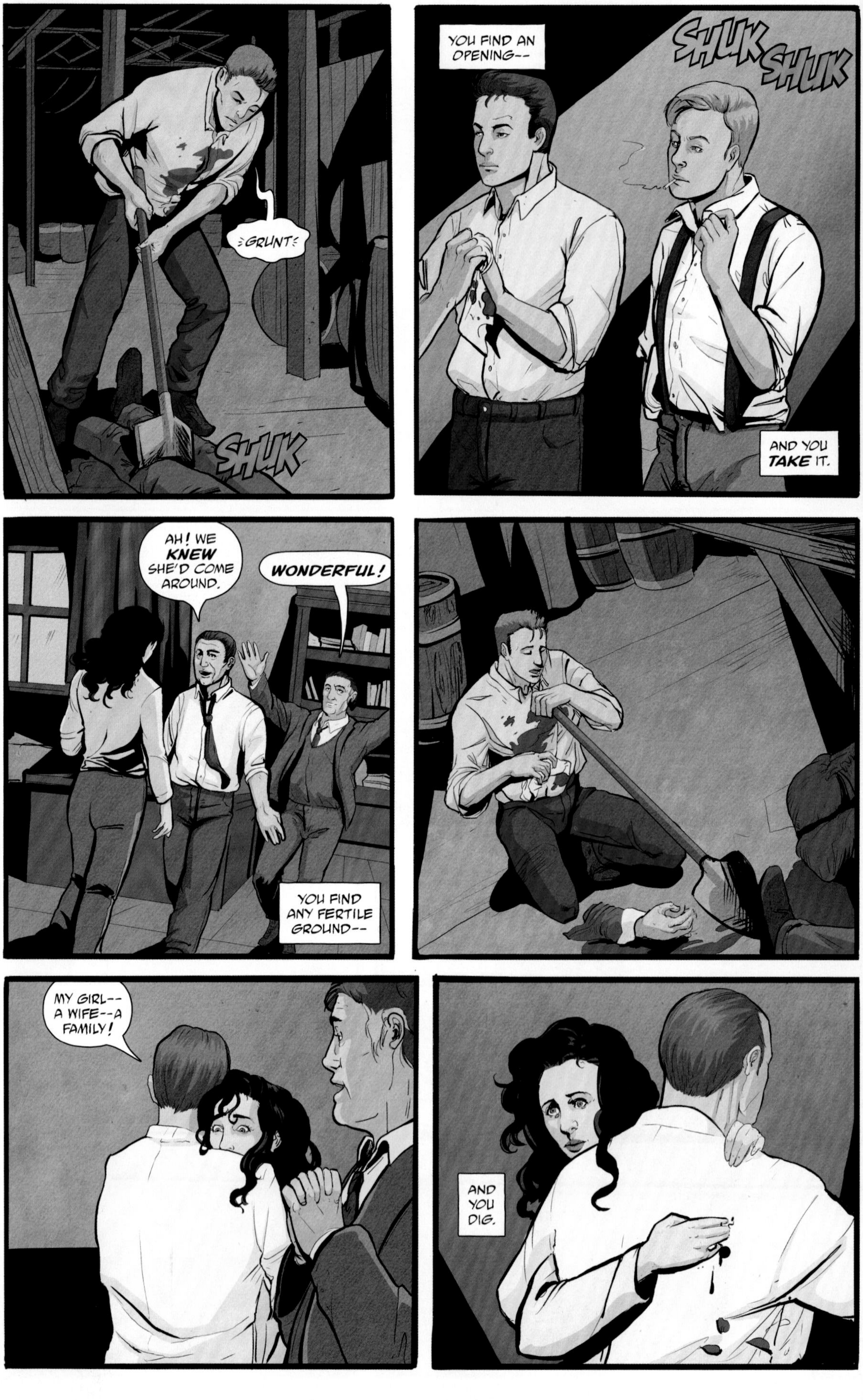
GRUNT
SHUK
YOU FIND AN OPENING--
SHUK SHUK
AND YOU TAKE IT.
AH! WE KNEW SHE'D COME AROUND.
WONDERFUL!
YOU FIND ANY FERTILE GROUND--
MY GIRL--A WIFE--A FAMILY!
AND YOU DIG.

CHAPTER
THREE

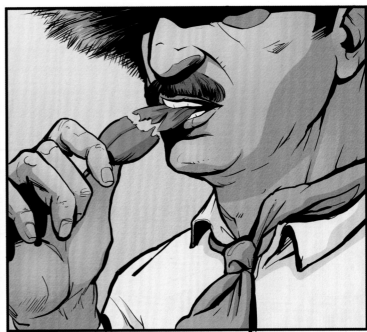

1853

PERU.

1900 AMERICA.

MIRACLE MAGICAL MIRACULOUS YOUTHFUL MARVELOUS RADIANT SPLENDID.

FOUNTAIN OF YOUTH

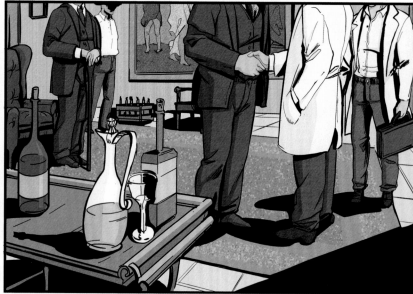

FOUNTAIN OF YOUTH

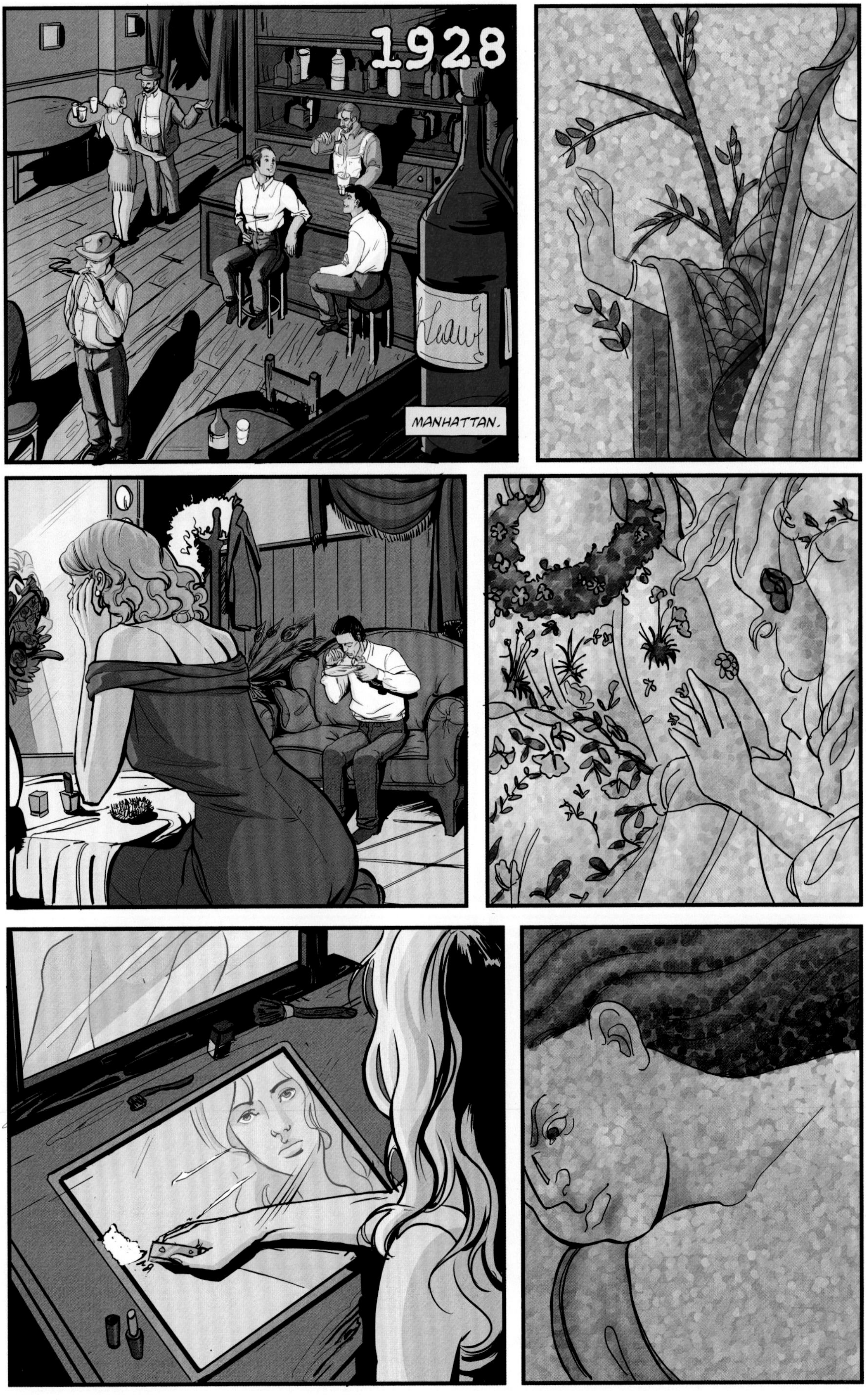
1928
MANHATTAN.

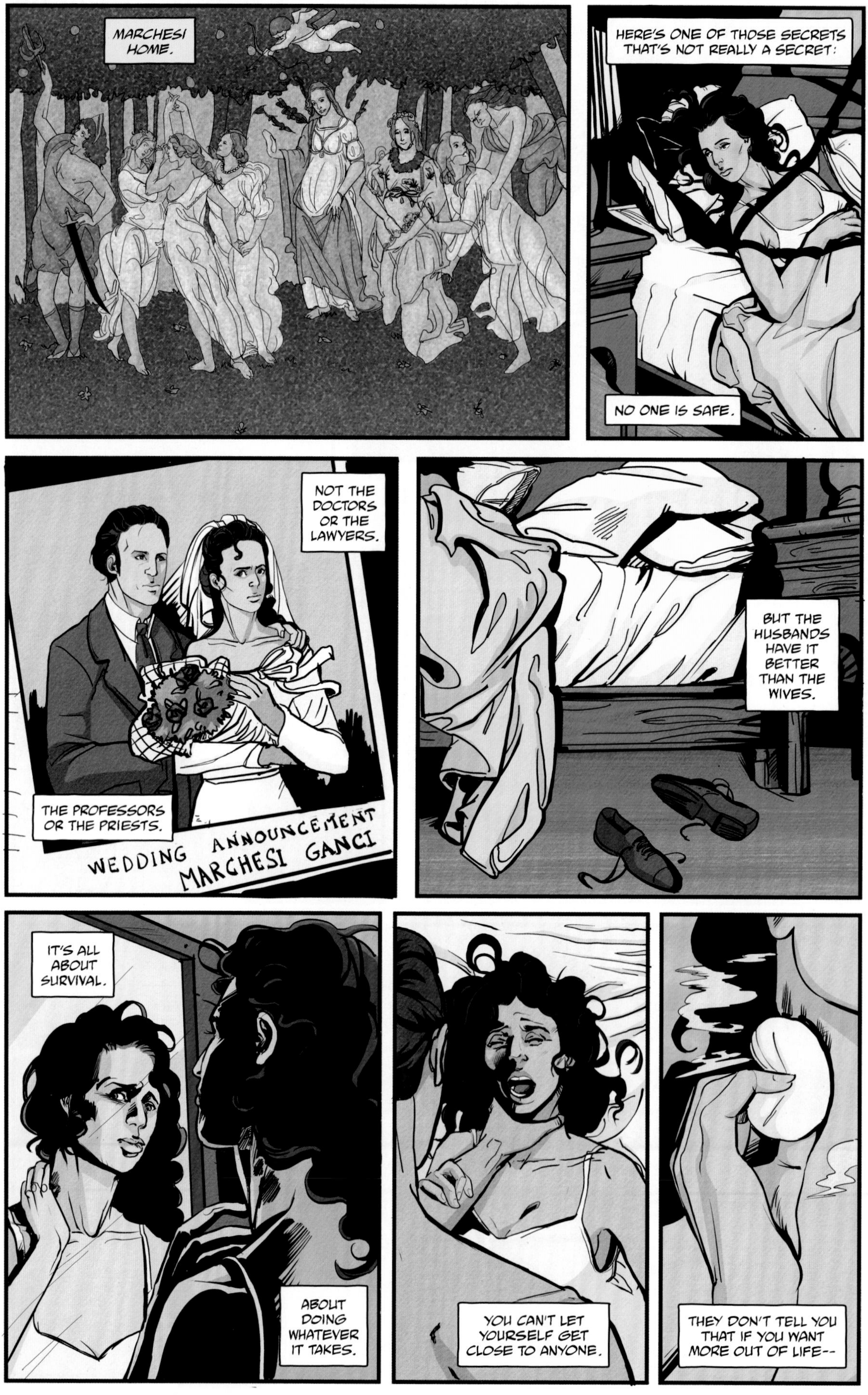
MARCHESI HOME.
HERE'S ONE OF THOSE SECRETS THAT'S NOT REALLY A SECRET:
NO ONE IS SAFE.
NOT THE DOCTORS OR THE LAWYERS.
THE PROFESSORS OR THE PRIESTS.
WEDDING ANNOUNCEMENT
MARCHESI GANCI
BUT THE HUSBANDS HAVE IT BETTER THAN THE WIVES.
IT'S ALL ABOUT SURVIVAL.
ABOUT DOING WHATEVER IT TAKES.
YOU CAN'T LET YOURSELF GET CLOSE TO ANYONE.
THEY DON'T TELL YOU THAT IF YOU WANT MORE OUT OF LIFE--

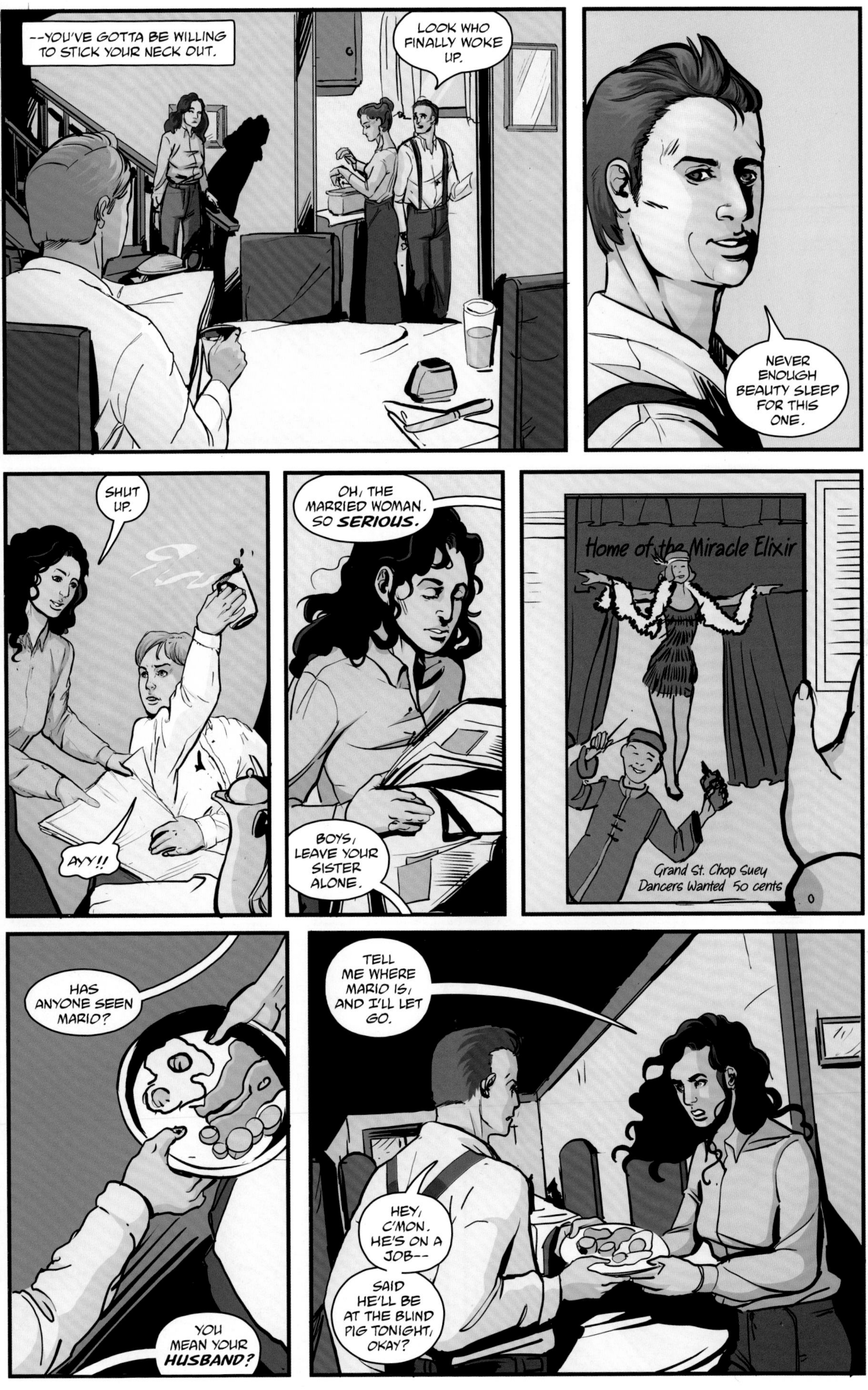
--YOU'VE GOTTA BE WILLING TO STICK YOUR NECK OUT.
LOOK WHO FINALLY WOKE UP.
NEVER ENOUGH BEAUTY SLEEP FOR THIS ONE.
SHUT UP.
AYY!!
OH, THE MARRIED WOMAN. SO **SERIOUS.**
BOYS, LEAVE YOUR SISTER ALONE.
Home of the Miracle Elixir
Grand St. Chop Suey
Dancers Wanted 50 cents
HAS ANYONE SEEN MARIO?
YOU MEAN YOUR **HUSBAND?**
TELL ME WHERE MARIO IS, AND I'LL LET GO.
HEY, C'MON. HE'S ON A JOB--
SAID HE'LL BE AT THE BLIND PIG TONIGHT, OKAY?

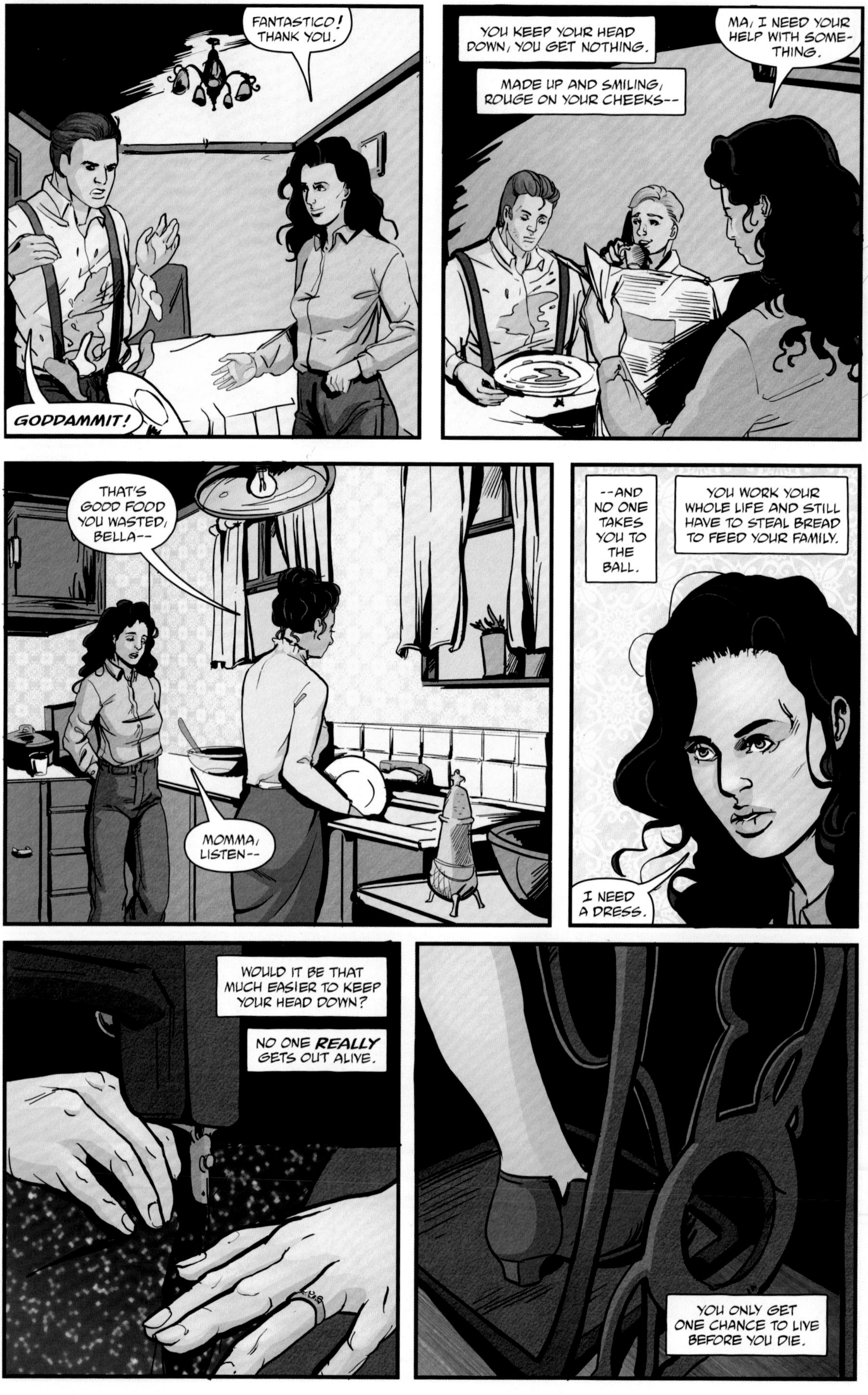

FANTASTICO! THANK YOU.
GODDAMMIT!
YOU KEEP YOUR HEAD DOWN, YOU GET NOTHING.
MA, I NEED YOUR HELP WITH SOME-THING.
MADE UP AND SMILING, ROUGE ON YOUR CHEEKS--
THAT'S GOOD FOOD YOU WASTED, BELLA--
MOMMA, LISTEN--
--AND NO ONE TAKES YOU TO THE BALL.
YOU WORK YOUR WHOLE LIFE AND STILL HAVE TO STEAL BREAD TO FEED YOUR FAMILY.
I NEED A DRESS.
WOULD IT BE THAT MUCH EASIER TO KEEP YOUR HEAD DOWN?
NO ONE **REALLY** GETS OUT ALIVE.
YOU ONLY GET ONE CHANCE TO LIVE BEFORE YOU DIE.

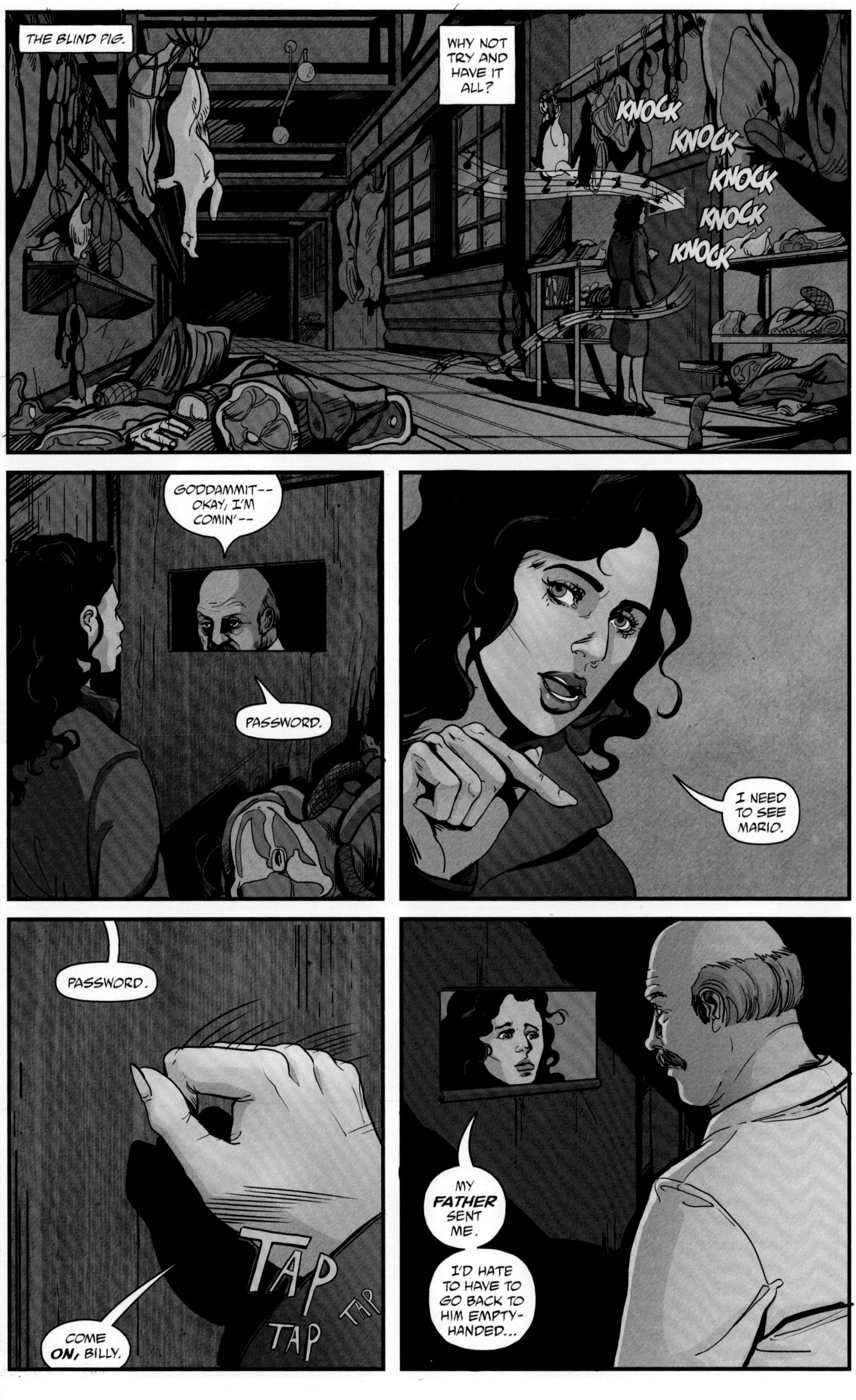
THE BLIND PIG.
WHY NOT TRY AND HAVE IT ALL?
KNOCK
KNOCK
KNOCK
KNOCK
KNOCK
GODDAMMIT-- OKAY, I'M COMIN'--
PASSWORD.
I NEED TO SEE MARIO.
PASSWORD.
TAP
TAP
TAP
COME ON, BILLY.
MY FATHER SENT ME.
I'D HATE TO HAVE TO GO BACK TO HIM EMPTY-HANDED...

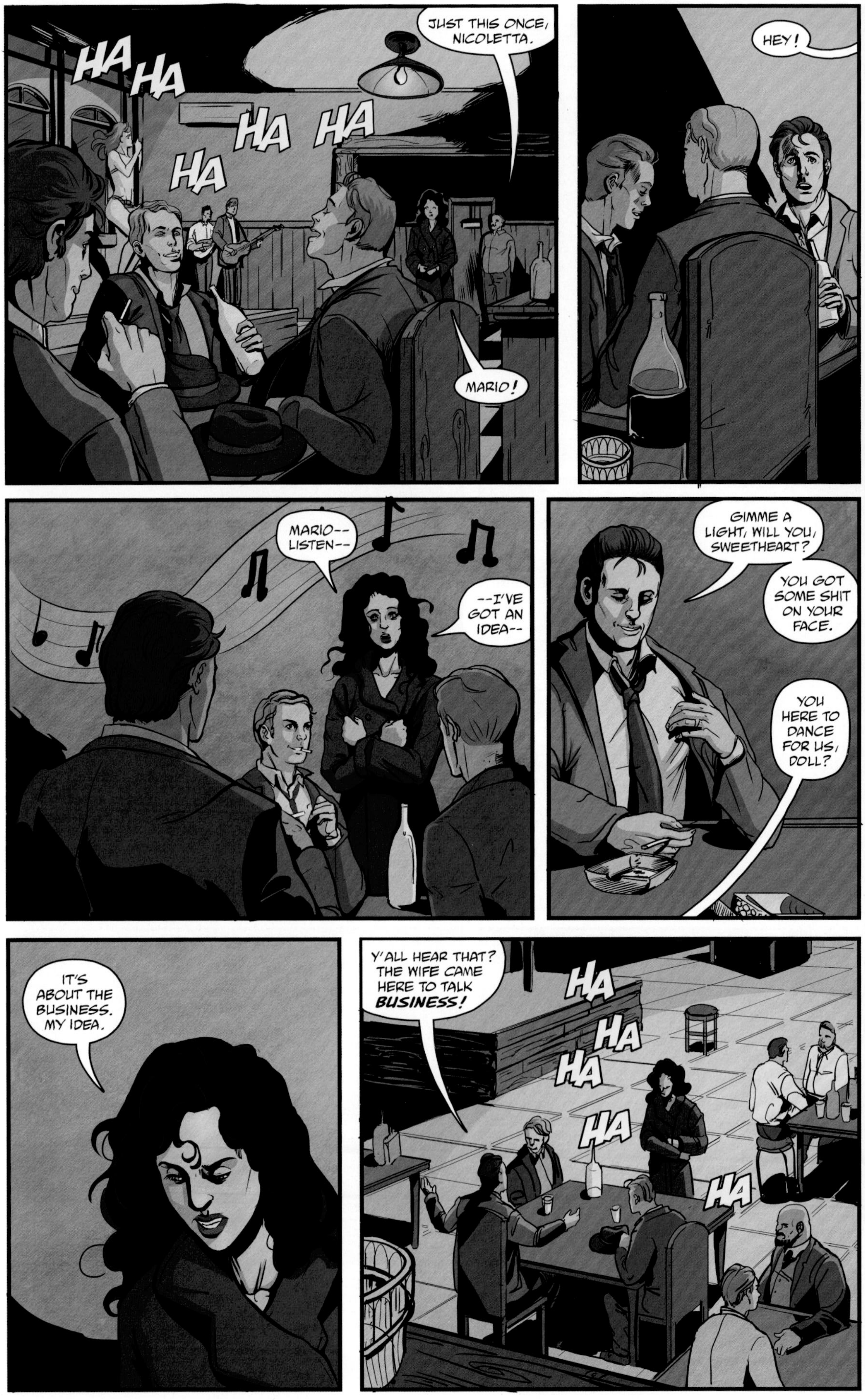
HA HA
JUST THIS ONCE, NICOLETTA.
HA HA HA
HA
MARIO!
HEY!
MARIO-- LISTEN--
--I'VE GOT AN IDEA--
GIMME A LIGHT, WILL YOU, SWEETHEART?
YOU GOT SOME SHIT ON YOUR FACE.
YOU HERE TO DANCE FOR US, DOLL?
IT'S ABOUT THE BUSINESS. MY IDEA.
Y'ALL HEAR THAT? THE WIFE CAME HERE TO TALK BUSINESS!
HA
HA
HA
HA
HA

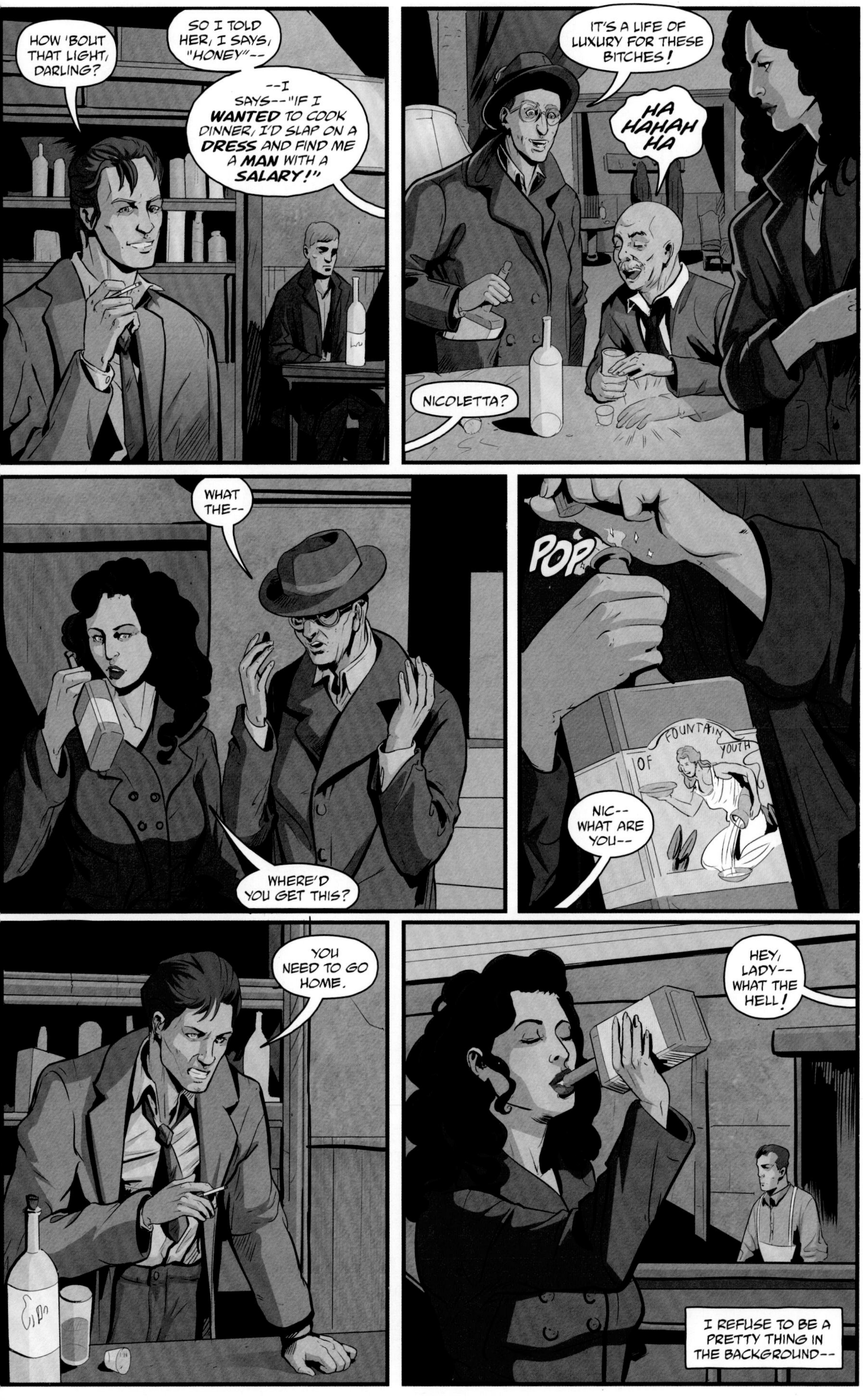
HOW 'BOUT THAT LIGHT, DARLING?
SO I TOLD HER, I SAYS, "HONEY"--
--I SAYS--"IF I WANTED TO COOK DINNER, I'D SLAP ON A DRESS AND FIND ME A MAN WITH A SALARY!"
IT'S A LIFE OF LUXURY FOR THESE BITCHES!
HA HAHAH HA
NICOLETTA?
WHAT THE--
WHERE'D YOU GET THIS?
POP
FOUNTAIN OF YOUTH
NIC-- WHAT ARE YOU--
YOU NEED TO GO HOME.
HEY, LADY-- WHAT THE HELL!
I REFUSE TO BE A PRETTY THING IN THE BACKGROUND--

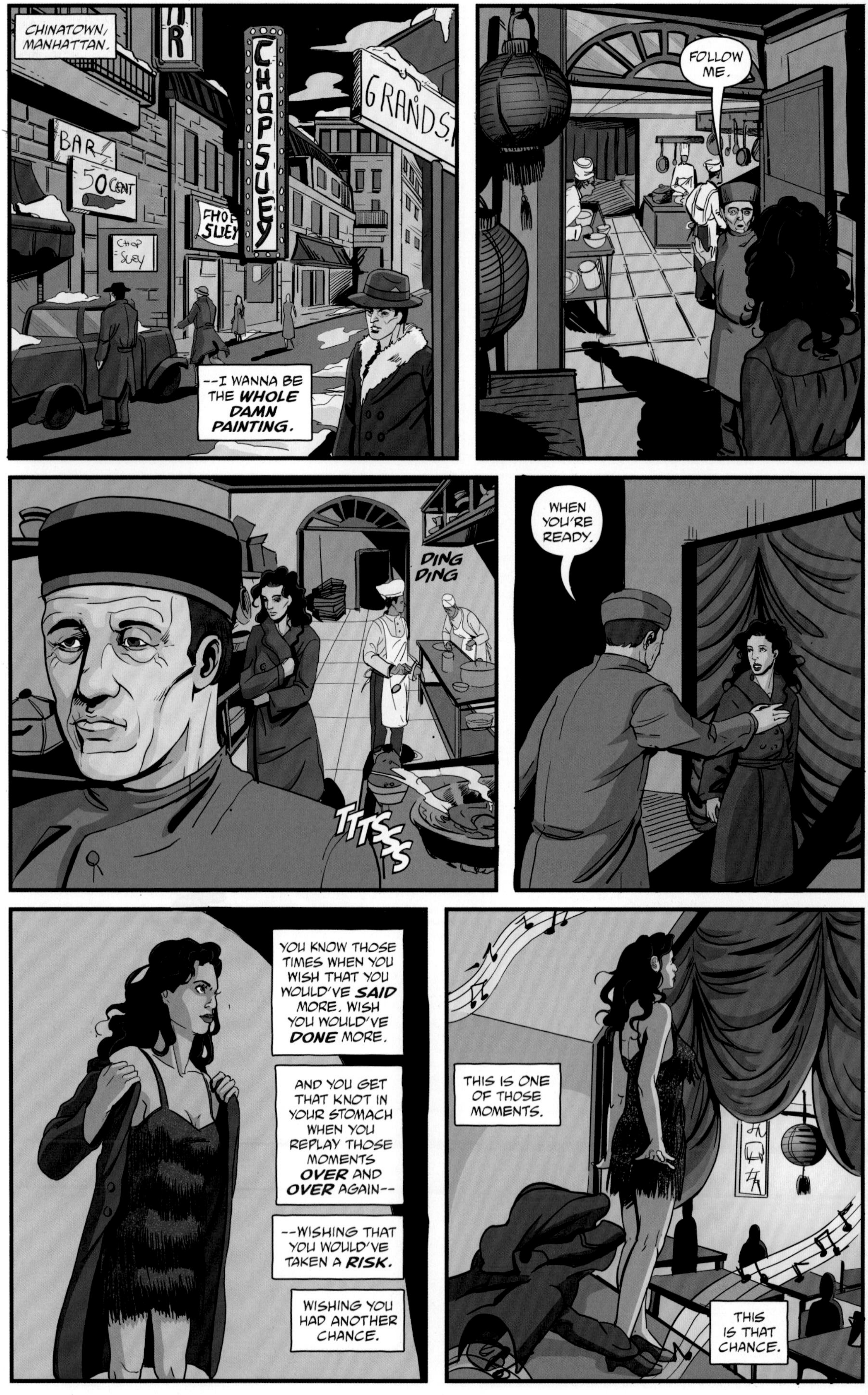
CHINATOWN, MANHATTAN.
BAR
50 CENT
CHOP SUEY
CHOP SUEY
GRAND ST.
--I WANNA BE THE WHOLE DAMN PAINTING.
FOLLOW ME.
DING DING
TTTSSS
WHEN YOU'RE READY.
YOU KNOW THOSE TIMES WHEN YOU WISH THAT YOU WOULD'VE SAID MORE. WISH YOU WOULD'VE DONE MORE.
AND YOU GET THAT KNOT IN YOUR STOMACH WHEN YOU REPLAY THOSE MOMENTS OVER AND OVER AGAIN--
--WISHING THAT YOU WOULD'VE TAKEN A RISK.
WISHING YOU HAD ANOTHER CHANCE.
THIS IS ONE OF THOSE MOMENTS.
THIS IS THAT CHANCE.

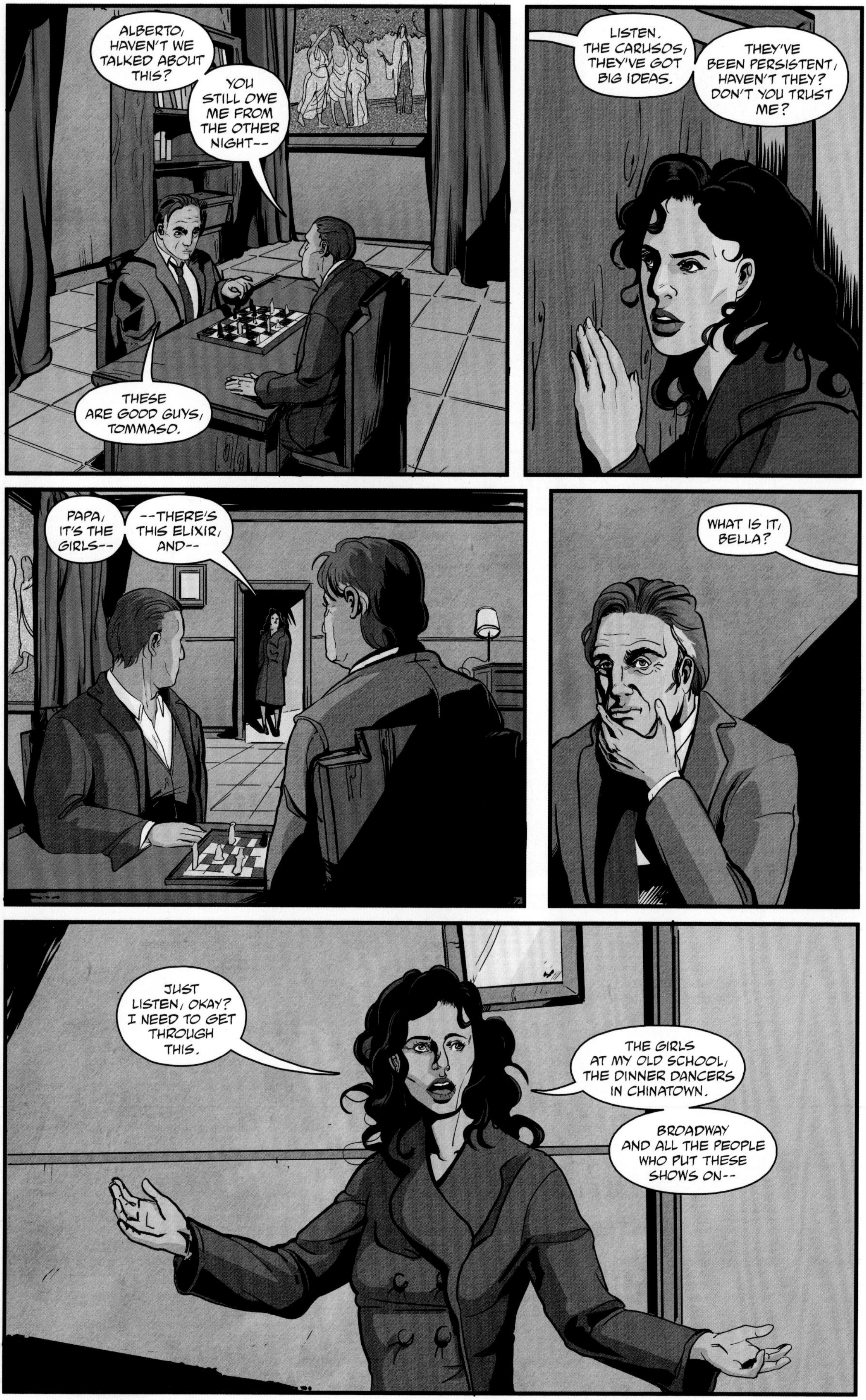
ALBERTO, HAVEN'T WE TALKED ABOUT THIS?
YOU STILL OWE ME FROM THE OTHER NIGHT--
THESE ARE GOOD GUYS, TOMMASO.
LISTEN. THE CARUSOS, THEY'VE GOT BIG IDEAS.
THEY'VE BEEN PERSISTENT, HAVEN'T THEY? DON'T YOU TRUST ME?
PAPA, IT'S THE GIRLS--
--THERE'S THIS ELIXIR, AND--
WHAT IS IT, BELLA?
JUST LISTEN, OKAY? I NEED TO GET THROUGH THIS.
THE GIRLS AT MY OLD SCHOOL, THE DINNER DANCERS IN CHINATOWN.
BROADWAY AND ALL THE PEOPLE WHO PUT THESE SHOWS ON--

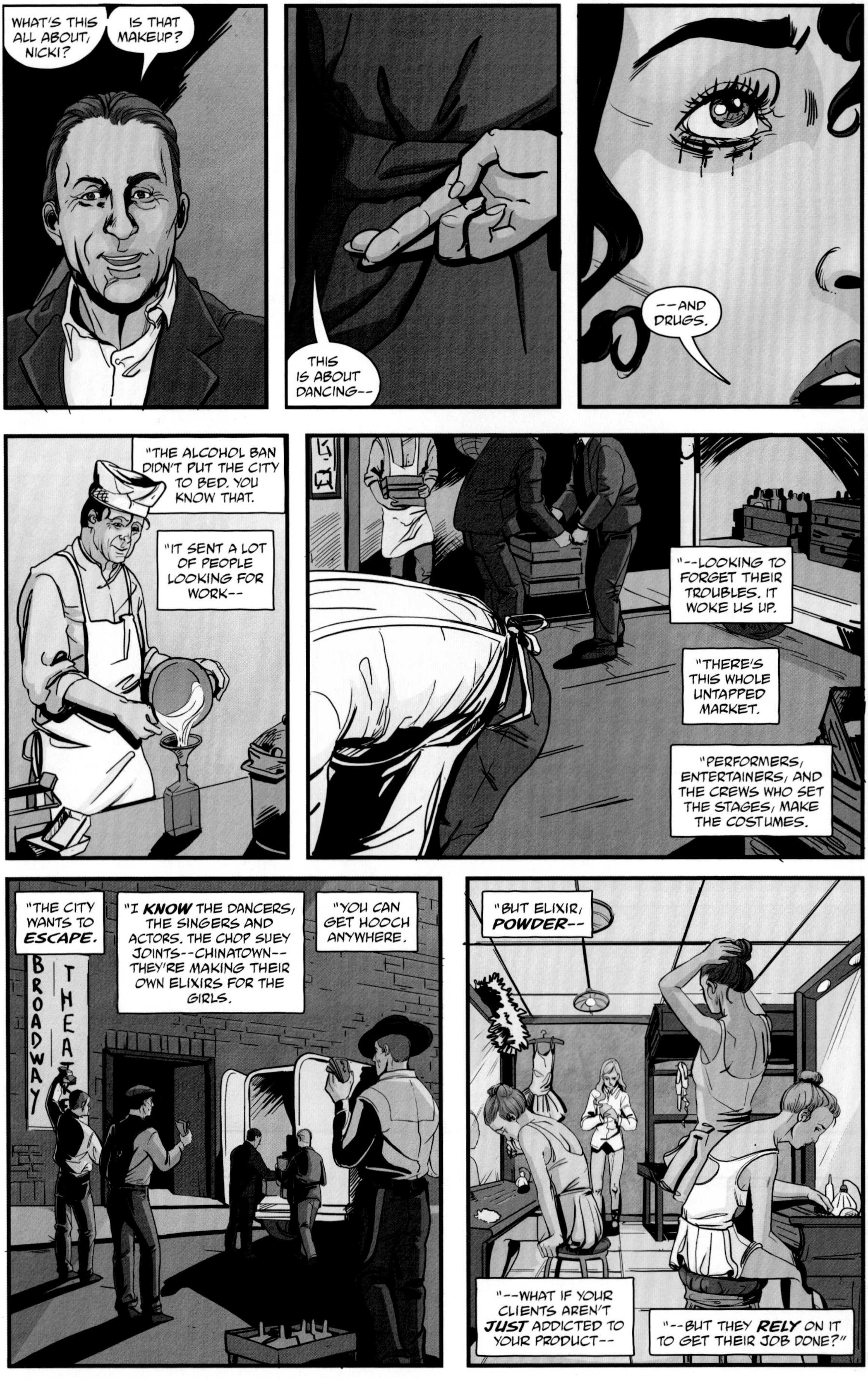

WHAT'S THIS ALL ABOUT, NICKI?
IS THAT MAKEUP?
THIS IS ABOUT DANCING--
--AND DRUGS.
"THE ALCOHOL BAN DIDN'T PUT THE CITY TO BED. YOU KNOW THAT.
"IT SENT A LOT OF PEOPLE LOOKING FOR WORK--
"--LOOKING TO FORGET THEIR TROUBLES. IT WOKE US UP.
"THERE'S THIS WHOLE UNTAPPED MARKET.
"PERFORMERS, ENTERTAINERS, AND THE CREWS WHO SET THE STAGES, MAKE THE COSTUMES.
"THE CITY WANTS TO **ESCAPE.**
"I **KNOW** THE DANCERS, THE SINGERS AND ACTORS. THE CHOP SUEY JOINTS--CHINATOWN--THEY'RE MAKING THEIR OWN ELIXIRS FOR THE GIRLS.
"YOU CAN GET HOOCH ANYWHERE.
BROADWAY
THEAT
"BUT ELIXIR, **POWDER**--
"--WHAT IF YOUR CLIENTS AREN'T **JUST** ADDICTED TO YOUR PRODUCT--
"--BUT THEY **RELY** ON IT TO GET THEIR JOB DONE?"

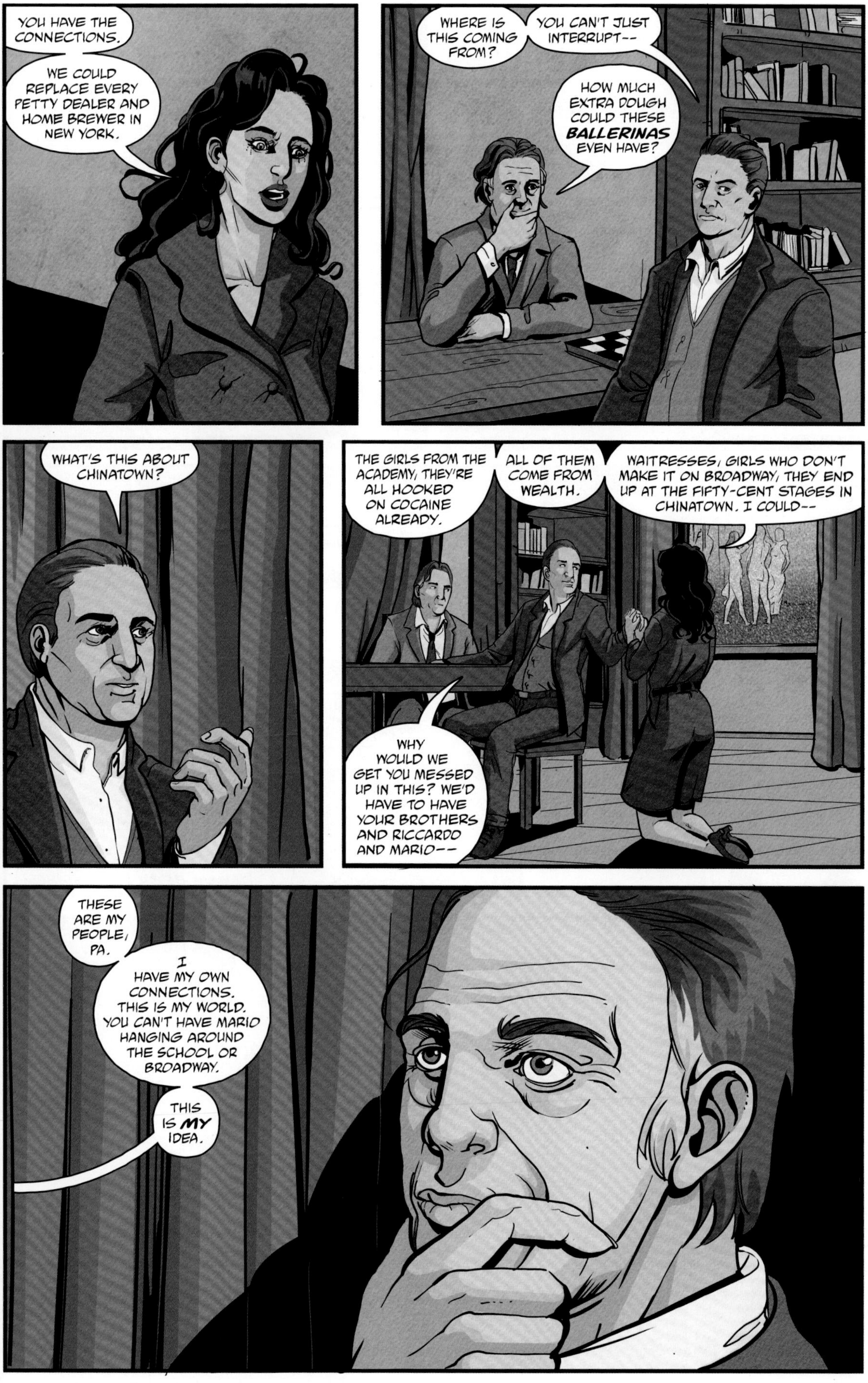
YOU HAVE THE CONNECTIONS.
WE COULD REPLACE EVERY PETTY DEALER AND HOME BREWER IN NEW YORK.
WHERE IS THIS COMING FROM?
YOU CAN'T JUST INTERRUPT--
HOW MUCH EXTRA DOUGH COULD THESE **BALLERINAS** EVEN HAVE?
WHAT'S THIS ABOUT CHINATOWN?
THE GIRLS FROM THE ACADEMY, THEY'RE ALL HOOKED ON COCAINE ALREADY.
ALL OF THEM COME FROM WEALTH.
WAITRESSES, GIRLS WHO DON'T MAKE IT ON BROADWAY, THEY END UP AT THE FIFTY-CENT STAGES IN CHINATOWN. I COULD--
WHY WOULD WE GET YOU MESSED UP IN THIS? WE'D HAVE TO HAVE YOUR BROTHERS AND RICCARDO AND MARIO--
THESE ARE MY PEOPLE, PA.
I HAVE MY OWN CONNECTIONS. THIS IS MY WORLD. YOU CAN'T HAVE MARIO HANGING AROUND THE SCHOOL OR BROADWAY.
THIS IS **MY** IDEA.

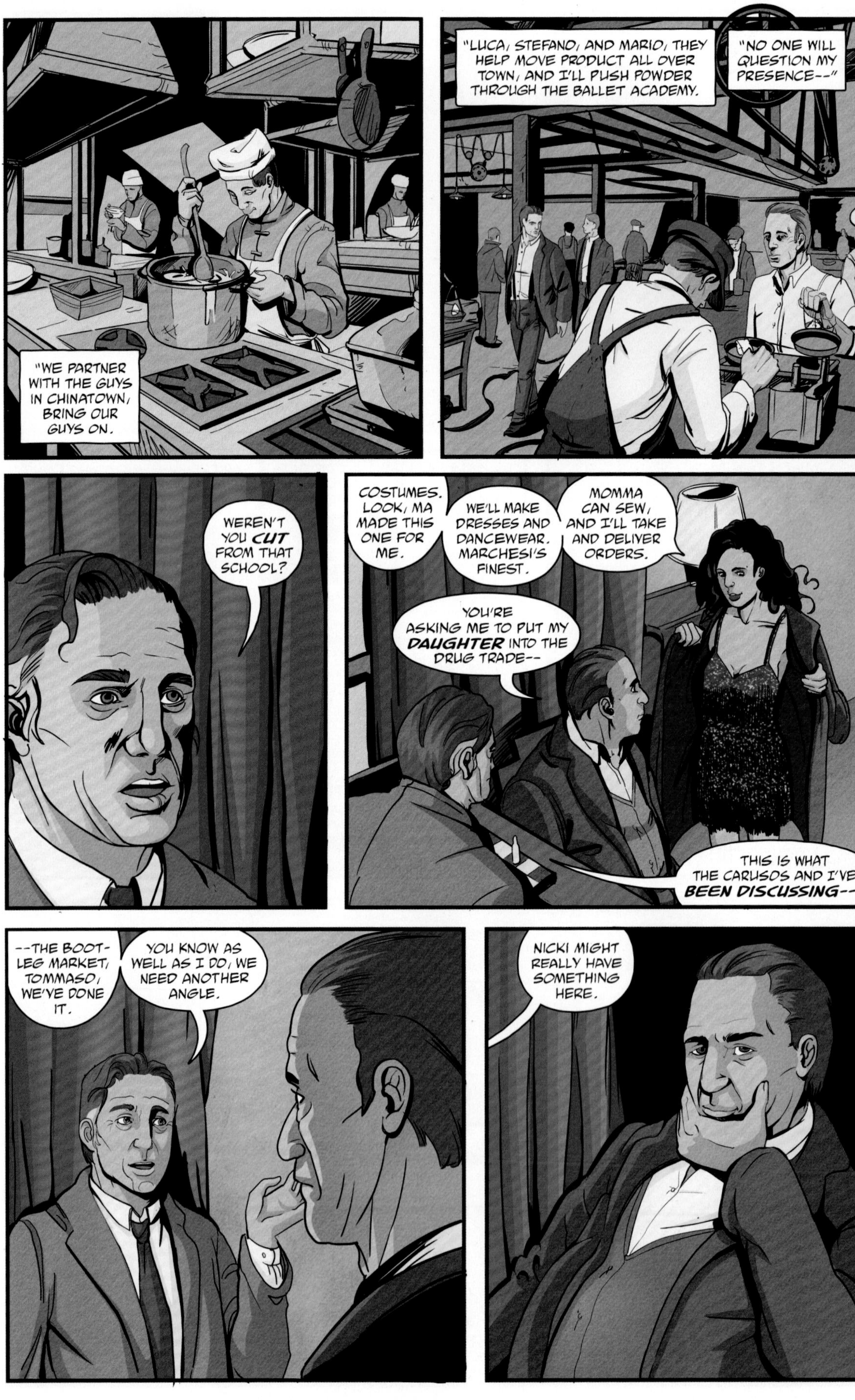
"WE PARTNER WITH THE GUYS IN CHINATOWN, BRING OUR GUYS ON.
"LUCA, STEFANO, AND MARIO, THEY HELP MOVE PRODUCT ALL OVER TOWN, AND I'LL PUSH POWDER THROUGH THE BALLET ACADEMY.
"NO ONE WILL QUESTION MY PRESENCE--"
WEREN'T YOU **CUT** FROM THAT SCHOOL?
COSTUMES. LOOK, MA MADE THIS ONE FOR ME.
WE'LL MAKE DRESSES AND DANCEWEAR. MARCHESI'S FINEST.
MOMMA CAN SEW, AND I'LL TAKE AND DELIVER ORDERS.
YOU'RE ASKING ME TO PUT MY **DAUGHTER** INTO THE DRUG TRADE--
THIS IS WHAT THE CARUSOS AND I'VE **BEEN DISCUSSING**--
--THE BOOTLEG MARKET, TOMMASO, WE'VE DONE IT.
YOU KNOW AS WELL AS I DO, WE NEED ANOTHER ANGLE.
NICKI MIGHT REALLY HAVE SOMETHING HERE.

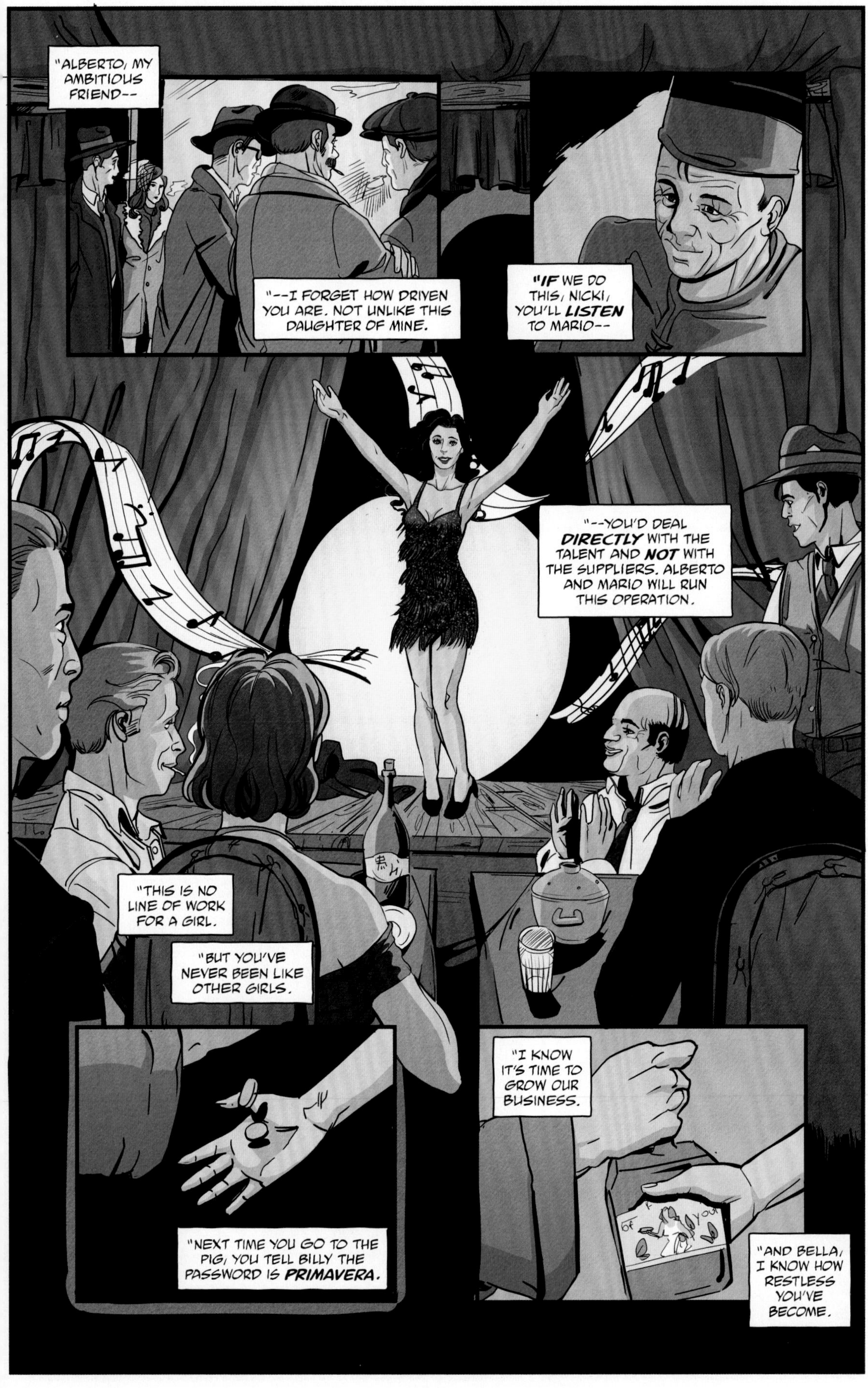
"ALBERTO, MY AMBITIOUS FRIEND--
"--I FORGET HOW DRIVEN YOU ARE. NOT UNLIKE THIS DAUGHTER OF MINE.
"IF WE DO THIS, NICKI, YOU'LL LISTEN TO MARIO--
"--YOU'D DEAL DIRECTLY WITH THE TALENT AND NOT WITH THE SUPPLIERS. ALBERTO AND MARIO WILL RUN THIS OPERATION.
"THIS IS NO LINE OF WORK FOR A GIRL.
"BUT YOU'VE NEVER BEEN LIKE OTHER GIRLS.
"NEXT TIME YOU GO TO THE PIG, YOU TELL BILLY THE PASSWORD IS PRIMAVERA.
"I KNOW IT'S TIME TO GROW OUR BUSINESS.
"AND BELLA, I KNOW HOW RESTLESS YOU'VE BECOME.

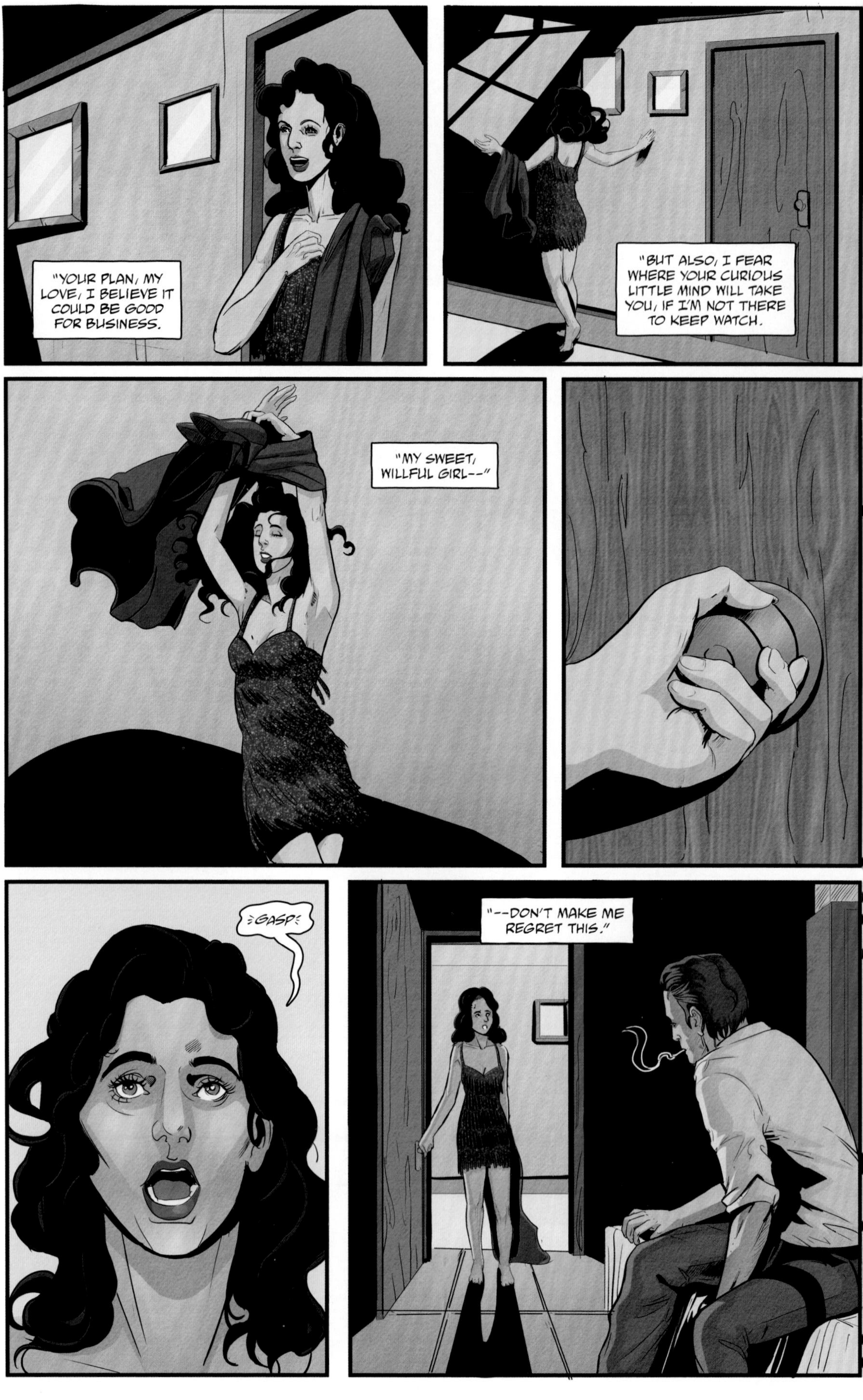
"YOUR PLAN, MY LOVE, I BELIEVE IT COULD BE GOOD FOR BUSINESS.
"BUT ALSO, I FEAR WHERE YOUR CURIOUS LITTLE MIND WILL TAKE YOU, IF I'M NOT THERE TO KEEP WATCH.
"MY SWEET, WILLFUL GIRL--"
GASP
"--DON'T MAKE ME REGRET THIS."

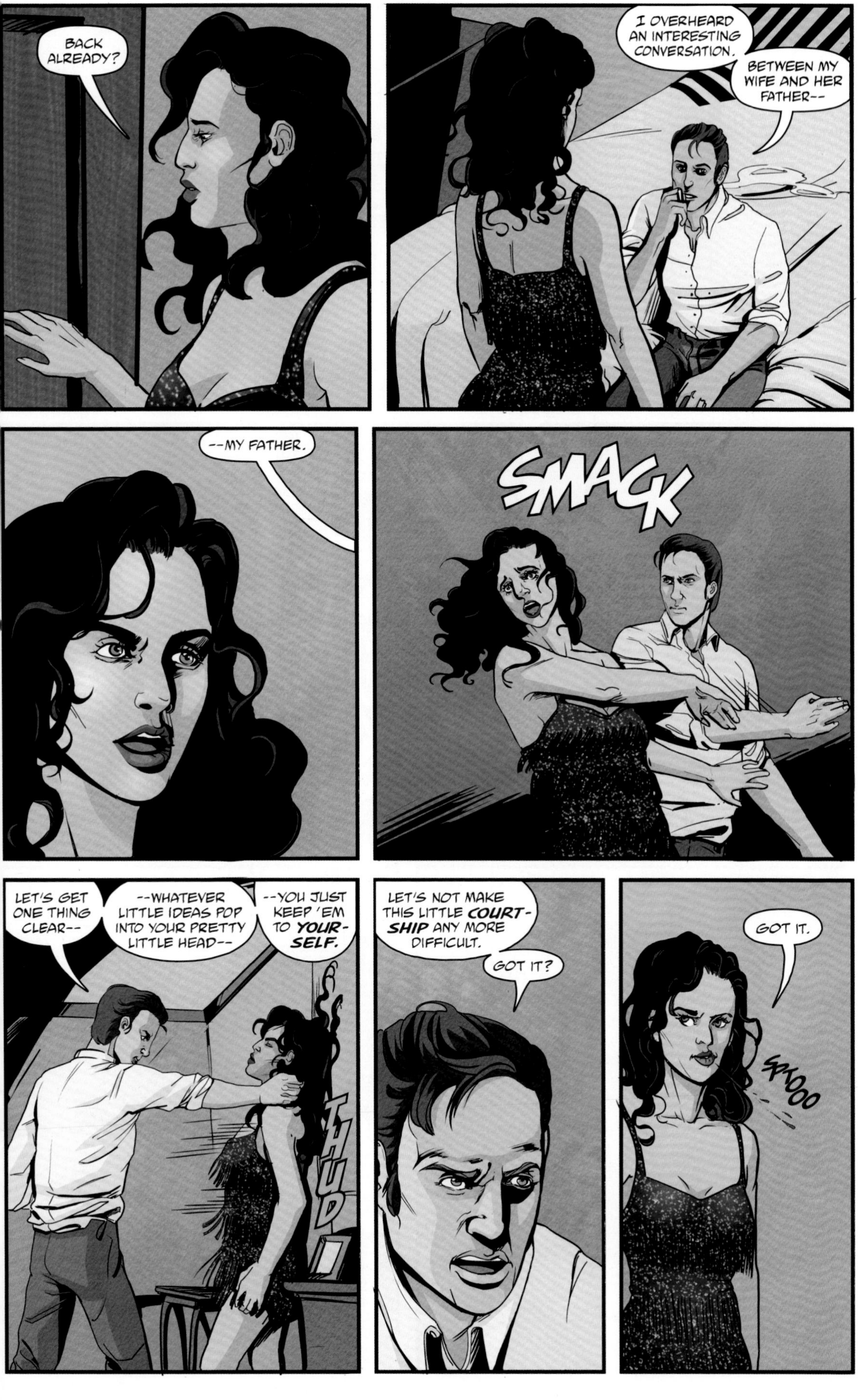
BACK ALREADY?
I OVERHEARD AN INTERESTING CONVERSATION.
BETWEEN MY WIFE AND HER FATHER--
--MY FATHER.
SMACK
LET'S GET ONE THING CLEAR--
--WHATEVER LITTLE IDEAS POP INTO YOUR PRETTY LITTLE HEAD--
--YOU JUST KEEP 'EM TO YOURSELF.
THUD
LET'S NOT MAKE THIS LITTLE COURTSHIP ANY MORE DIFFICULT.
GOT IT?
GOT IT.
SPTOOO

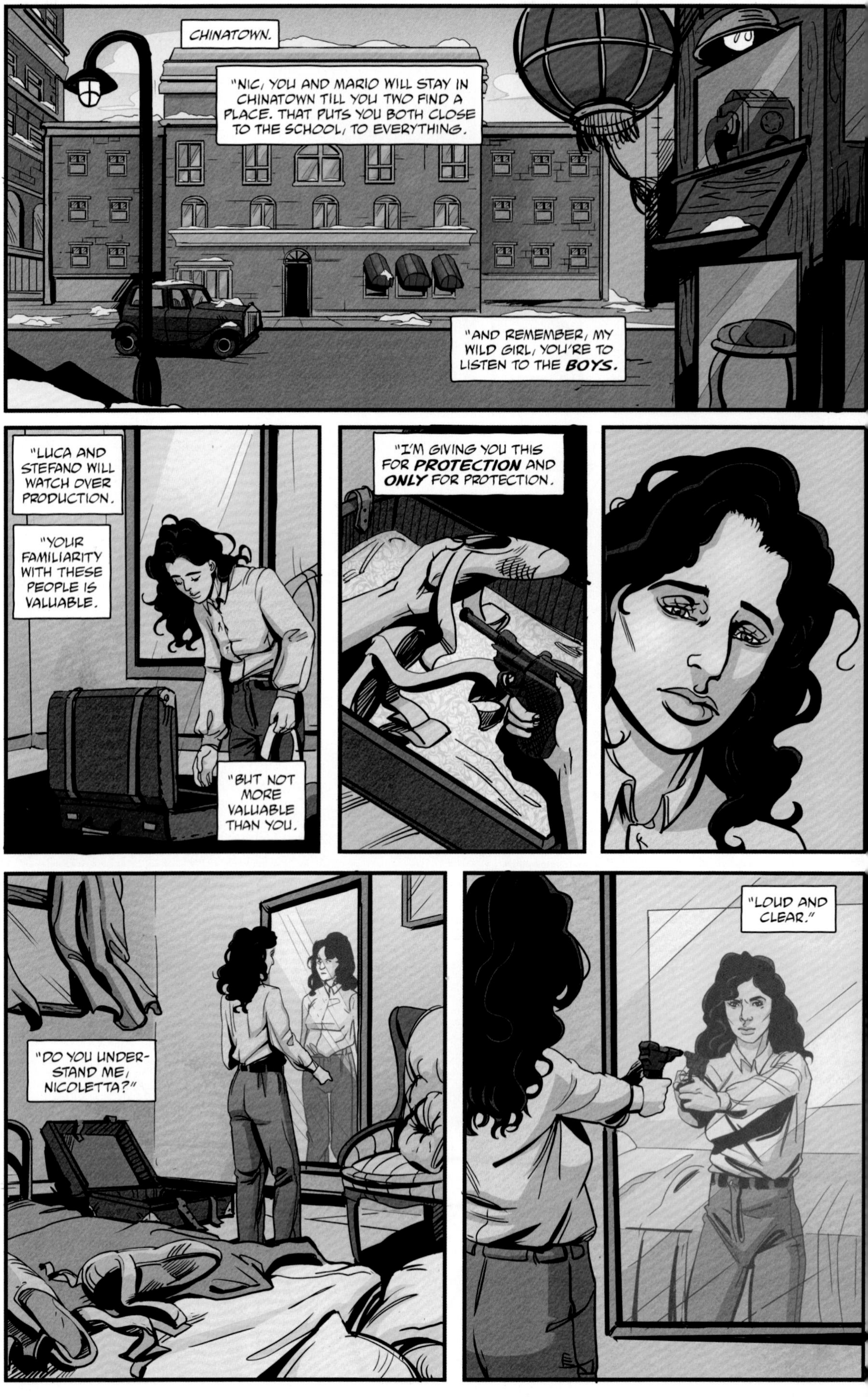
CHINATOWN.
"NIC, YOU AND MARIO WILL STAY IN CHINATOWN TILL YOU TWO FIND A PLACE. THAT PUTS YOU BOTH CLOSE TO THE SCHOOL, TO EVERYTHING.
"AND REMEMBER, MY WILD GIRL, YOU'RE TO LISTEN TO THE BOYS.
"LUCA AND STEFANO WILL WATCH OVER PRODUCTION.
"YOUR FAMILIARITY WITH THESE PEOPLE IS VALUABLE.
"BUT NOT MORE VALUABLE THAN YOU.
"I'M GIVING YOU THIS FOR PROTECTION AND ONLY FOR PROTECTION.
"DO YOU UNDERSTAND ME, NICOLETTA?"
"LOUD AND CLEAR."

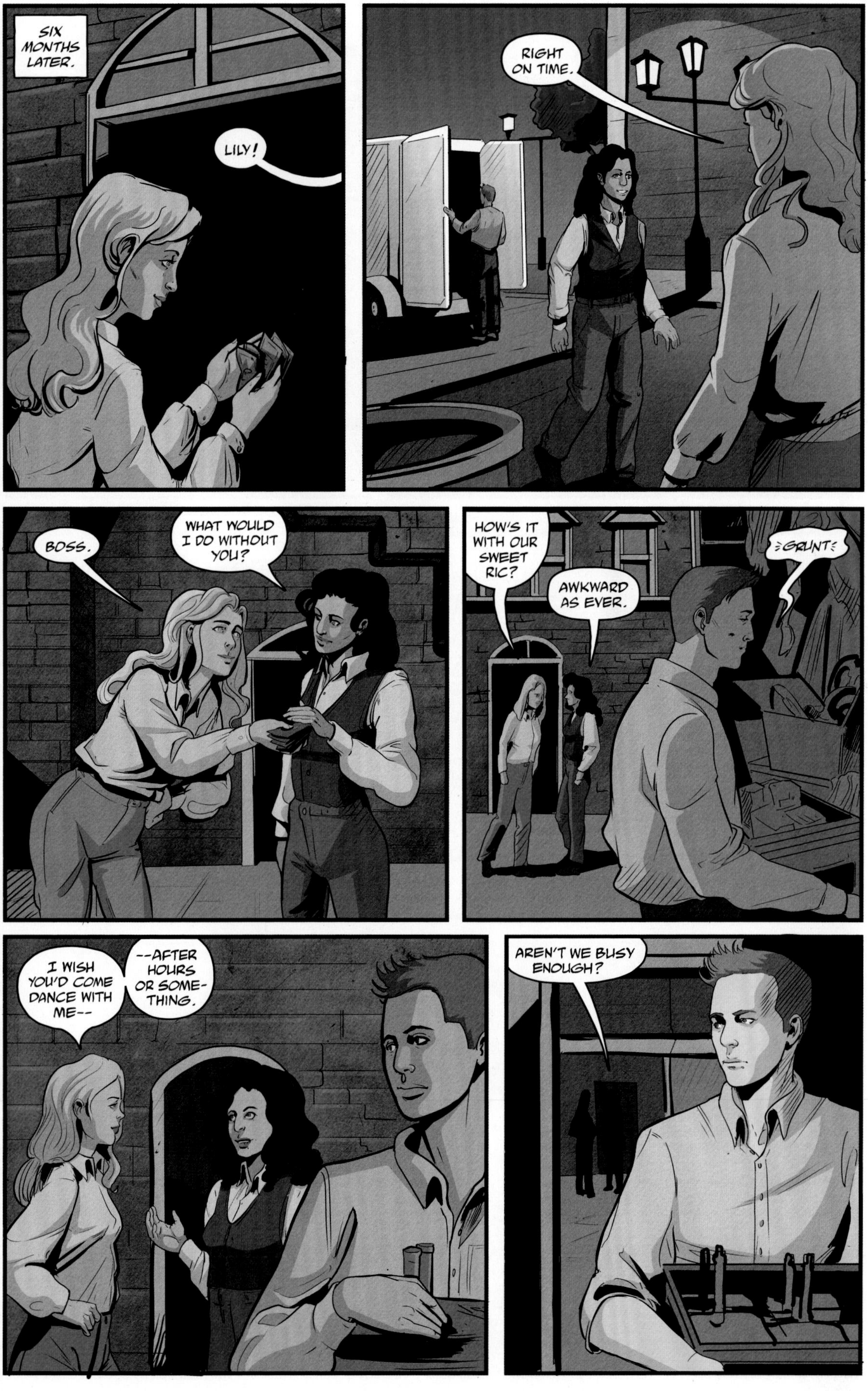
SIX MONTHS LATER.
LILY!
RIGHT ON TIME.
BOSS.
WHAT WOULD I DO WITHOUT YOU?
HOW'S IT WITH OUR SWEET RIC?
AWKWARD AS EVER.
GRUNT
I WISH YOU'D COME DANCE WITH ME--
--AFTER HOURS OR SOME-THING.
AREN'T WE BUSY ENOUGH?

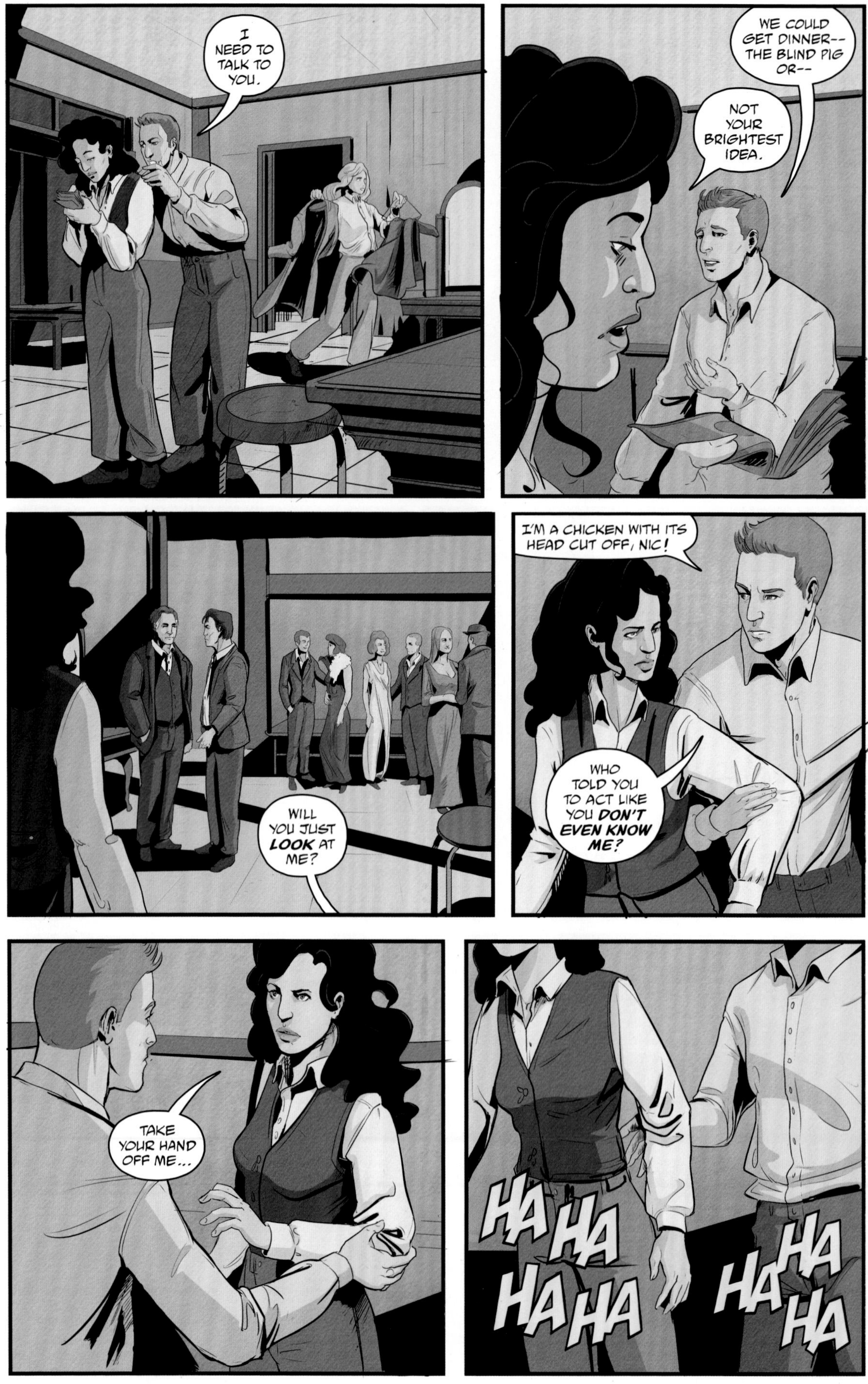

I NEED TO TALK TO YOU.
WE COULD GET DINNER-- THE BLIND PIG OR--
NOT YOUR BRIGHTEST IDEA.
WILL YOU JUST LOOK AT ME?
I'M A CHICKEN WITH ITS HEAD CUT OFF, NIC!
WHO TOLD YOU TO ACT LIKE YOU DON'T EVEN KNOW ME?
TAKE YOUR HAND OFF ME...
HA HA HA HA HA
HA HA HA HA

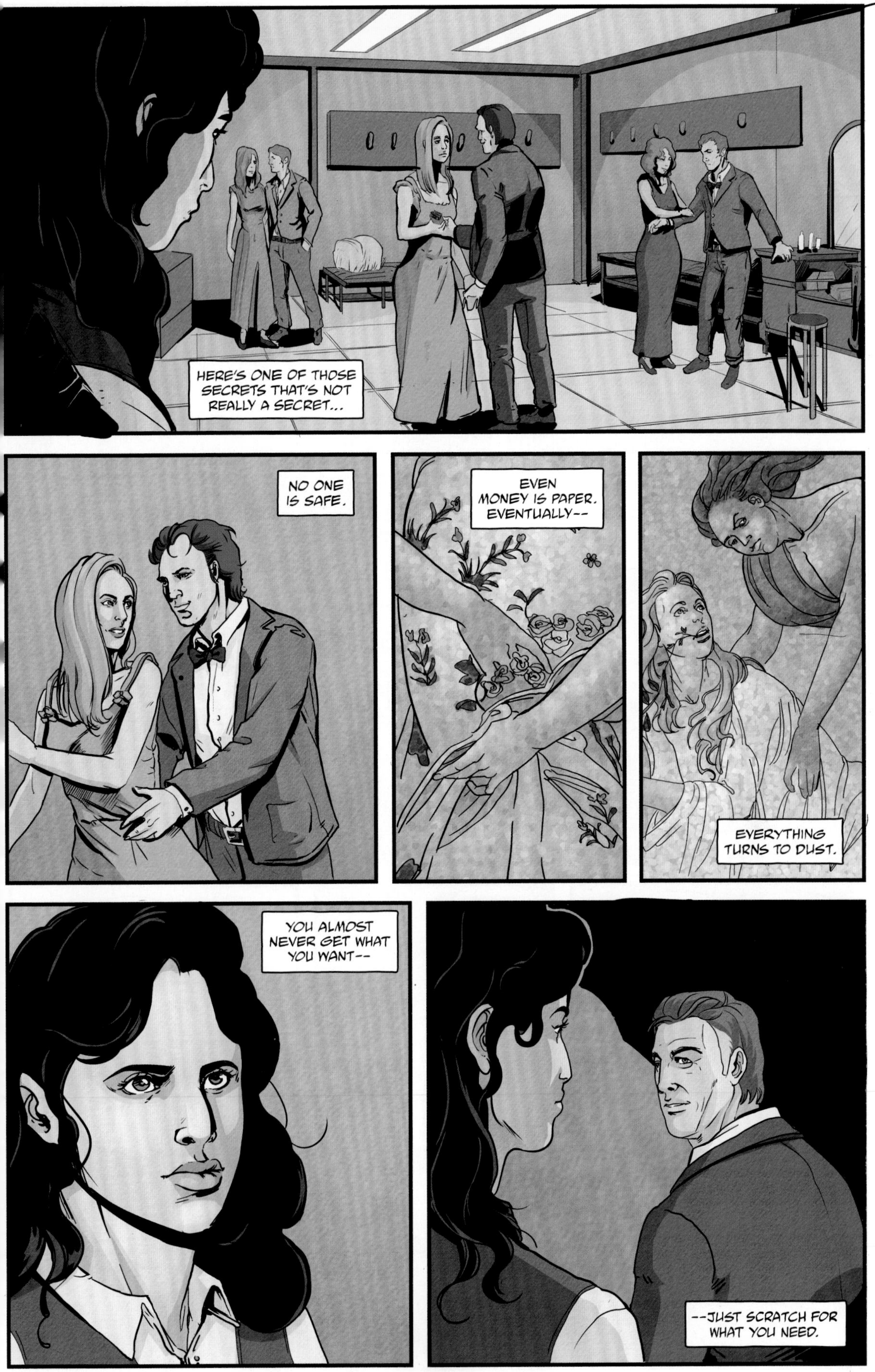
HERE'S ONE OF THOSE SECRETS THAT'S NOT REALLY A SECRET...
NO ONE IS SAFE.
EVEN MONEY IS PAPER. EVENTUALLY--
EVERYTHING TURNS TO DUST.
YOU ALMOST NEVER GET WHAT YOU WANT--
--JUST SCRATCH FOR WHAT YOU NEED.

YOU'VE GOTTA BE WILLING TO STICK YOUR NECK OUT.

MY FATHER KNOW ABOUT YOUR LATE-NIGHT VISITS TO CLIENTS?

ALL BUSINESS IS GOOD BUSINESS, LOVELY.

YOUR FATHER JUST ISN'T AS *AMBITIOUS* AS HE SHOULD BE.

AND WHAT HE DOESN'T KNOW CAN'T KILL HIM.

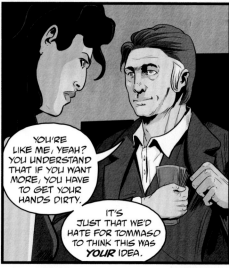

YOU'RE LIKE ME, YEAH? YOU UNDERSTAND THAT IF YOU WANT MORE, YOU HAVE TO GET YOUR HANDS DIRTY.

IT'S JUST THAT WE'D HATE FOR TOMMASO TO THINK THIS WAS *YOUR* IDEA.

THESE ARE *YOUR* GIRLS, AFTER ALL.

I'M SURE WE CAN WORK SOMETHING OUT, NIC.

IN THE MEANTIME, WE'LL JUST CUT YOU IN.

COST OF DOING BUSINESS, RIGHT?

RIGHT.

CHAPTER
FOUR

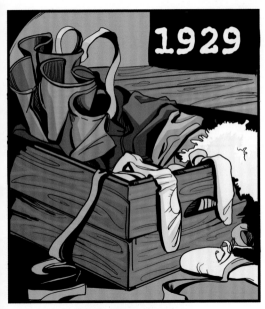

1929

MARCHESI HOME.

SO NO ONE TELLS ME ANYTHING ANYMORE?

THIS WAS *MY* IDEA. *MINE.* WE'VE NEVER WORKED WITH THESE CARUSOS BEFORE--

"*NOTHING* YOU DO IS SEPARATE FROM THIS FAMILY! YOU DON'T EXIST IN THIS WORLD WITHOUT *MY* SAY.

"IF ALBERTO TRUSTS THESE GUYS--"

--THEN WE DO. *YOU* DO.

"OKAY. FINE, SURE.

"BUT JUST SO YOU KNOW, I'VE GOT THE MADAME BREATHING DOWN MY NECK ABOUT HER GIRLS.

"THEY'RE NOT SHOWING UP FOR REHEARSALS."

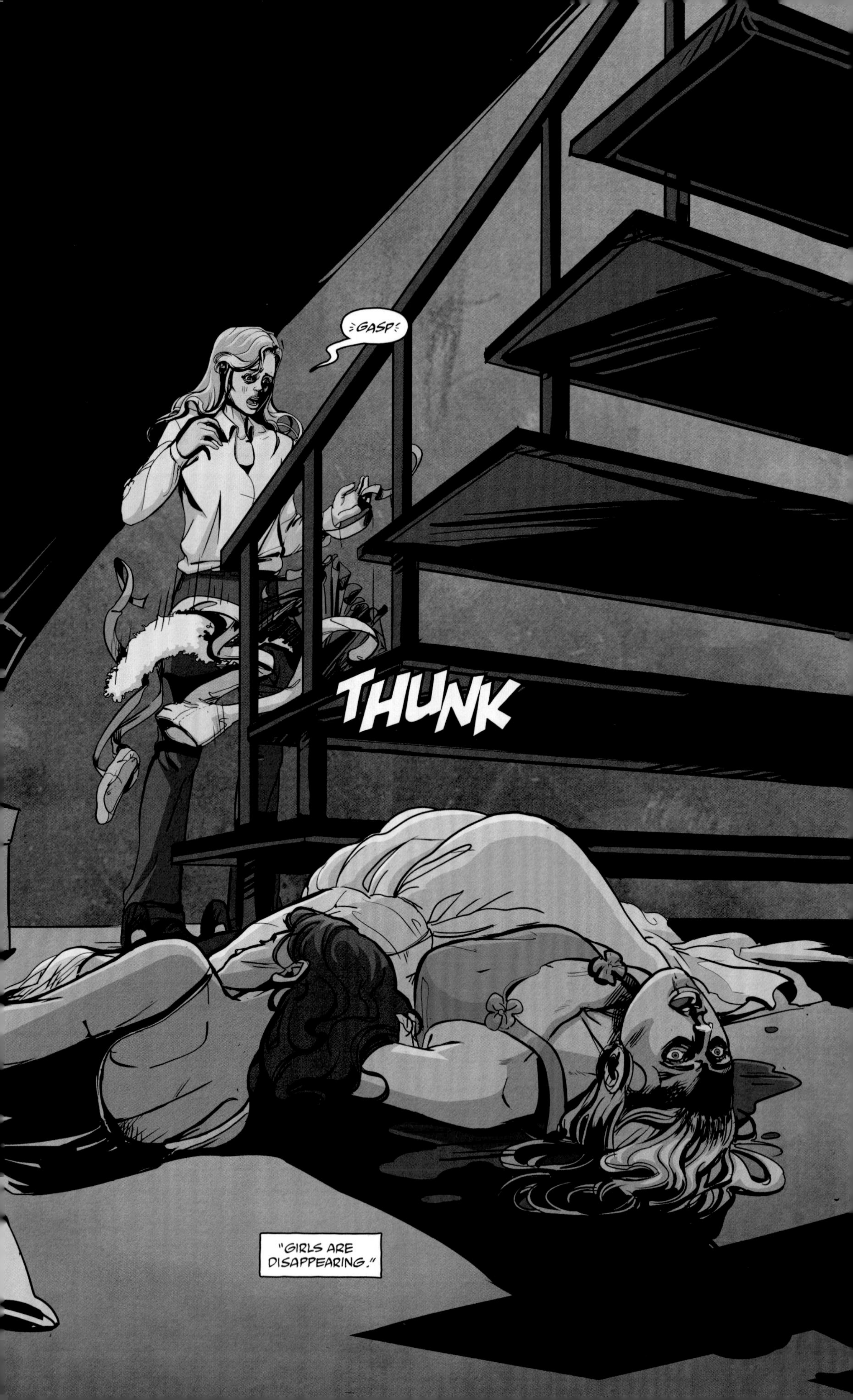
GASP
THUNK
"GIRLS ARE DISAPPEARING."

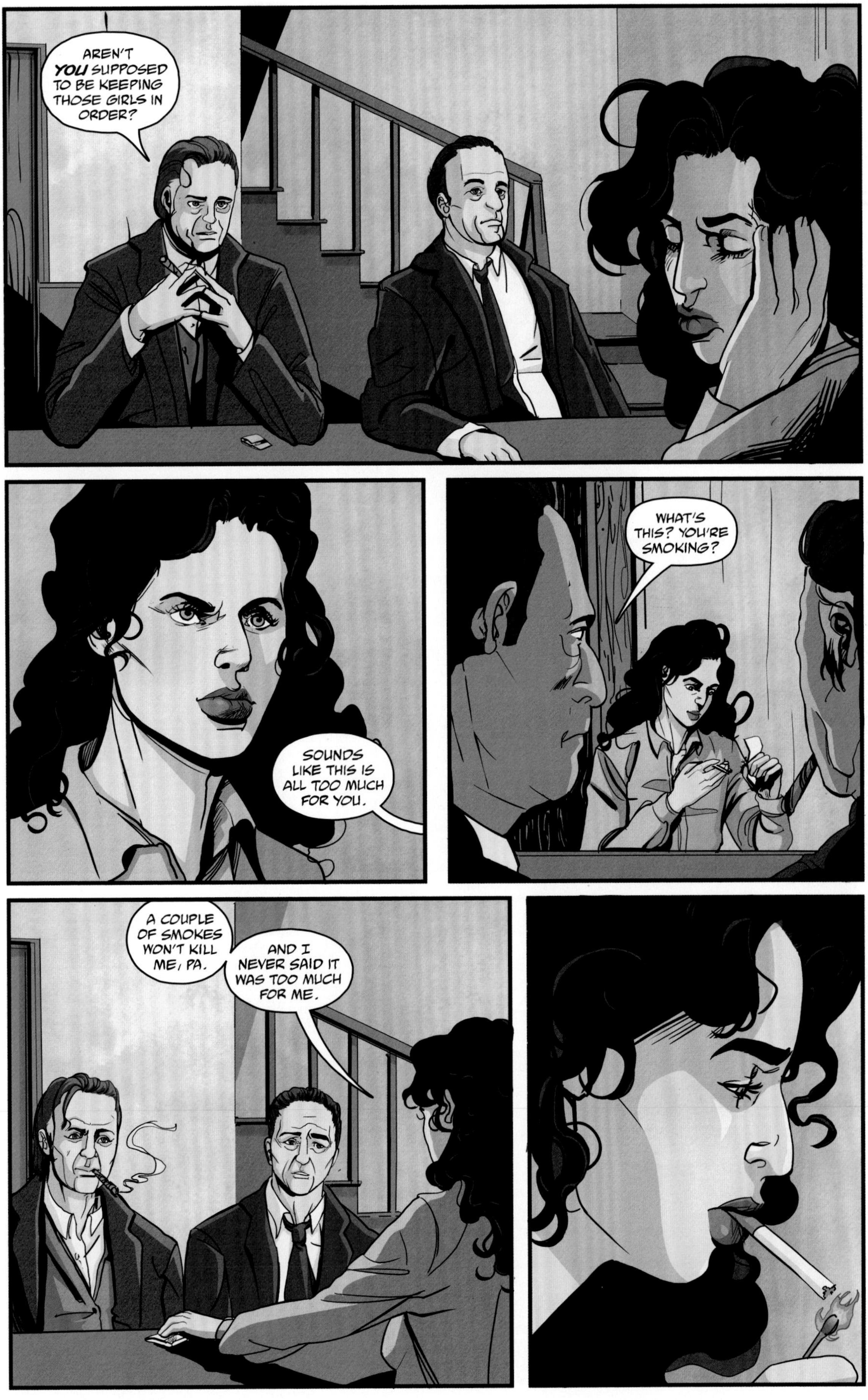

AREN'T YOU SUPPOSED TO BE KEEPING THOSE GIRLS IN ORDER?
SOUNDS LIKE THIS IS ALL TOO MUCH FOR YOU.
WHAT'S THIS? YOU'RE SMOKING?
A COUPLE OF SMOKES WON'T KILL ME, PA.
AND I NEVER SAID IT WAS TOO MUCH FOR ME.

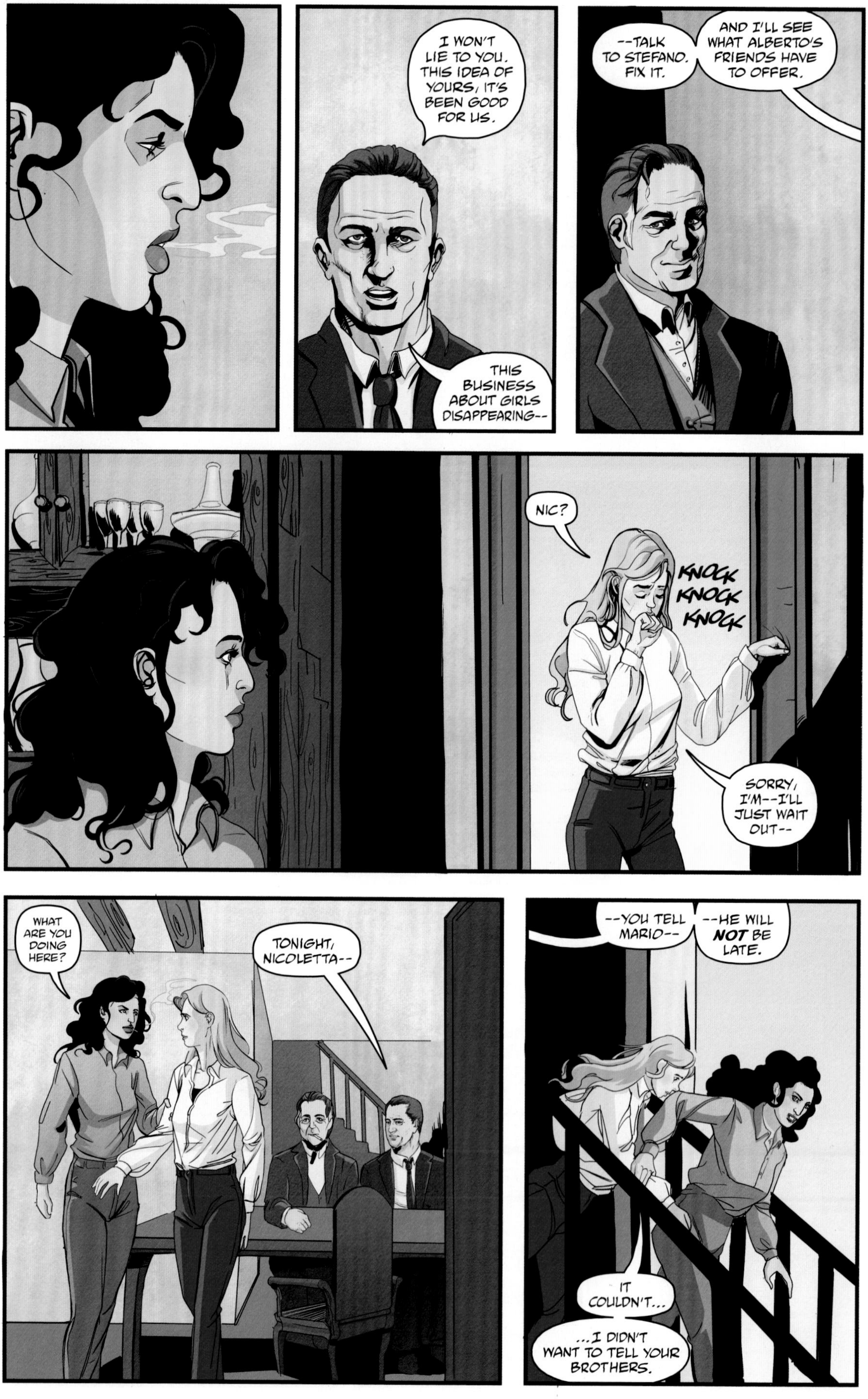
I WON'T LIE TO YOU. THIS IDEA OF YOURS, IT'S BEEN GOOD FOR US.
THIS BUSINESS ABOUT GIRLS DISAPPEARING--
--TALK TO STEFANO. FIX IT.
AND I'LL SEE WHAT ALBERTO'S FRIENDS HAVE TO OFFER.
NIC?
KNOCK KNOCK KNOCK
SORRY, I'M--I'LL JUST WAIT OUT--
WHAT ARE YOU DOING HERE?
TONIGHT, NICOLETTA--
--YOU TELL MARIO--
--HE WILL **NOT** BE LATE.
IT COULDN'T...
...I DIDN'T WANT TO TELL YOUR BROTHERS.

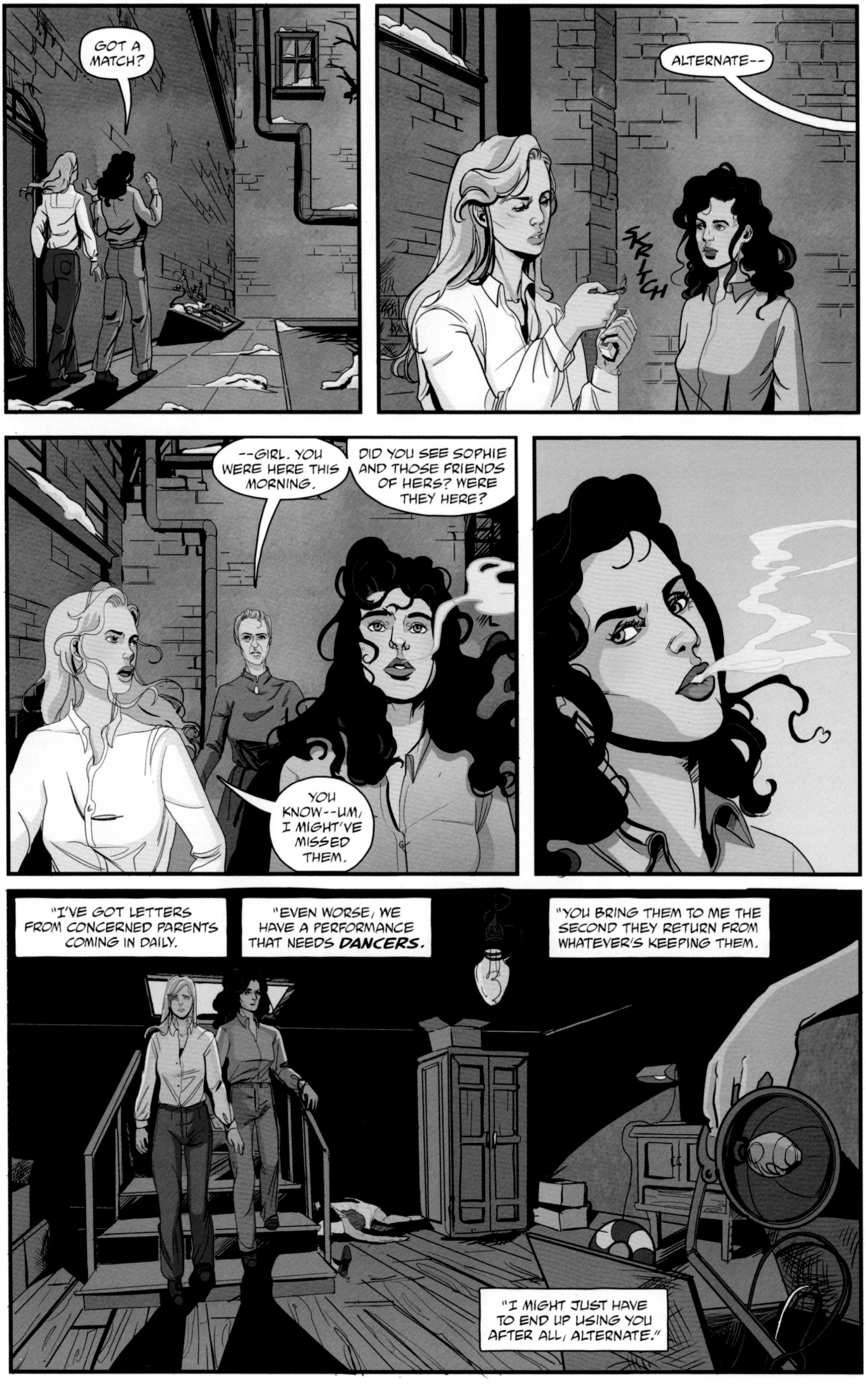
GOT A MATCH?
ALTERNATE--
SKRITCH
--GIRL. YOU WERE HERE THIS MORNING.
DID YOU SEE SOPHIE AND THOSE FRIENDS OF HERS? WERE THEY HERE?
YOU KNOW--UM, I MIGHT'VE MISSED THEM.
"I'VE GOT LETTERS FROM CONCERNED PARENTS COMING IN DAILY.
"EVEN WORSE, WE HAVE A PERFORMANCE THAT NEEDS **DANCERS.**
"YOU BRING THEM TO ME THE SECOND THEY RETURN FROM WHATEVER'S KEEPING THEM.
"I MIGHT JUST HAVE TO END UP USING YOU AFTER ALL, ALTERNATE."

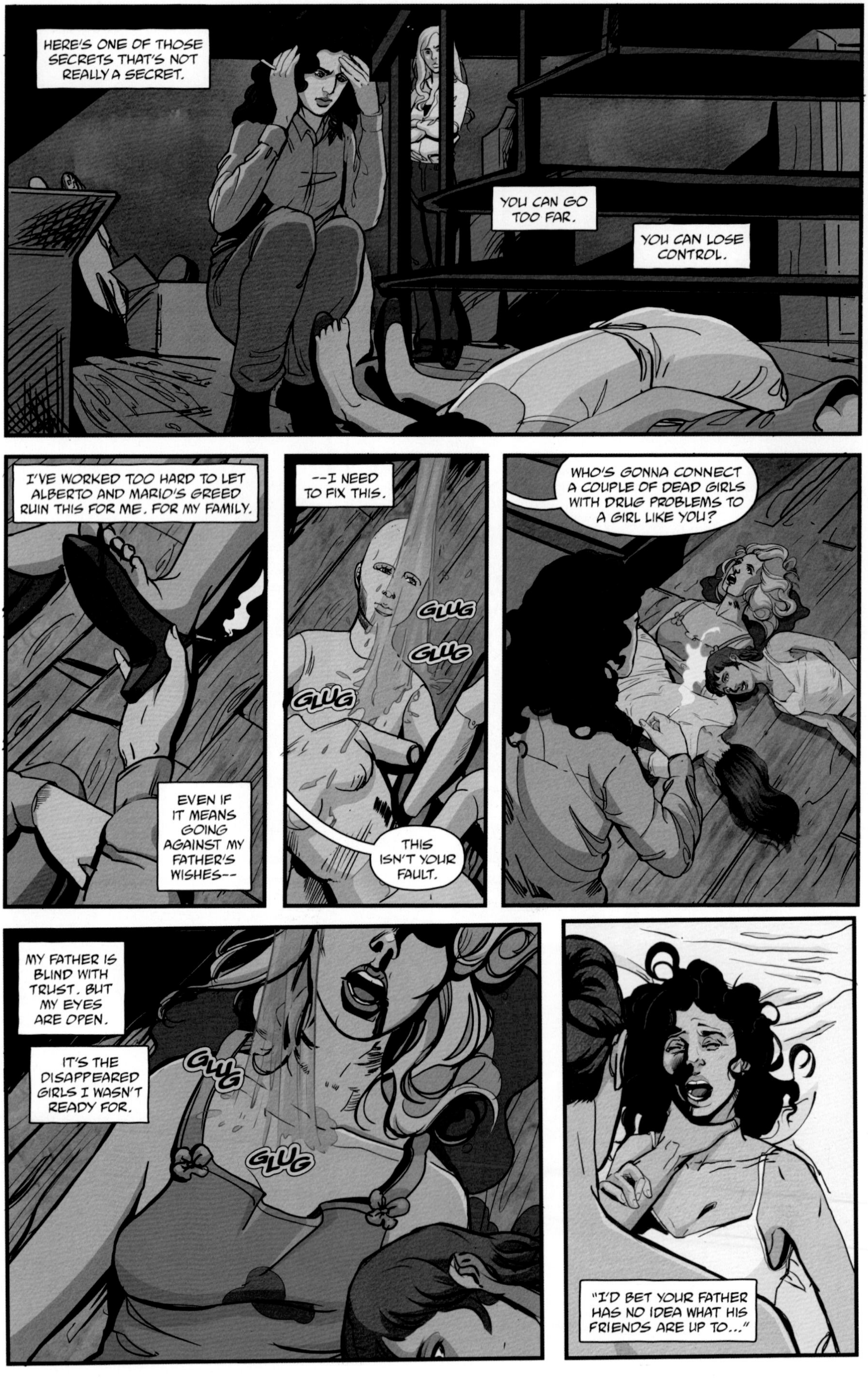
HERE'S ONE OF THOSE SECRETS THAT'S NOT REALLY A SECRET.
YOU CAN GO TOO FAR.
YOU CAN LOSE CONTROL.
I'VE WORKED TOO HARD TO LET ALBERTO AND MARIO'S GREED RUIN THIS FOR ME. FOR MY FAMILY.
EVEN IF IT MEANS GOING AGAINST MY FATHER'S WISHES--
--I NEED TO FIX THIS.
GLUG
GLUG
GLUG
THIS ISN'T YOUR FAULT.
WHO'S GONNA CONNECT A COUPLE OF DEAD GIRLS WITH DRUG PROBLEMS TO A GIRL LIKE YOU?
MY FATHER IS BLIND WITH TRUST. BUT MY EYES ARE OPEN.
IT'S THE DISAPPEARED GIRLS I WASN'T READY FOR.
GLUG
GLUG
"I'D BET YOUR FATHER HAS NO IDEA WHAT HIS FRIENDS ARE UP TO..."

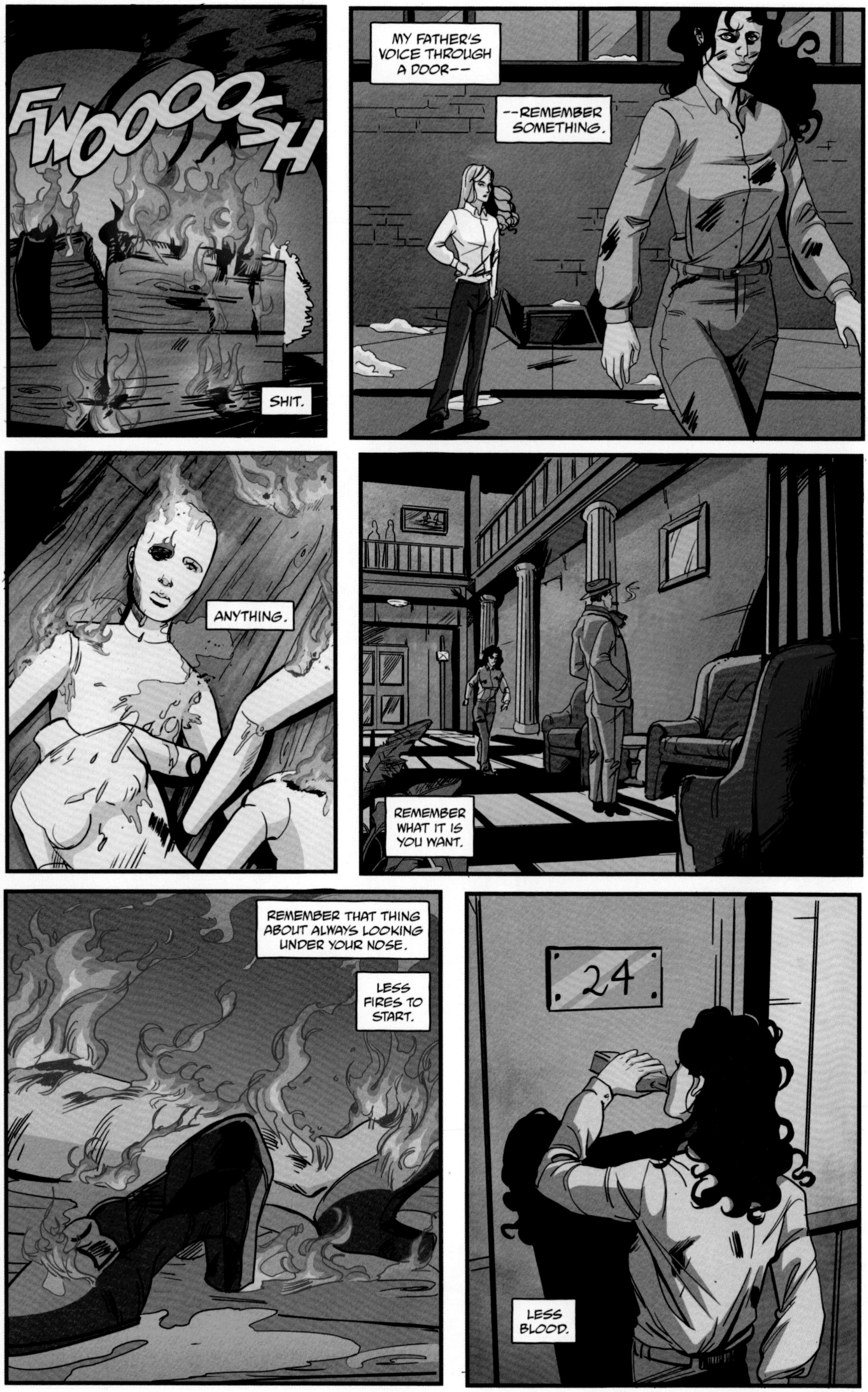
FWOOOOSH
SHIT.
MY FATHER'S VOICE THROUGH A DOOR--
--REMEMBER SOMETHING.
ANYTHING.
REMEMBER WHAT IT IS YOU WANT.
REMEMBER THAT THING ABOUT ALWAYS LOOKING UNDER YOUR NOSE.
LESS FIRES TO START.
24
LESS BLOOD.

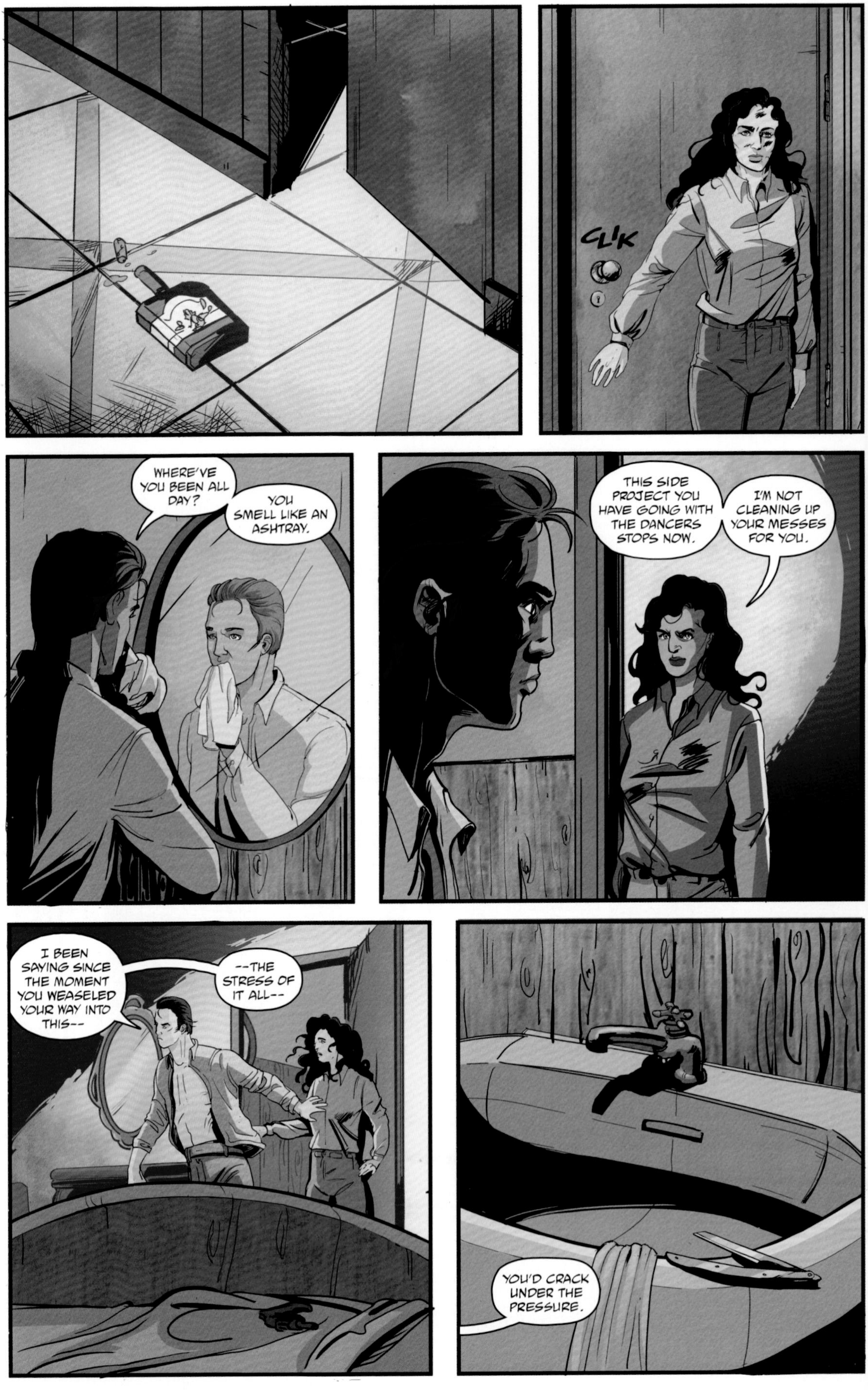
CLIK
WHERE'VE YOU BEEN ALL DAY?
YOU SMELL LIKE AN ASHTRAY.
THIS SIDE PROJECT YOU HAVE GOING WITH THE DANCERS STOPS NOW.
I'M NOT CLEANING UP YOUR MESSES FOR YOU.
I BEEN SAYING SINCE THE MOMENT YOU WEASELED YOUR WAY INTO THIS--
--THE STRESS OF IT ALL--
YOU'D CRACK UNDER THE PRESSURE.

YOU CAN'T-- TELL MY FATHER THAT THIS LITTLE **SIDE GIG** IS GONNA GET US ALL LOCKED UP.

YOU THINK I'M STUPID? THESE ARE **POWERFUL, IMPORTANT** FAMILIES, LOOKING FOR THEIR **DAUGHTERS.**

NO, NIC, THAT'S **JUST IT.** I THINK YOU KNOW **EXACTLY** WHAT'S GOING ON.

AND I THINK THAT EXTRA **CASH** IN YOUR POCKET AND THE POCKETS OF THOSE LITTLE **SLUT FRIENDS** OF YOURS FEELS PRETTY GOOD, DON'T IT?

DON'T GET ALL HOLY ON ME NOW.

I HAD TO BURN MY OWN--

AND WHO SAID YOU HAVE ANY POWER HERE, HUH? YOU'RE GONNA LEAVE THIS ISSUE ALONE...

AND YOU'RE NOT GONNA RUN OFF TO **DADDY** TO RAT, NEITHER.

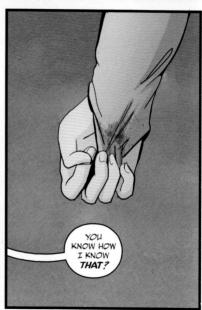

YOU KNOW HOW I KNOW **THAT?**

'CAUSE LITTLE GIRLS LIKE YOU DO WHAT THEY'RE TOLD...

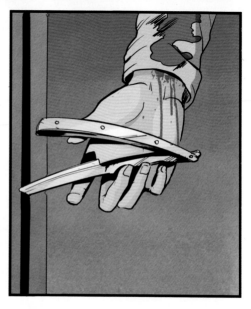

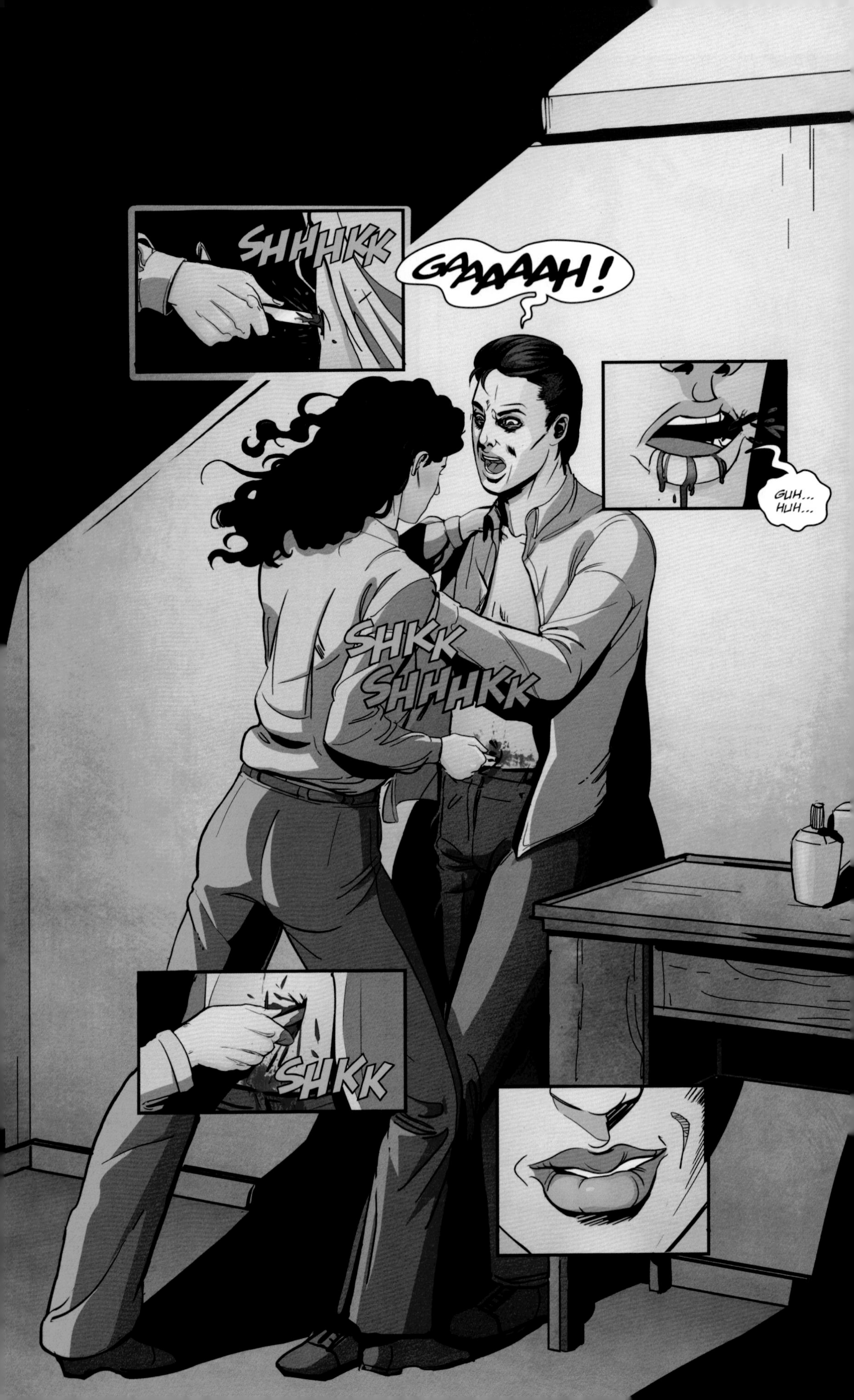
SHHHKK
GAAAAAH!
GUH... HUH...
SHKK
SHHHKK
SHKK

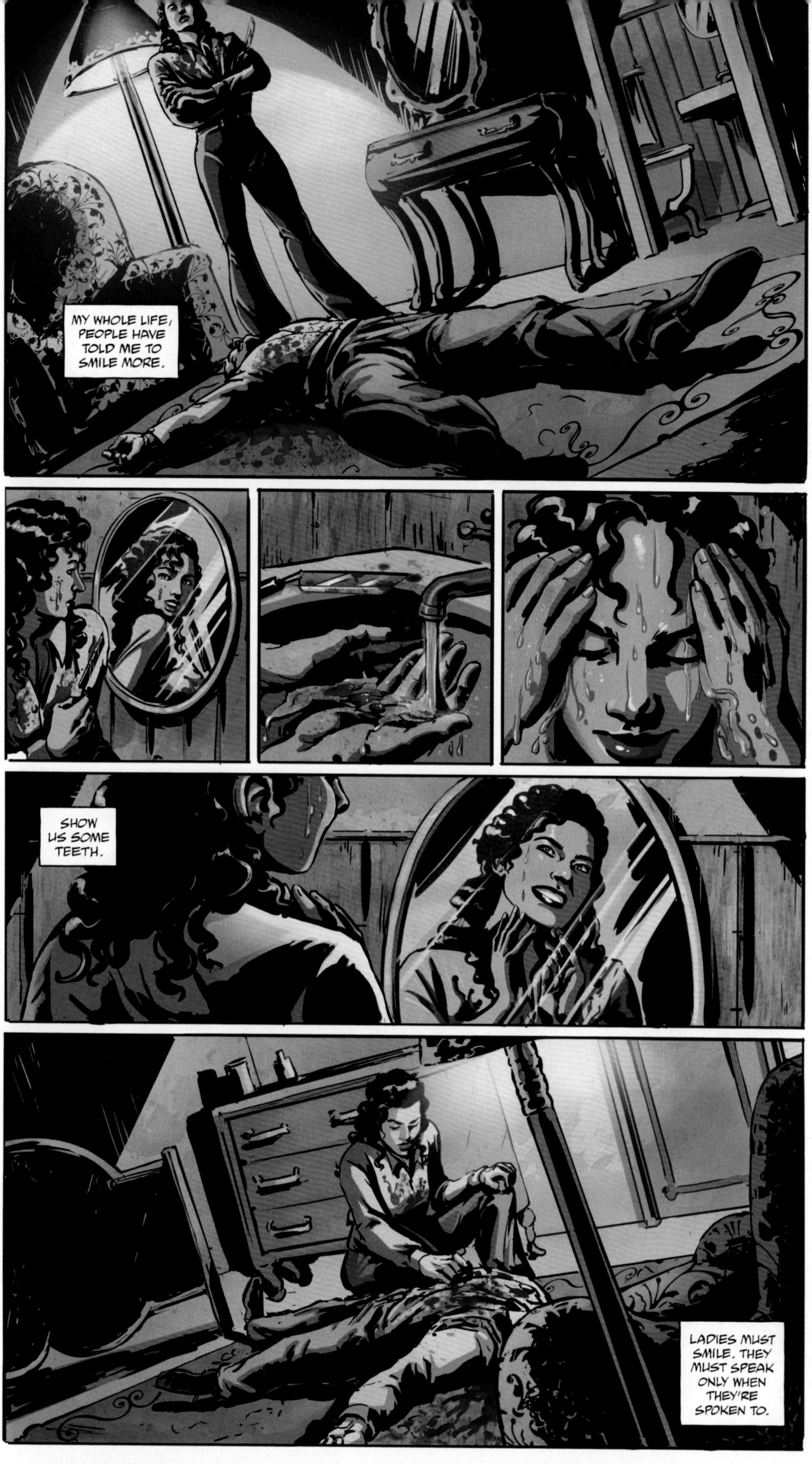
MY WHOLE LIFE, PEOPLE HAVE TOLD ME TO SMILE MORE.
SHOW US SOME TEETH.
LADIES MUST SMILE. THEY MUST SPEAK ONLY WHEN THEY'RE SPOKEN TO.

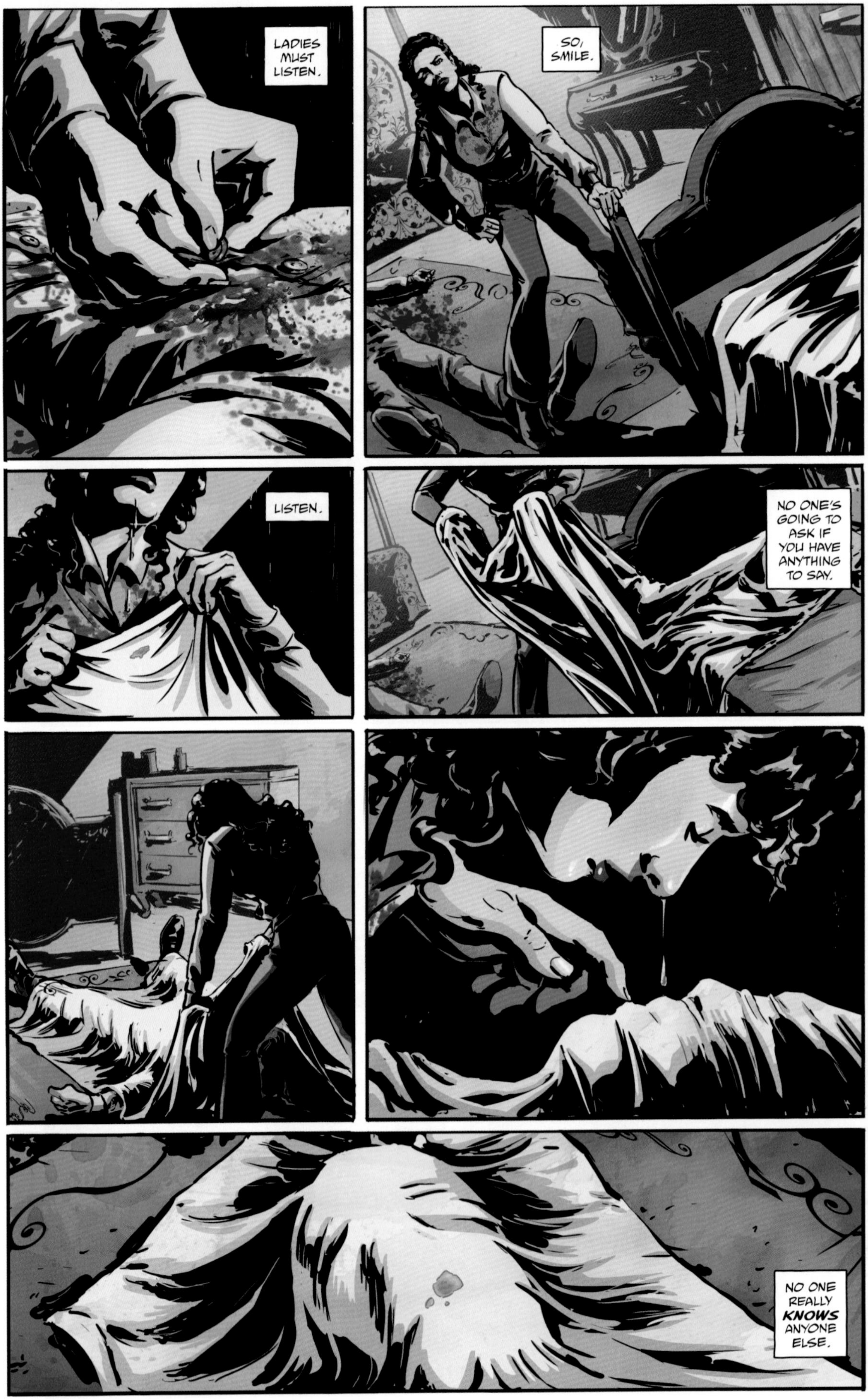
LADIES MUST LISTEN.
SO, SMILE.
LISTEN.
NO ONE'S GOING TO ASK IF YOU HAVE ANYTHING TO SAY.
NO ONE REALLY **KNOWS** ANYONE ELSE.

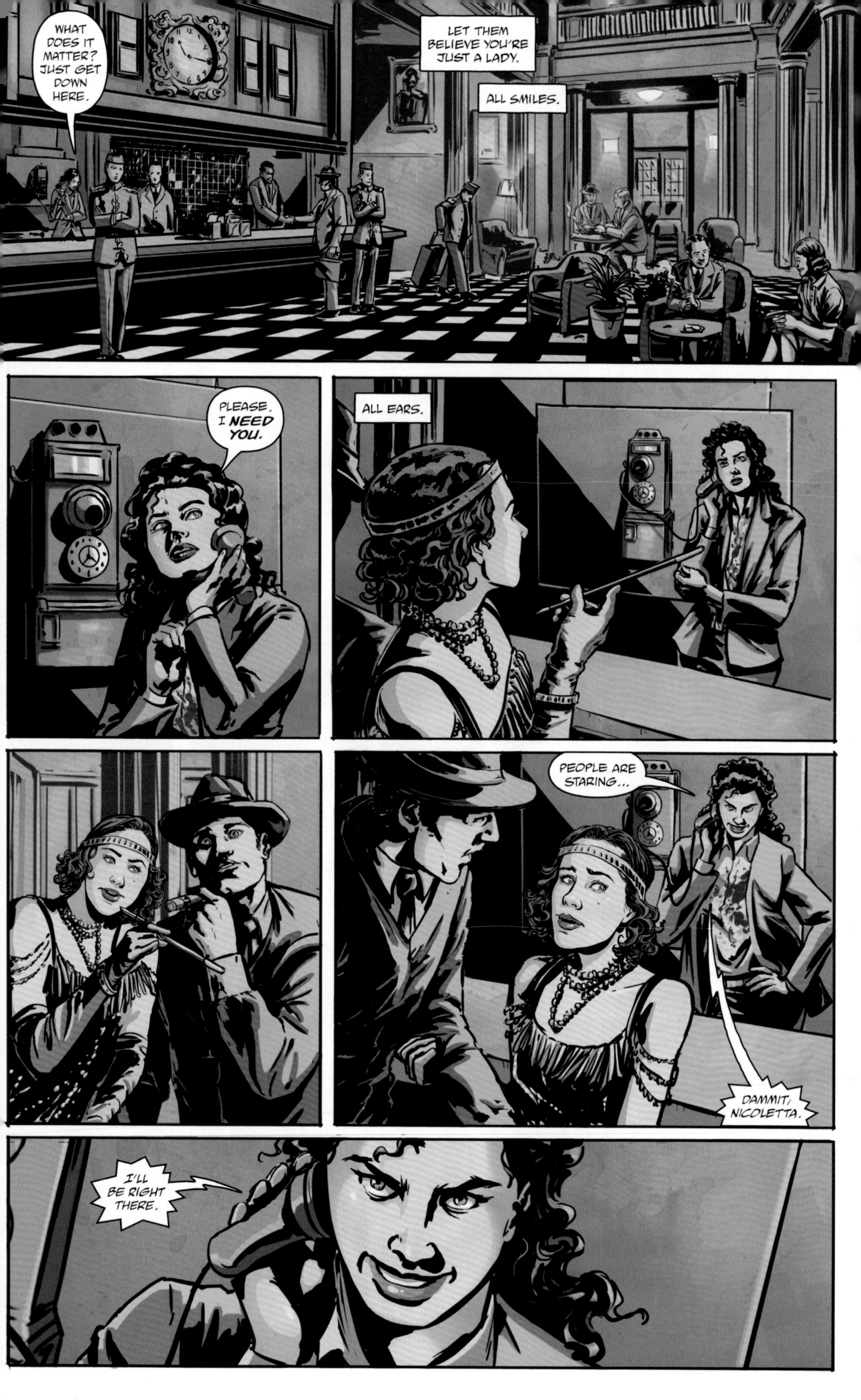
WHAT DOES IT MATTER? JUST GET DOWN HERE.
LET THEM BELIEVE YOU'RE JUST A LADY.
ALL SMILES.
PLEASE. I NEED YOU.
ALL EARS.
PEOPLE ARE STARING...
DAMMIT, NICOLETTA.
I'LL BE RIGHT THERE.

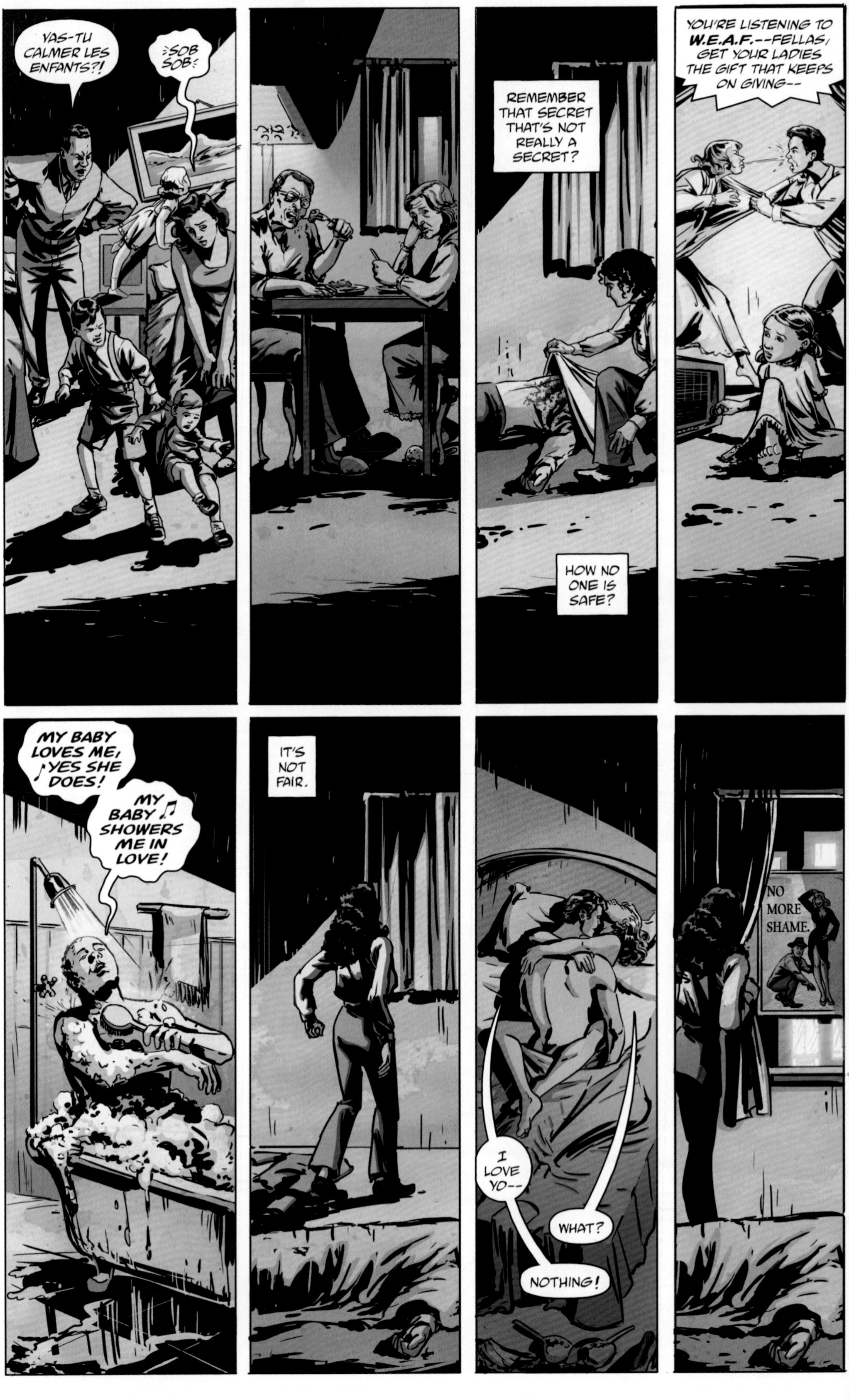

VAS-TU CALMER LES ENFANTS?!
SOB SOB
REMEMBER THAT SECRET THAT'S NOT REALLY A SECRET?
HOW NO ONE IS SAFE?
YOU'RE LISTENING TO W.E.A.F.--FELLAS, GET YOUR LADIES THE GIFT THAT KEEPS ON GIVING--
MY BABY LOVES ME, YES SHE DOES!
MY BABY SHOWERS ME IN LOVE!
IT'S NOT FAIR.
I LOVE YO--
WHAT?
NOTHING!
NO MORE SHAME.

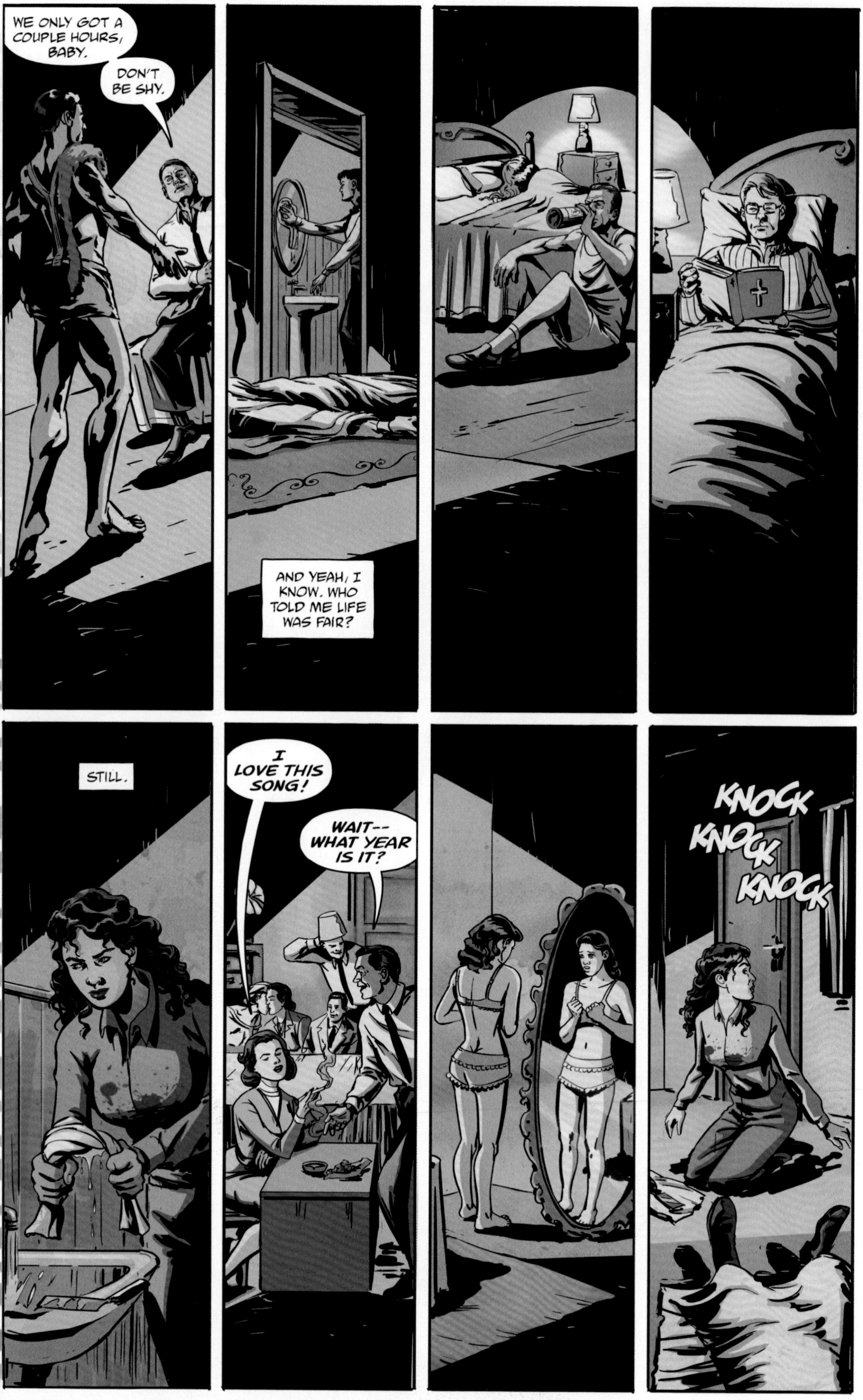
WE ONLY GOT A COUPLE HOURS, BABY.
DON'T BE SHY.
AND YEAH, I KNOW. WHO TOLD ME LIFE WAS FAIR?
STILL.
I LOVE THIS SONG!
WAIT-- WHAT YEAR IS IT?
KNOCK
KNOCK
KNOCK

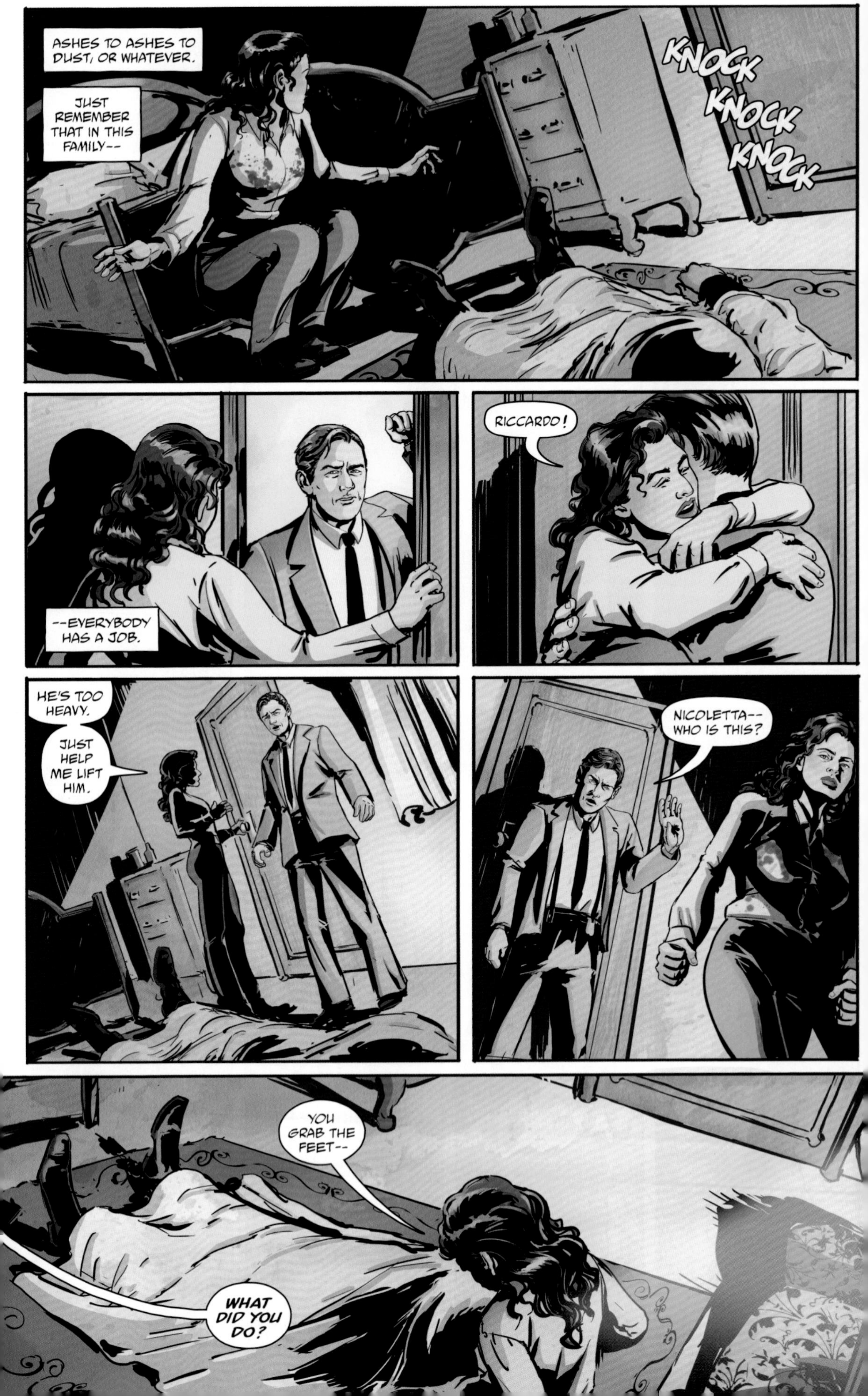
ASHES TO ASHES TO DUST, OR WHATEVER.
JUST REMEMBER THAT IN THIS FAMILY--
KNOCK KNOCK KNOCK
--EVERYBODY HAS A JOB.
RICCARDO!
HE'S TOO HEAVY.
JUST HELP ME LIFT HIM.
NICOLETTA-- WHO IS THIS?
YOU GRAB THE FEET--
WHAT DID YOU DO?

JUST **HELP** ME.

OH GOD. NIC, WHAT DID HE--?

THIS ISN'T **YOU**, NICOLETTA.

LOOK. I JUST NEED YOU TO--

NO! TH-THIS IS **INSANE**!

Y-YOU'RE NOT A KILLER.

YOU HATED HIM, ANY-WAY!

YOU DIDN'T BELONG WITH HIM! NONE OF THIS WOULD'VE HAPPENED IF--

YOU HAVE NO **IDEA** WHAT I AM.

COME ON, NIC. WE WERE KIDS.

THINGS HAVE CHANGED.

AND **WE** ARE NOT ANYTHING. JUST DO YOUR JOB AND **HELP** ME.

I CAN'T DO THIS WITH YOU ANYMORE.

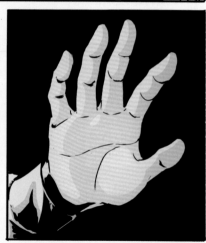

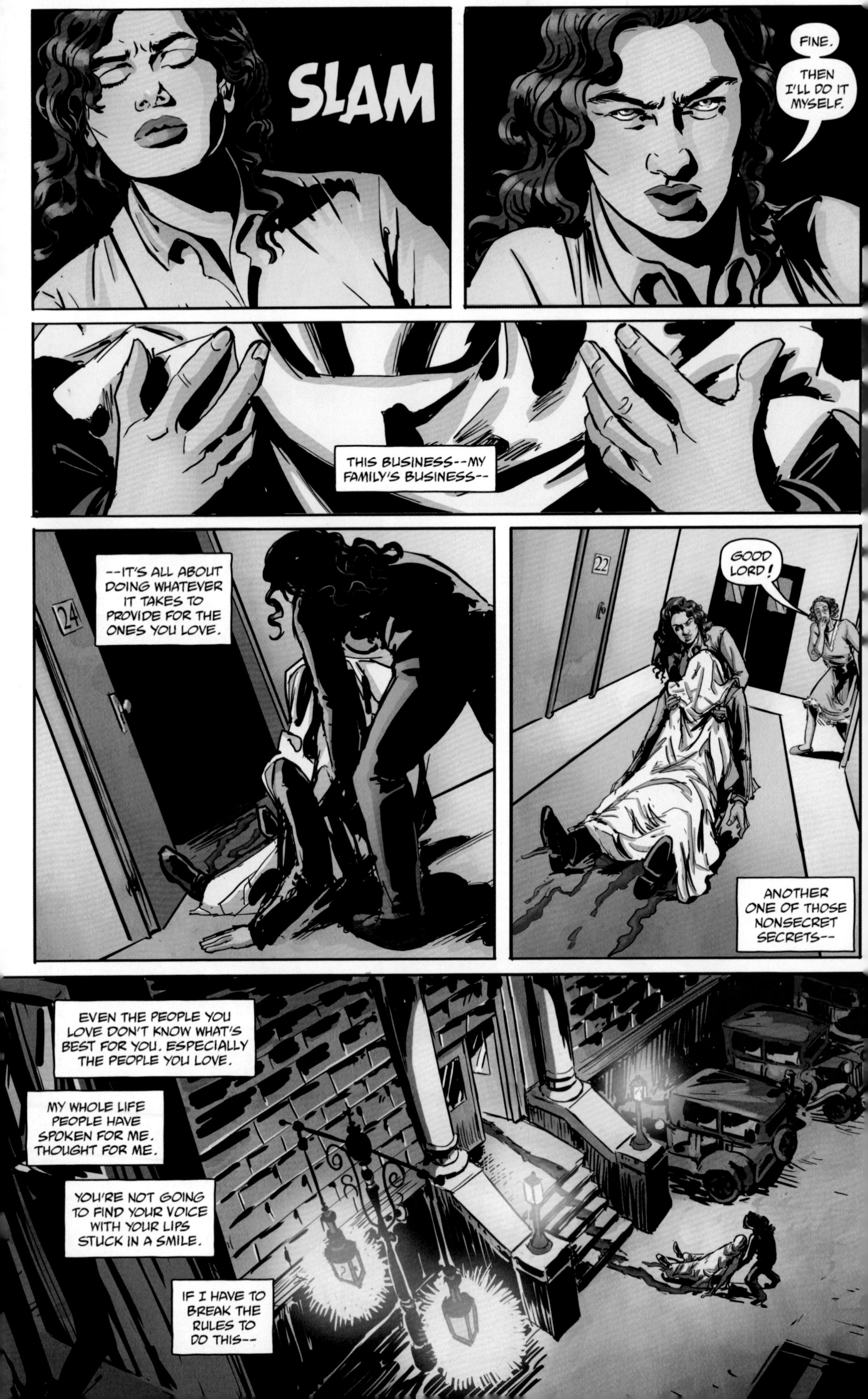
SLAM
FINE.
THEN I'LL DO IT MYSELF.
THIS BUSINESS--MY FAMILY'S BUSINESS--
--IT'S ALL ABOUT DOING WHATEVER IT TAKES TO PROVIDE FOR THE ONES YOU LOVE.
24
22
GOOD LORD!
ANOTHER ONE OF THOSE NONSECRET SECRETS--
EVEN THE PEOPLE YOU LOVE DON'T KNOW WHAT'S BEST FOR YOU. ESPECIALLY THE PEOPLE YOU LOVE.
MY WHOLE LIFE PEOPLE HAVE SPOKEN FOR ME. THOUGHT FOR ME.
YOU'RE NOT GOING TO FIND YOUR VOICE WITH YOUR LIPS STUCK IN A SMILE.
IF I HAVE TO BREAK THE RULES TO DO THIS--

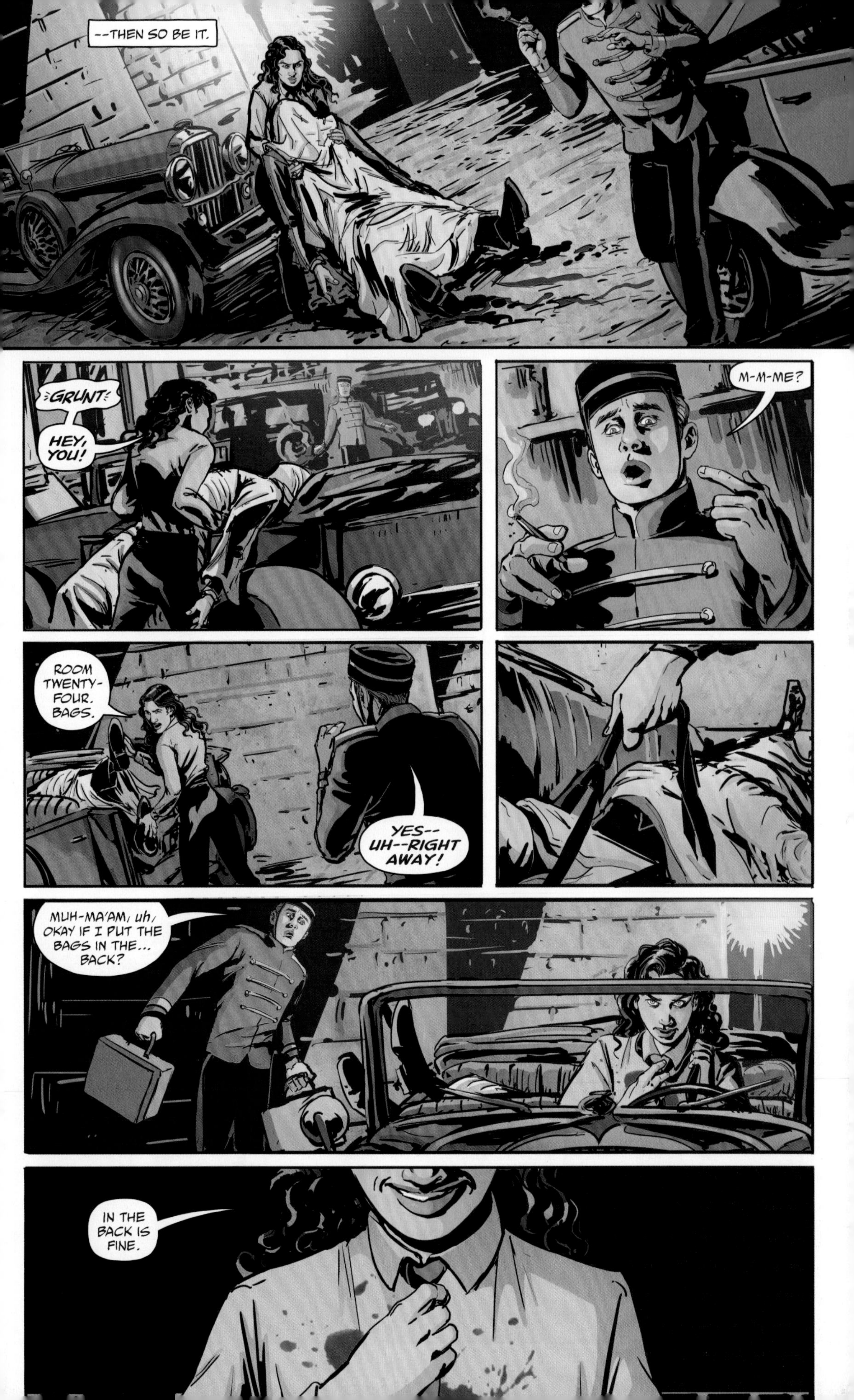
--THEN SO BE IT.
GRUNT
HEY, YOU!
M-M-ME?
ROOM TWENTY-FOUR. BAGS.
YES--UH--RIGHT AWAY!
MUH-MA'AM, uh, OKAY IF I PUT THE BAGS IN THE... BACK?
IN THE BACK IS FINE.

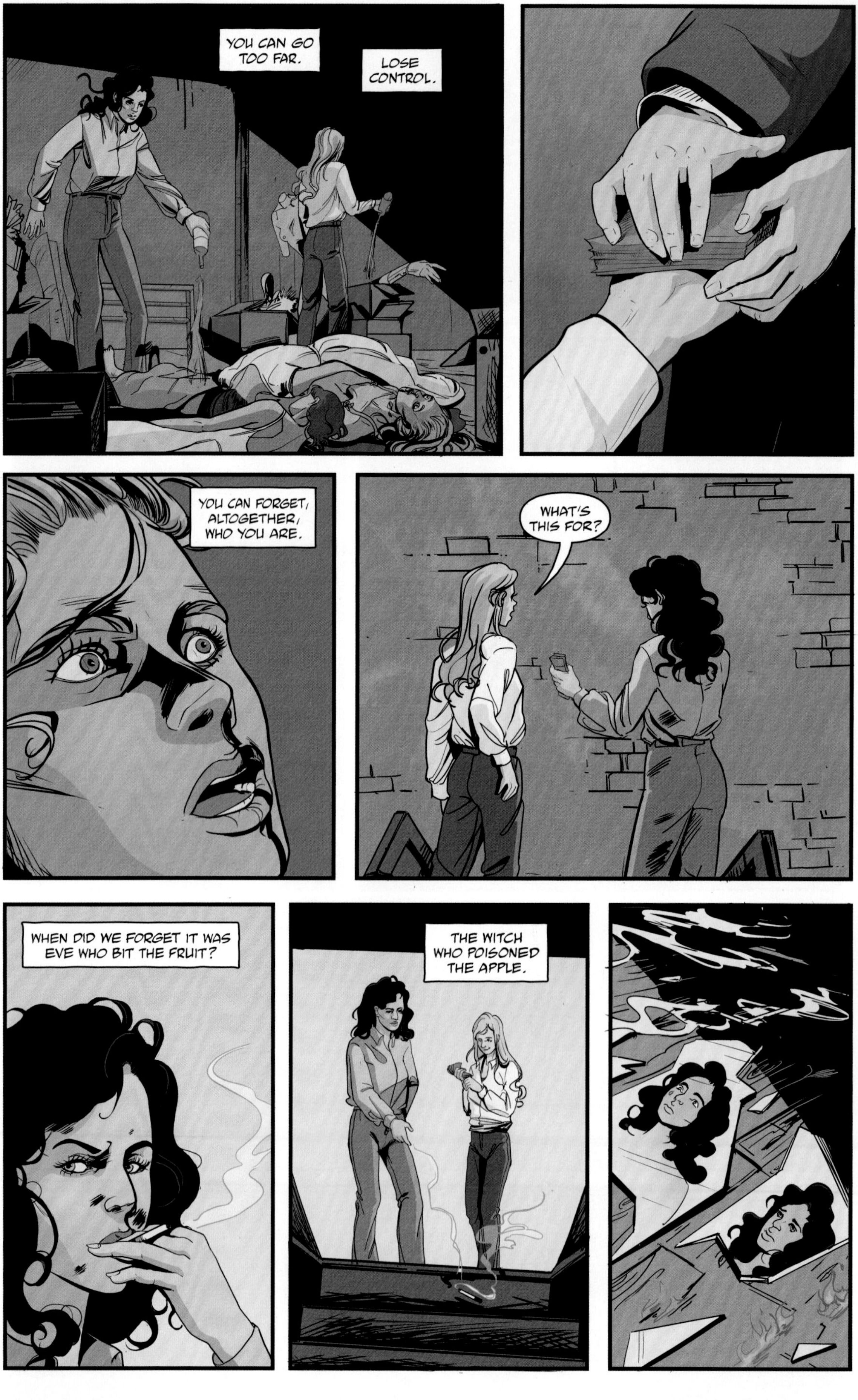
YOU CAN GO TOO FAR.
LOSE CONTROL.
YOU CAN FORGET, ALTOGETHER, WHO YOU ARE.
WHAT'S THIS FOR?
WHEN DID WE FORGET IT WAS EVE WHO BIT THE FRUIT?
THE WITCH WHO POISONED THE APPLE.

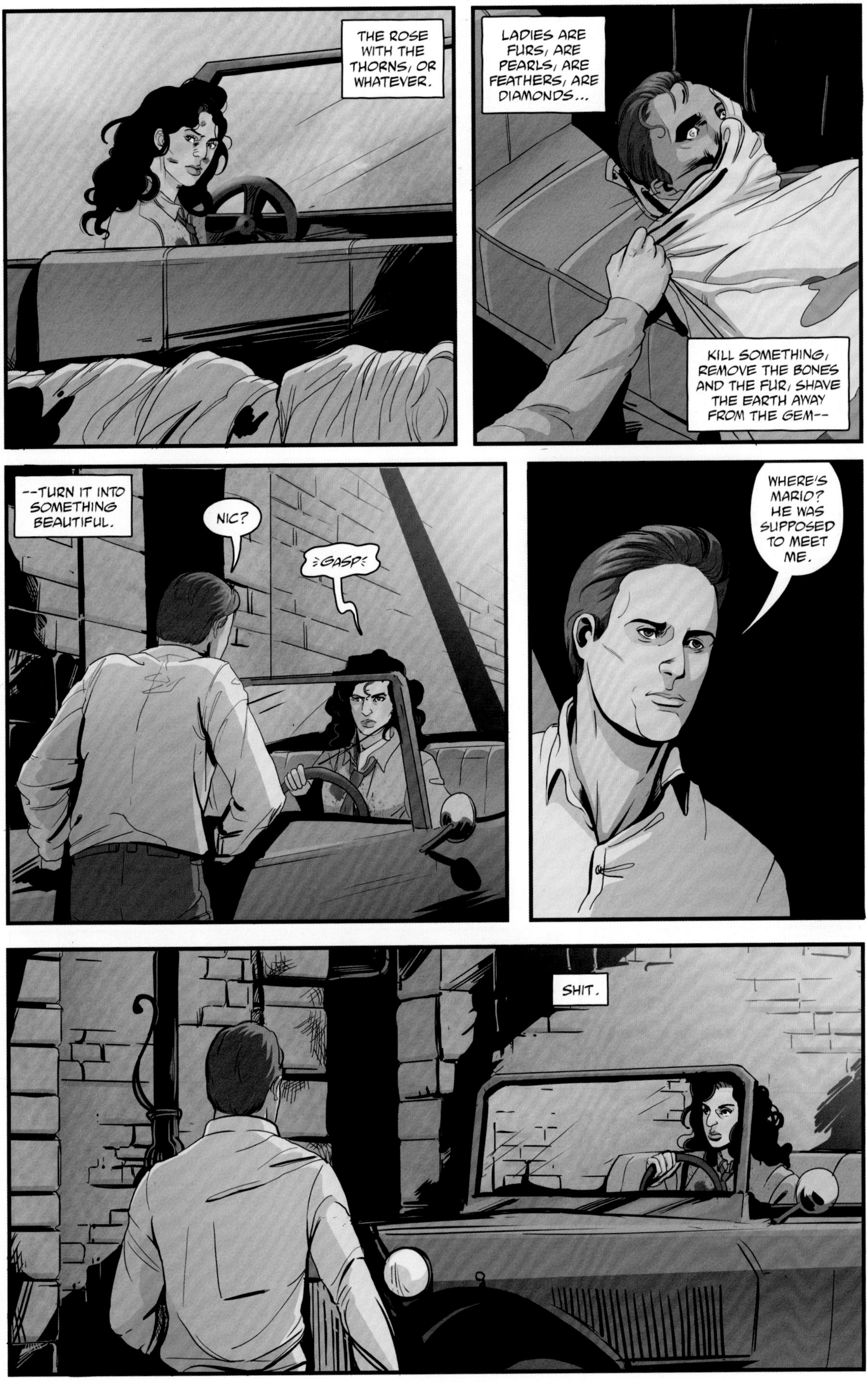
THE ROSE WITH THE THORNS, OR WHATEVER.
LADIES ARE FURS, ARE PEARLS, ARE FEATHERS, ARE DIAMONDS...
KILL SOMETHING, REMOVE THE BONES AND THE FUR, SHAVE THE EARTH AWAY FROM THE GEM--
--TURN IT INTO SOMETHING BEAUTIFUL.
NIC?
GASP
WHERE'S MARIO? HE WAS SUPPOSED TO MEET ME.
SHIT.

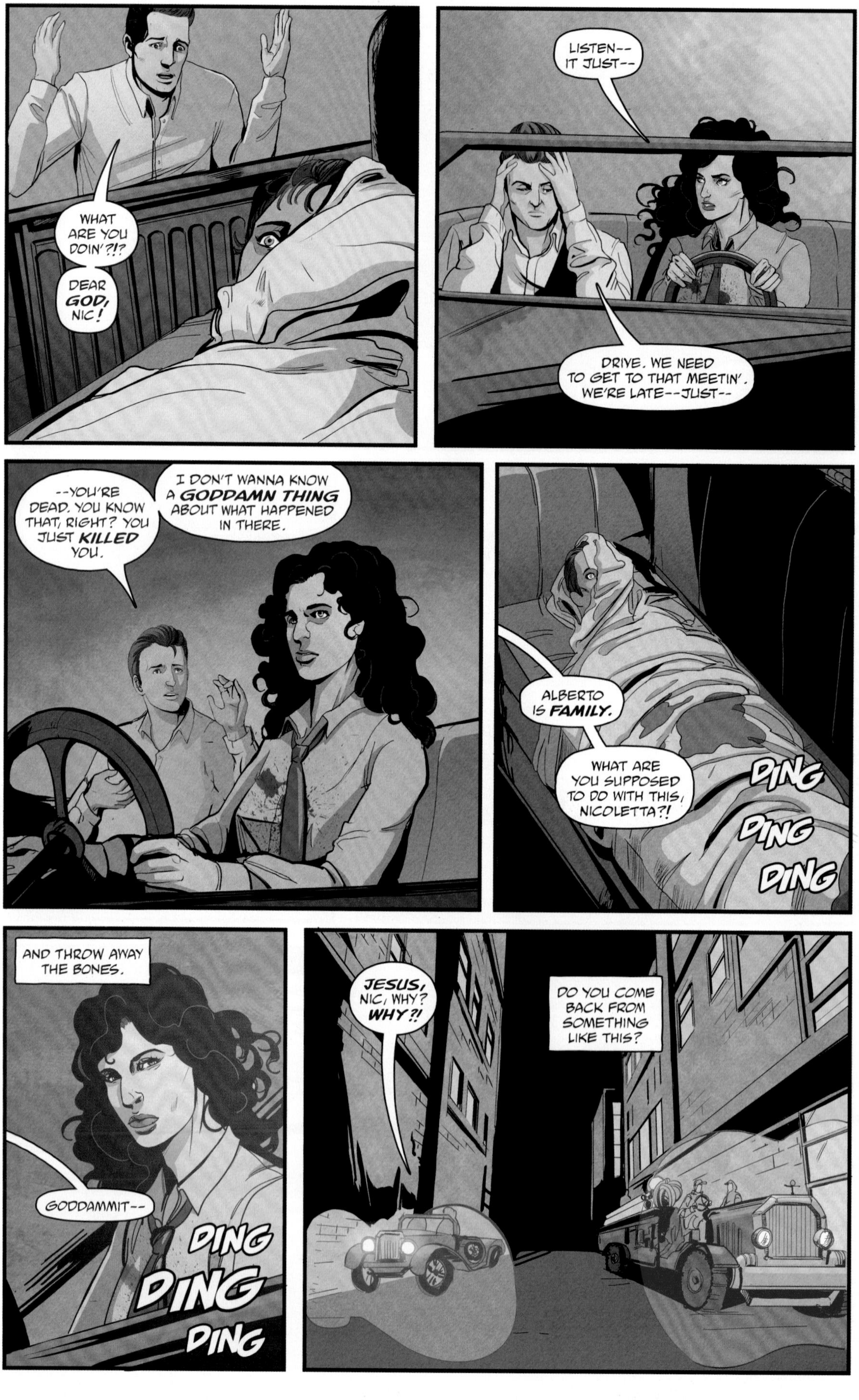
WHAT ARE YOU DOIN'?!?
DEAR GOD, NIC!
LISTEN-- IT JUST--
DRIVE. WE NEED TO GET TO THAT MEETIN'. WE'RE LATE--JUST--
--YOU'RE DEAD. YOU KNOW THAT, RIGHT? YOU JUST KILLED YOU.
I DON'T WANNA KNOW A GODDAMN THING ABOUT WHAT HAPPENED IN THERE.
ALBERTO IS FAMILY.
WHAT ARE YOU SUPPOSED TO DO WITH THIS, NICOLETTA?!
DING
DING
DING
AND THROW AWAY THE BONES.
GODDAMMIT--
DING
DING
DING
JESUS, NIC, WHY? WHY?!
DO YOU COME BACK FROM SOMETHING LIKE THIS?

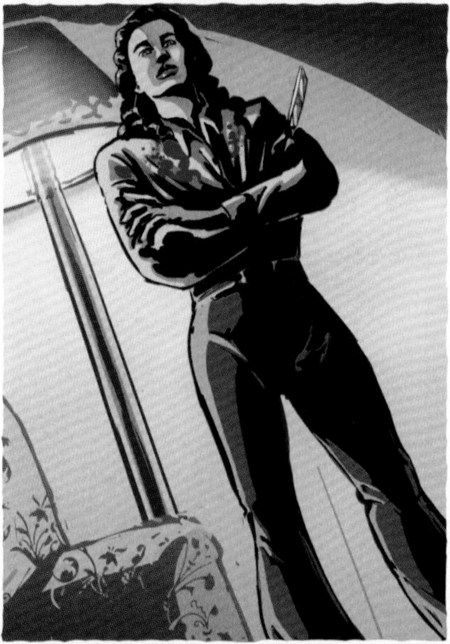

CHAPTER
FIVE

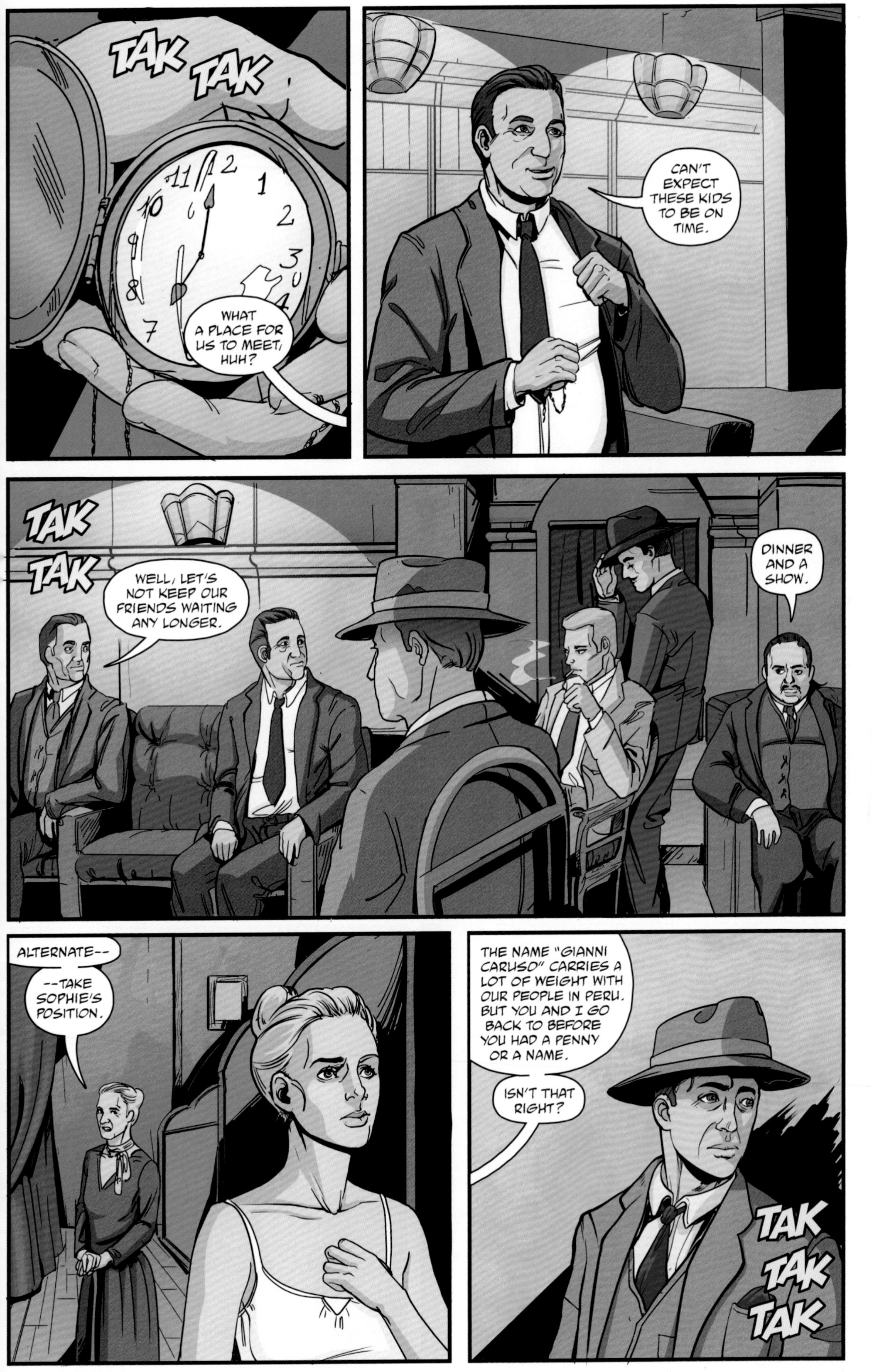
TAK TAK
WHAT A PLACE FOR US TO MEET, HUH?
CAN'T EXPECT THESE KIDS TO BE ON TIME.
TAK
TAK
WELL, LET'S NOT KEEP OUR FRIENDS WAITING ANY LONGER.
DINNER AND A SHOW.
ALTERNATE--
--TAKE SOPHIE'S POSITION.
THE NAME "GIANNI CARUSO" CARRIES A LOT OF WEIGHT WITH OUR PEOPLE IN PERU. BUT YOU AND I GO BACK TO BEFORE YOU HAD A PENNY OR A NAME.
ISN'T THAT RIGHT?
TAK
TAK
TAK

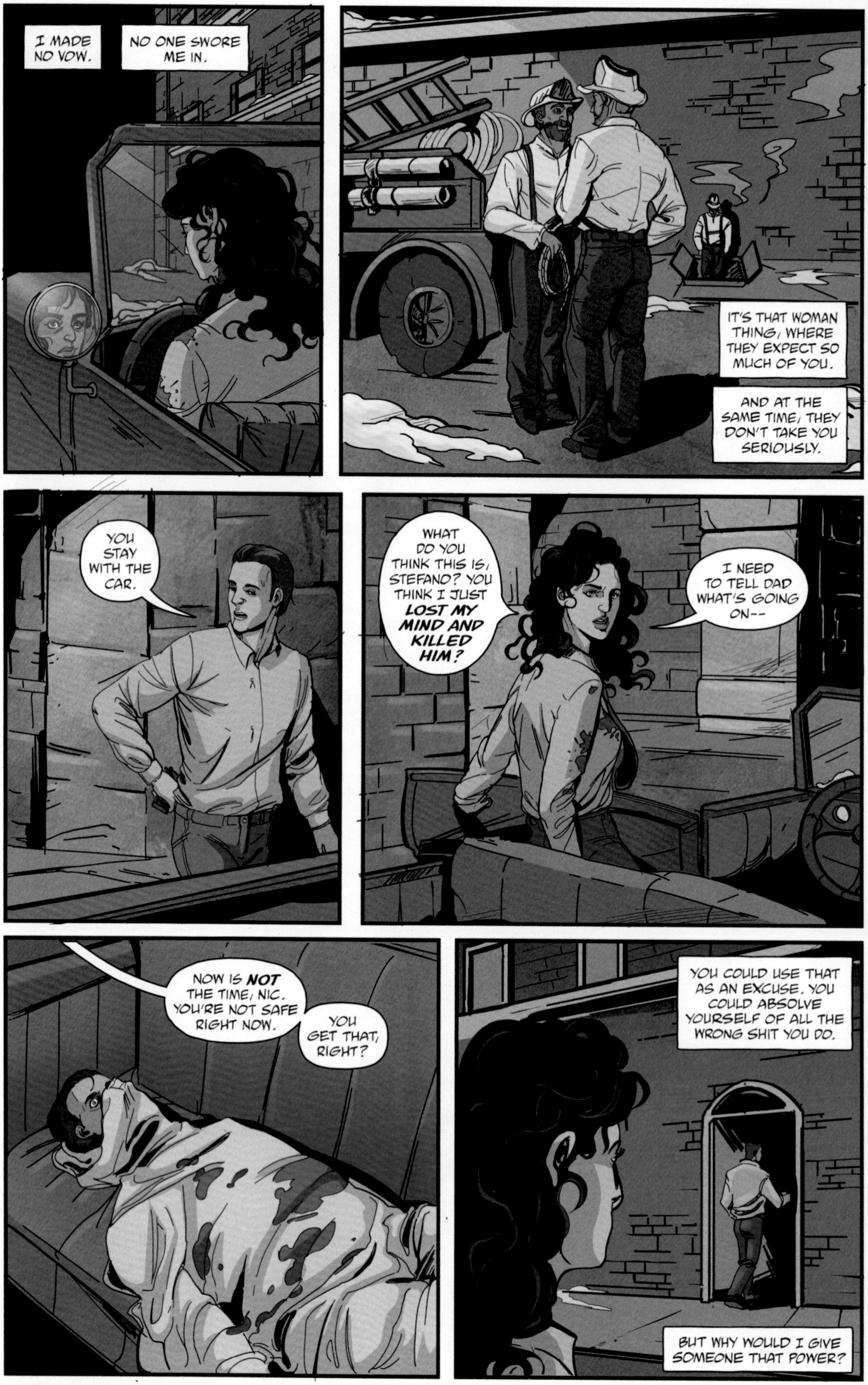

I MADE NO VOW.
NO ONE SWORE ME IN.
IT'S THAT WOMAN THING, WHERE THEY EXPECT SO MUCH OF YOU.
AND AT THE SAME TIME, THEY DON'T TAKE YOU SERIOUSLY.
YOU STAY WITH THE CAR.
WHAT DO YOU THINK THIS IS, STEFANO? YOU THINK I JUST **LOST MY MIND AND KILLED HIM?**
I NEED TO TELL DAD WHAT'S GOING ON--
NOW IS **NOT** THE TIME, NIC. YOU'RE NOT SAFE RIGHT NOW.
YOU GET THAT, RIGHT?
YOU COULD USE THAT AS AN EXCUSE. YOU COULD ABSOLVE YOURSELF OF ALL THE WRONG SHIT YOU DO.
BUT WHY WOULD I GIVE SOMEONE THAT POWER?

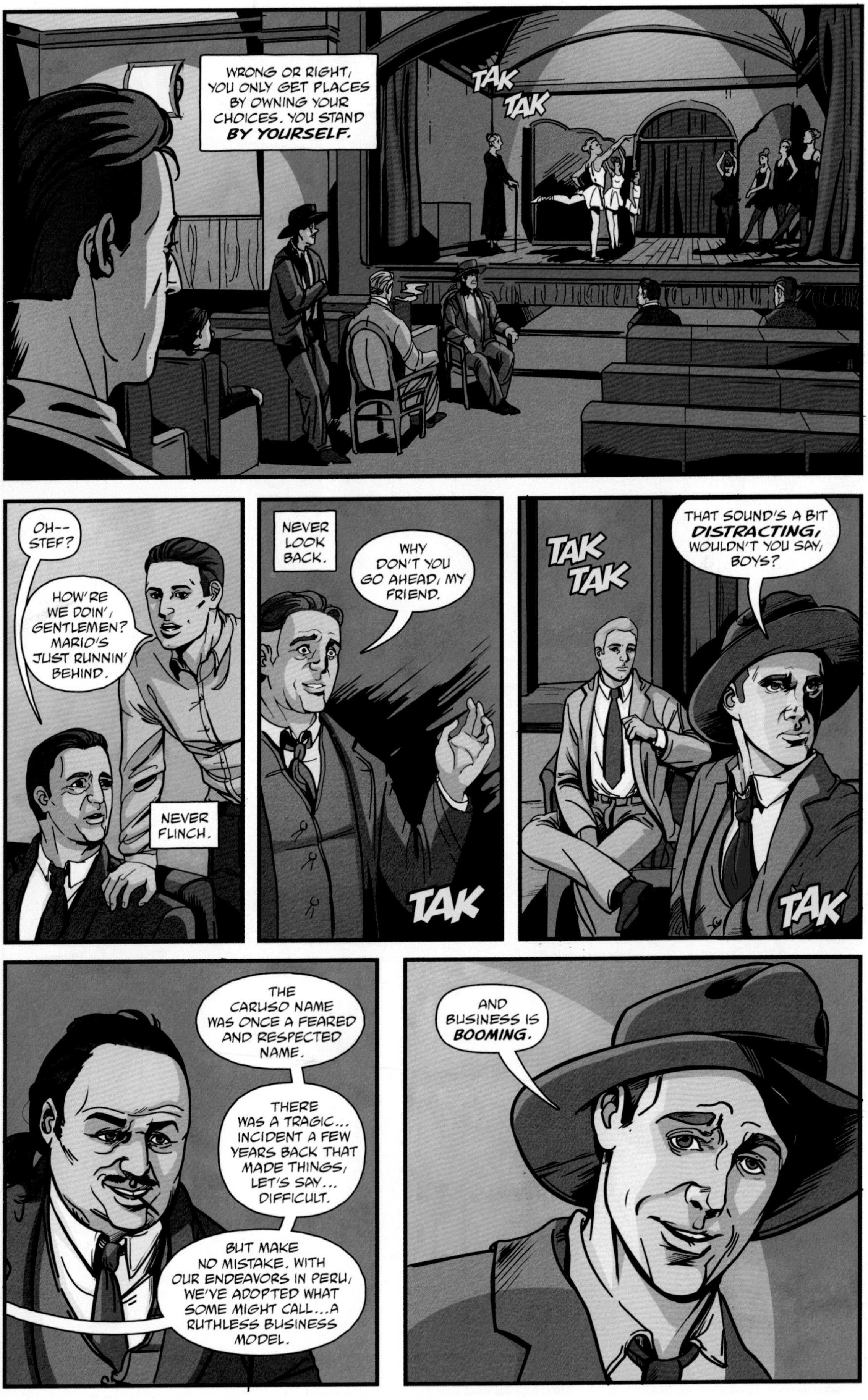
WRONG OR RIGHT, YOU ONLY GET PLACES BY OWNING YOUR CHOICES. YOU STAND **BY YOURSELF.**
TAK TAK
OH-- STEF?
HOW'RE WE DOIN', GENTLEMEN? MARIO'S JUST RUNNIN' BEHIND.
NEVER FLINCH.
NEVER LOOK BACK.
WHY DON'T YOU GO AHEAD, MY FRIEND.
TAK
TAK TAK
THAT SOUND'S A BIT ***DISTRACTING,*** WOULDN'T YOU SAY, BOYS?
TAK
THE CARUSO NAME WAS ONCE A FEARED AND RESPECTED NAME.
THERE WAS A TRAGIC... INCIDENT A FEW YEARS BACK THAT MADE THINGS, LET'S SAY... DIFFICULT.
BUT MAKE NO MISTAKE. WITH OUR ENDEAVORS IN PERU, WE'VE ADOPTED WHAT SOME MIGHT CALL...A RUTHLESS BUSINESS MODEL.
AND BUSINESS IS ***BOOMING.***

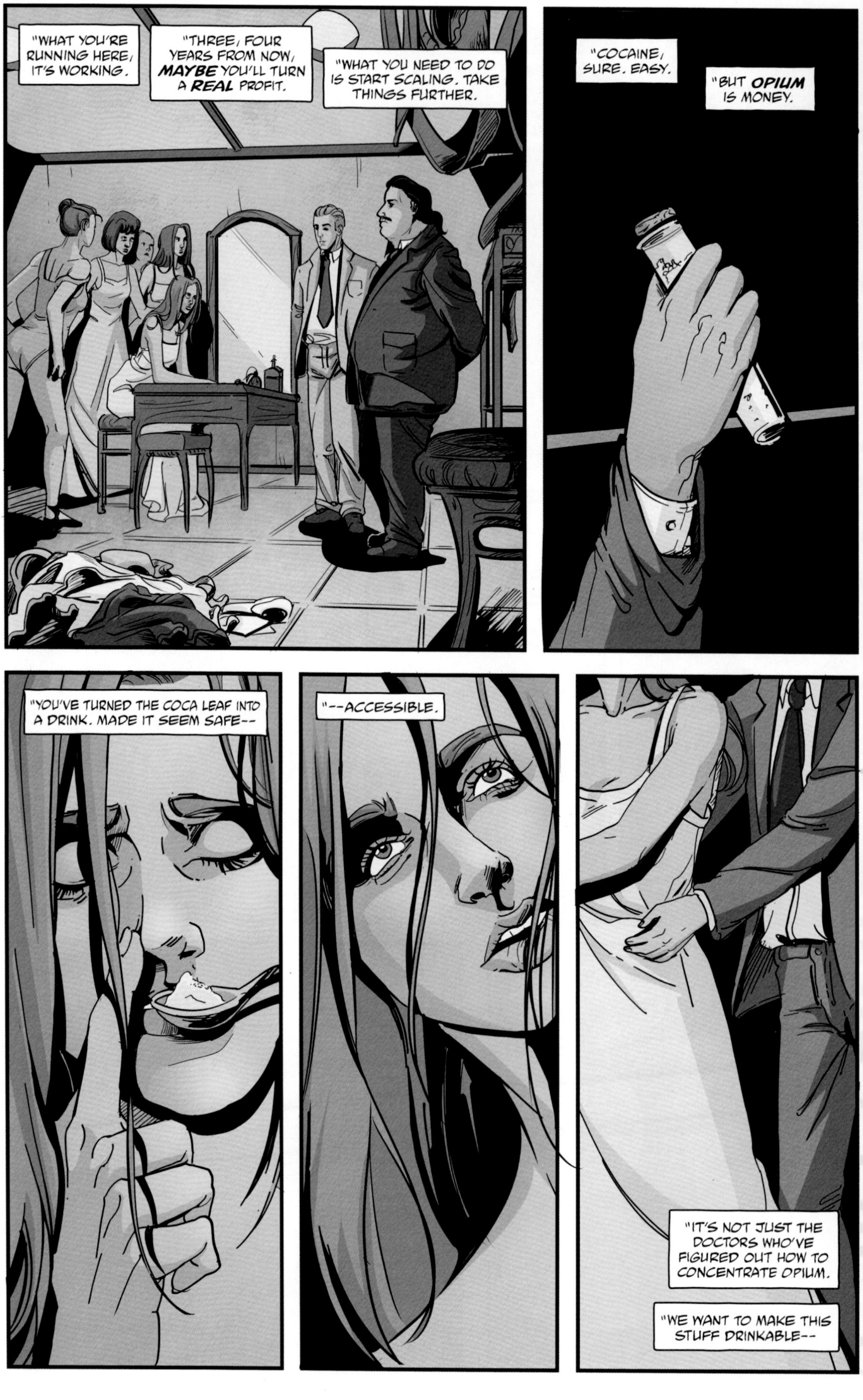
"WHAT YOU'RE RUNNING HERE, IT'S WORKING.
"THREE, FOUR YEARS FROM NOW, MAYBE YOU'LL TURN A REAL PROFIT.
"WHAT YOU NEED TO DO IS START SCALING. TAKE THINGS FURTHER.
"COCAINE, SURE. EASY.
"BUT OPIUM IS MONEY.
"YOU'VE TURNED THE COCA LEAF INTO A DRINK. MADE IT SEEM SAFE--
"--ACCESSIBLE.
"IT'S NOT JUST THE DOCTORS WHO'VE FIGURED OUT HOW TO CONCENTRATE OPIUM.
"WE WANT TO MAKE THIS STUFF DRINKABLE--

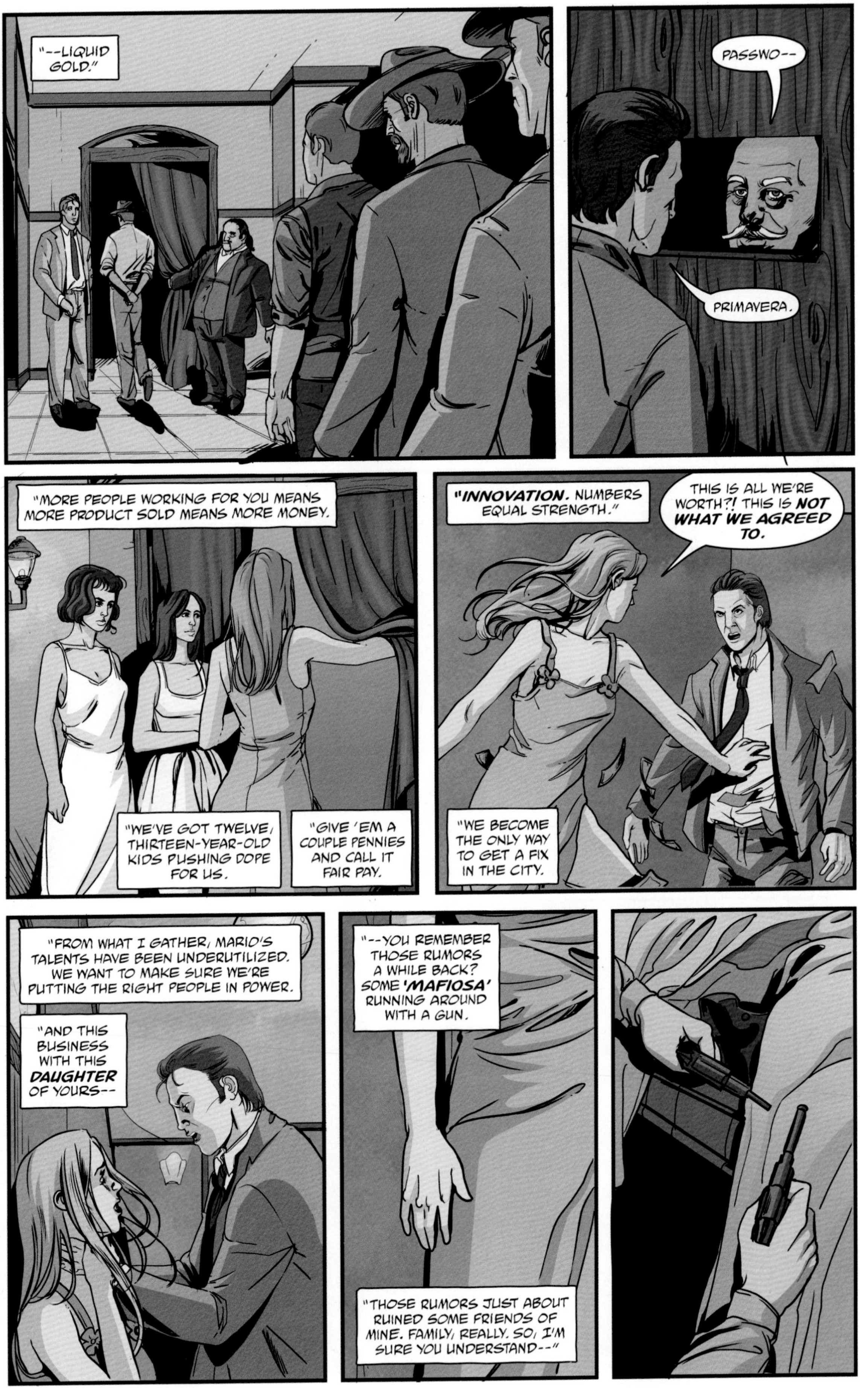
"--LIQUID GOLD."
PASSWO--
PRIMAVERA.
"MORE PEOPLE WORKING FOR YOU MEANS MORE PRODUCT SOLD MEANS MORE MONEY.
"WE'VE GOT TWELVE, THIRTEEN-YEAR-OLD KIDS PUSHING DOPE FOR US.
"GIVE 'EM A COUPLE PENNIES AND CALL IT FAIR PAY.
"**INNOVATION.** NUMBERS EQUAL STRENGTH."
THIS IS ALL WE'RE WORTH?! THIS IS **NOT WHAT WE AGREED TO.**
"WE BECOME THE ONLY WAY TO GET A FIX IN THE CITY.
"FROM WHAT I GATHER, MARIO'S TALENTS HAVE BEEN UNDERUTILIZED. WE WANT TO MAKE SURE WE'RE PUTTING THE RIGHT PEOPLE IN POWER.
"AND THIS BUSINESS WITH THIS ***DAUGHTER*** OF YOURS--
"--YOU REMEMBER THOSE RUMORS A WHILE BACK? SOME ***'MAFIOSA'*** RUNNING AROUND WITH A GUN.
"THOSE RUMORS JUST ABOUT RUINED SOME FRIENDS OF MINE. FAMILY, REALLY. SO, I'M SURE YOU UNDERSTAND--"

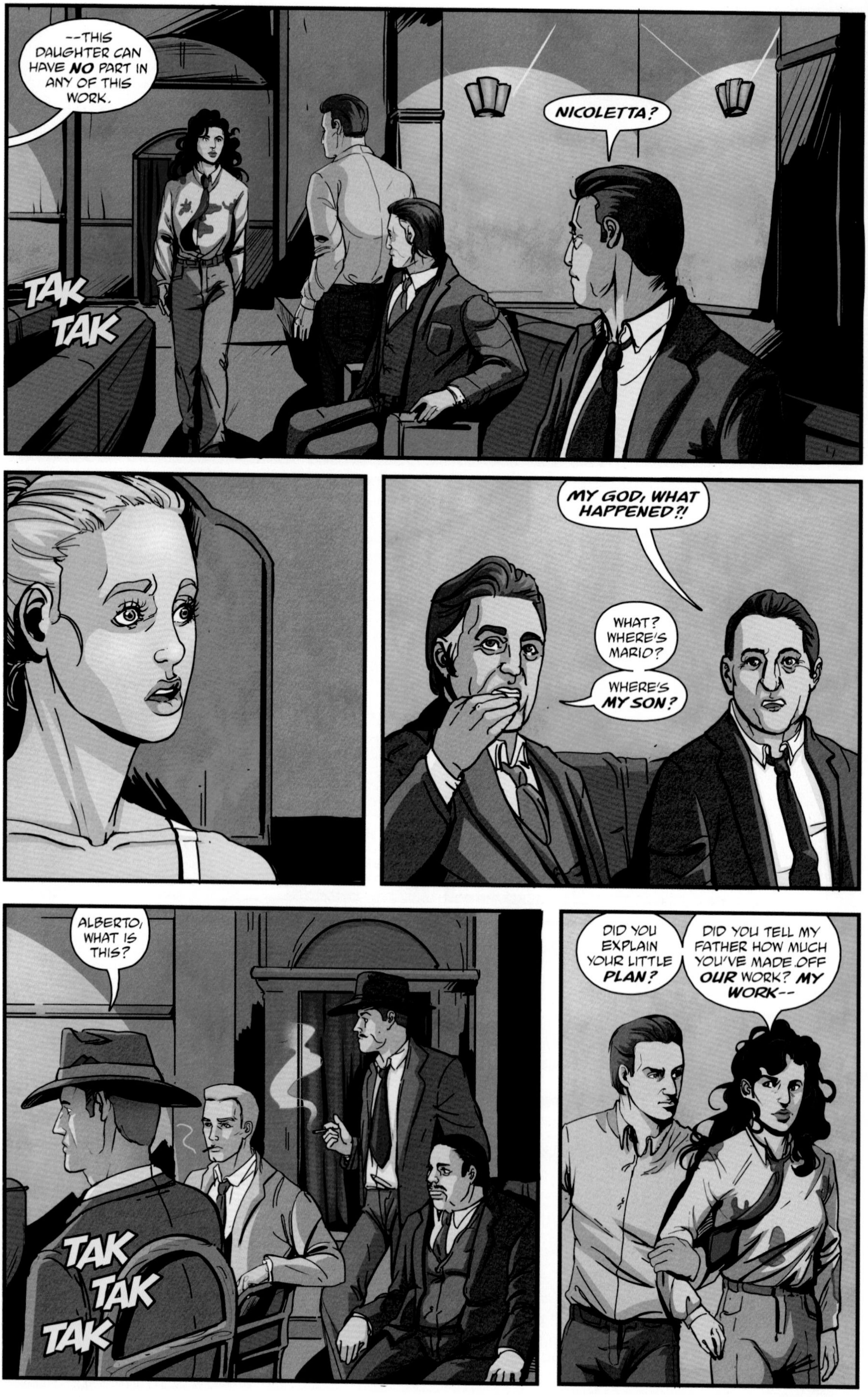
--THIS DAUGHTER CAN HAVE **NO** PART IN ANY OF THIS WORK.
TAK TAK
NICOLETTA?
MY GOD, WHAT HAPPENED?!
WHAT? WHERE'S MARIO?
WHERE'S **MY SON**?
ALBERTO, WHAT IS THIS?
TAK TAK TAK
DID YOU EXPLAIN YOUR LITTLE **PLAN**?
DID YOU TELL MY FATHER HOW MUCH YOU'VE MADE OFF **OUR** WORK? **MY WORK**--

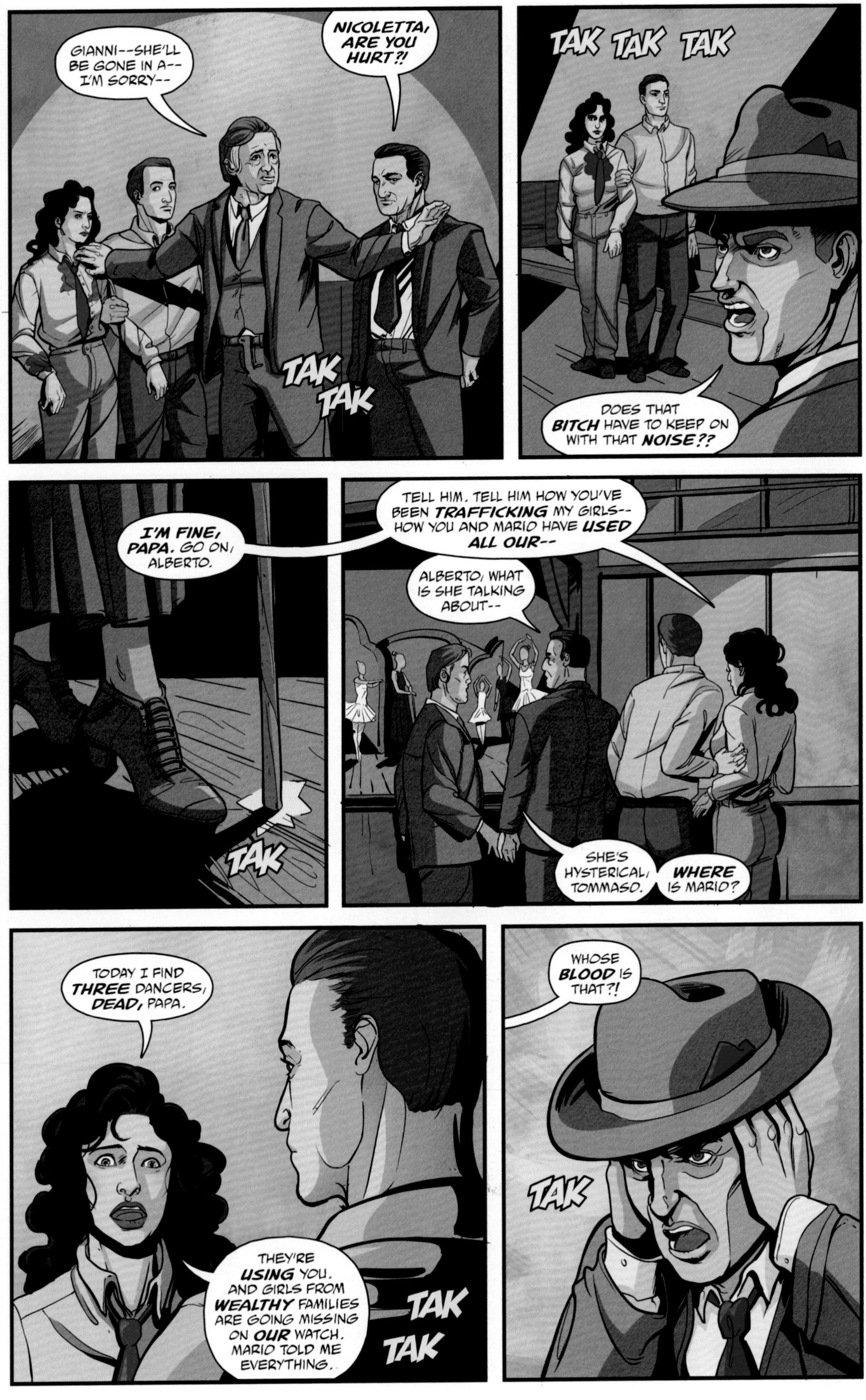
GIANNI--SHE'LL BE GONE IN A-- I'M SORRY--
NICOLETTA, ARE YOU HURT?!
TAK TAK
TAK TAK TAK
DOES THAT BITCH HAVE TO KEEP ON WITH THAT NOISE??
I'M FINE, PAPA. GO ON, ALBERTO.
TAK
TELL HIM. TELL HIM HOW YOU'VE BEEN TRAFFICKING MY GIRLS-- HOW YOU AND MARIO HAVE USED ALL OUR--
ALBERTO, WHAT IS SHE TALKING ABOUT--
SHE'S HYSTERICAL, TOMMASO.
WHERE IS MARIO?
TODAY I FIND THREE DANCERS, DEAD, PAPA.
THEY'RE USING YOU. AND GIRLS FROM WEALTHY FAMILIES ARE GOING MISSING ON OUR WATCH. MARIO TOLD ME EVERYTHING.
TAK TAK
WHOSE BLOOD IS THAT?!
TAK

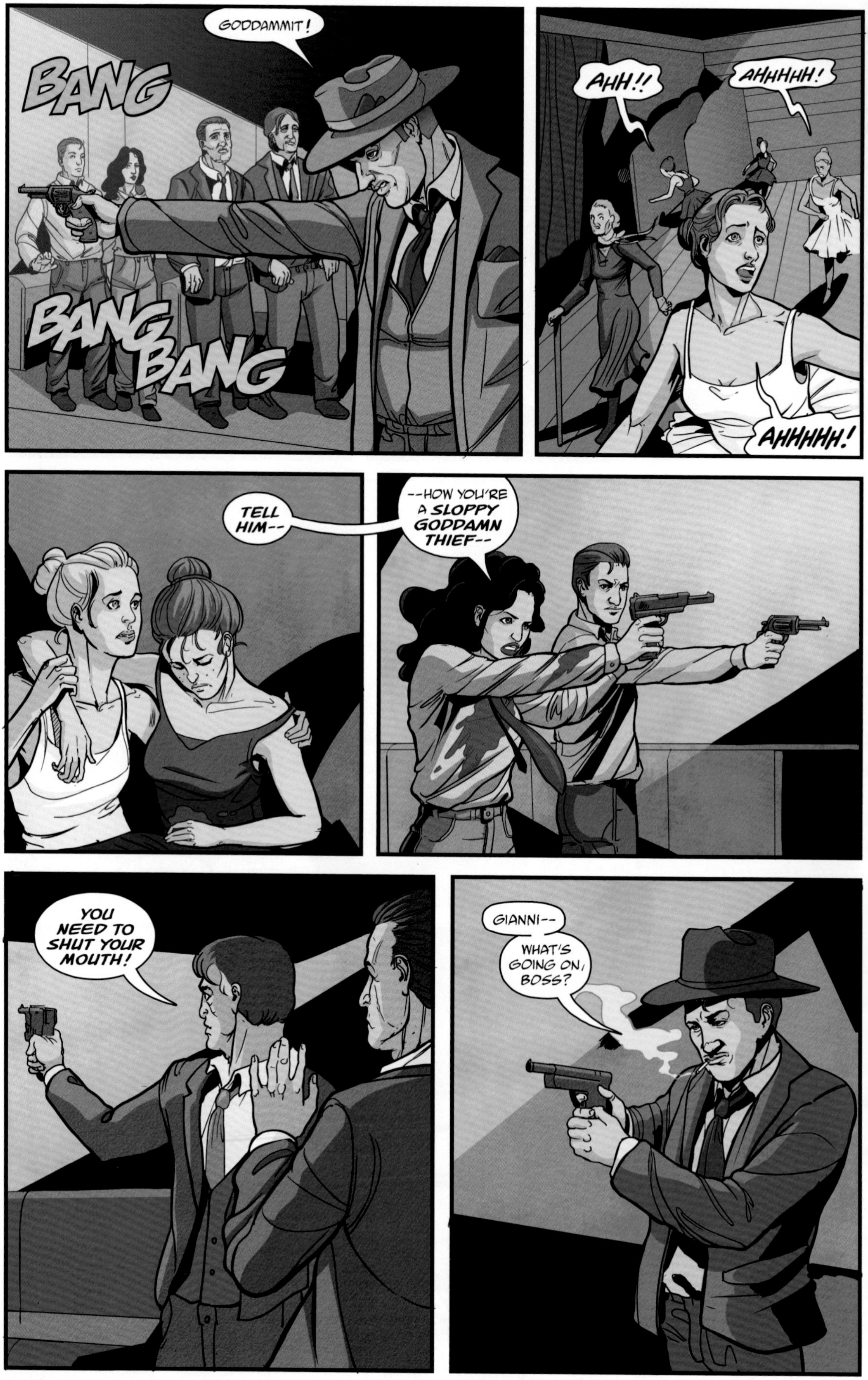
GODDAMMIT!
BANG
BANG
BANG
AHH!!
AHHHHH!
AHHHHH!
TELL HIM--
--HOW YOU'RE A SLOPPY GODDAMN THIEF--
YOU NEED TO SHUT YOUR MOUTH!
GIANNI--
WHAT'S GOING ON, BOSS?

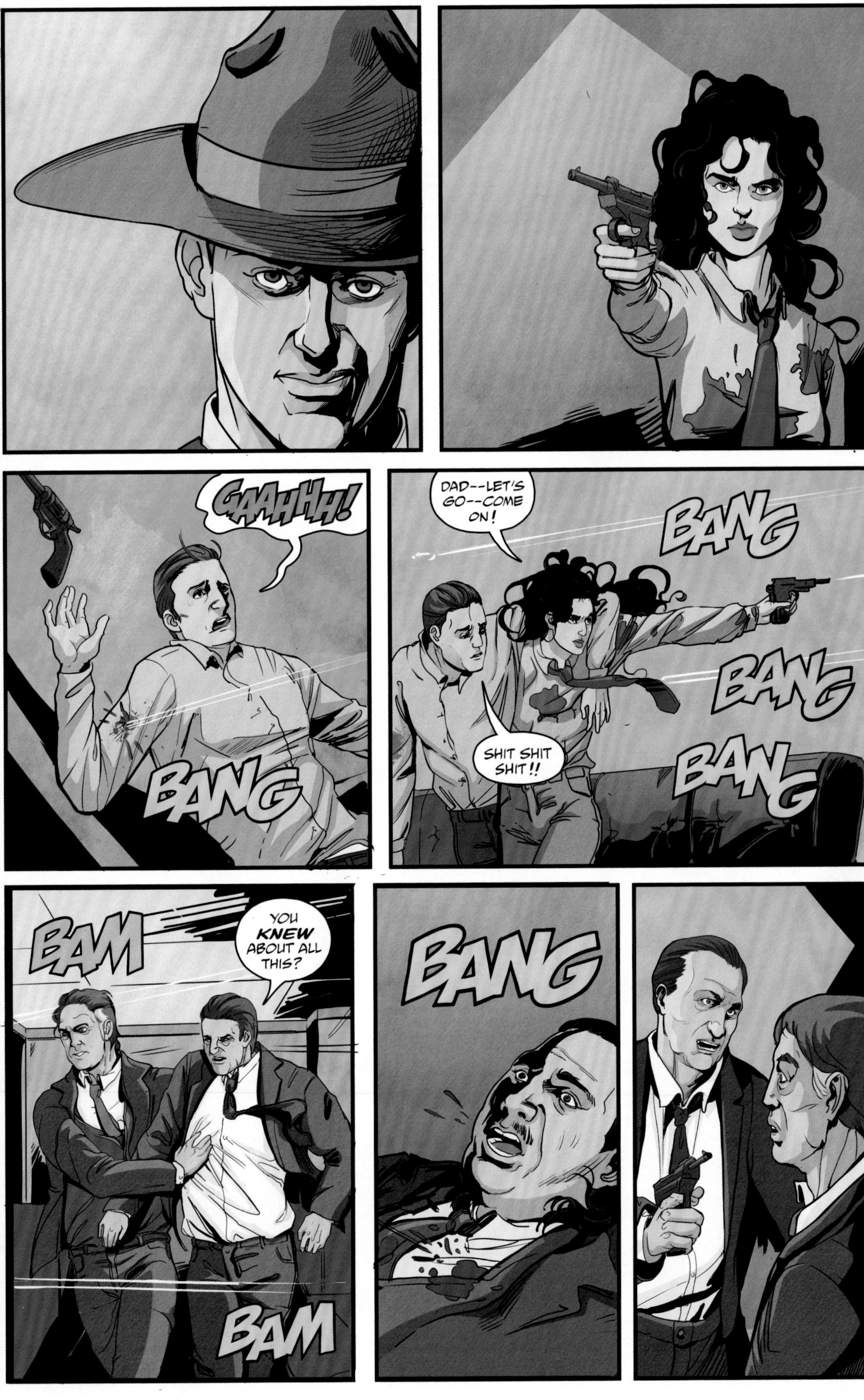
GAAHHH!
BANG
DAD--LET'S GO--COME ON!
BANG
BANG
BANG
SHIT SHIT SHIT!!
BAM
YOU KNEW ABOUT ALL THIS?
BAM
BANG

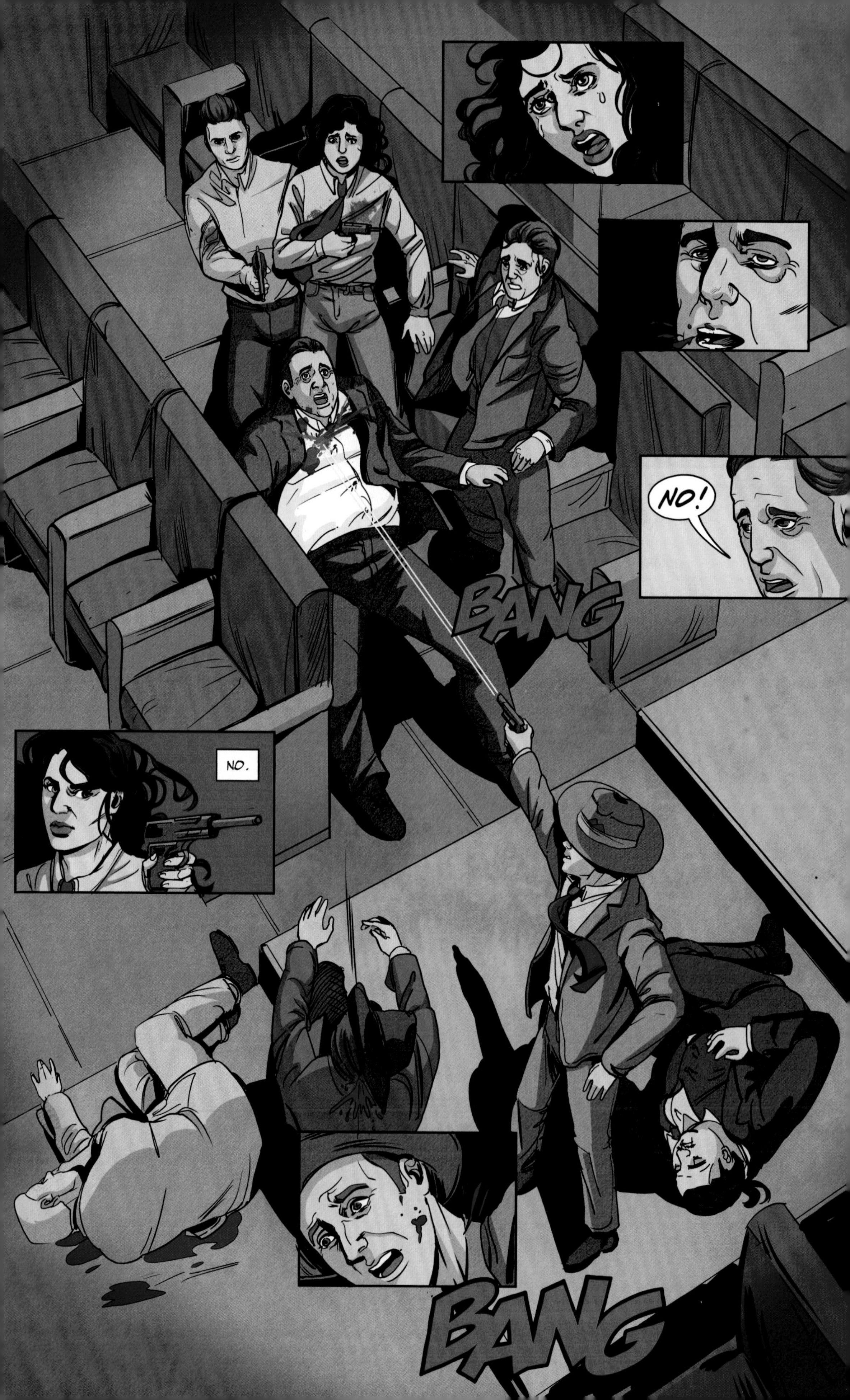
NO!
BANG
NO.
BANG

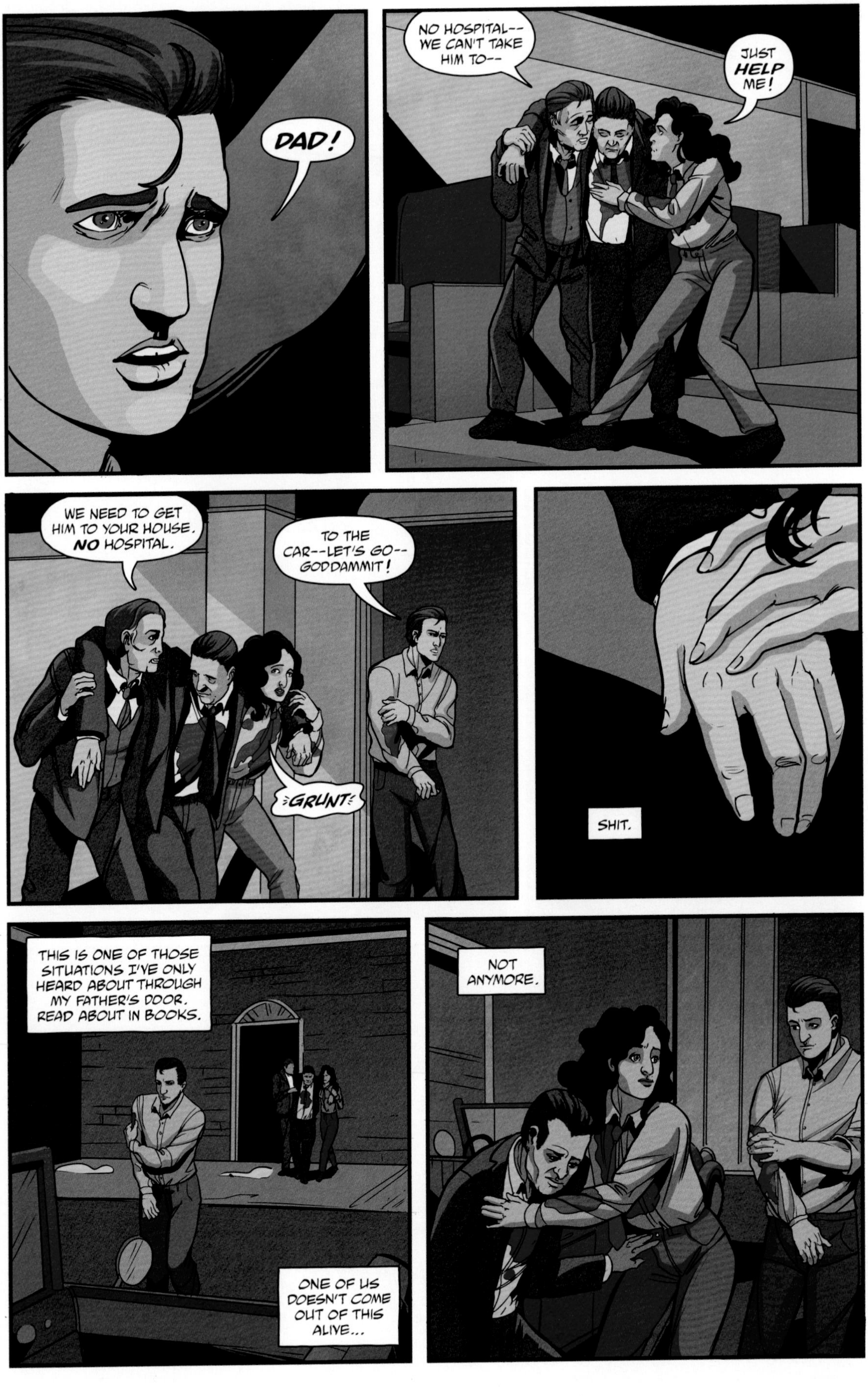
DAD!
NO HOSPITAL-- WE CAN'T TAKE HIM TO--
JUST HELP ME!
WE NEED TO GET HIM TO YOUR HOUSE. NO HOSPITAL.
TO THE CAR--LET'S GO-- GODDAMMIT!
GRUNT
SHIT.
THIS IS ONE OF THOSE SITUATIONS I'VE ONLY HEARD ABOUT THROUGH MY FATHER'S DOOR. READ ABOUT IN BOOKS.
NOT ANYMORE.
ONE OF US DOESN'T COME OUT OF THIS ALIVE...

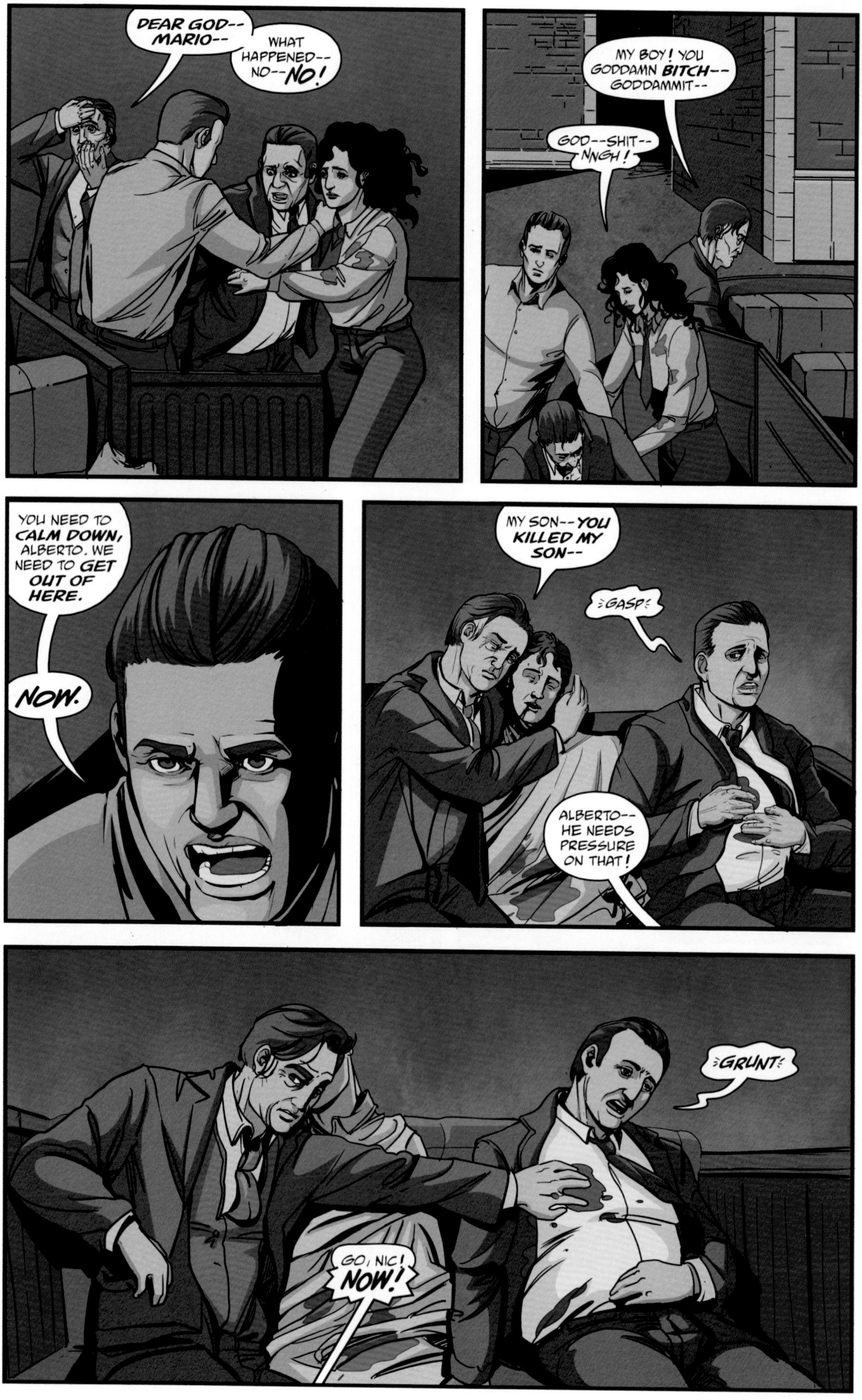

DEAR GOD--
MARIO--
WHAT HAPPENED--
NO--NO!
MY BOY! YOU GODDAMN BITCH--
GODDAMMIT--
GOD--SHIT--
NNGH!
YOU NEED TO CALM DOWN, ALBERTO. WE NEED TO GET OUT OF HERE.
NOW.
MY SON--YOU KILLED MY SON--
GASP
ALBERTO--
HE NEEDS PRESSURE ON THAT!
GRUNT
GO, NIC!
NOW!

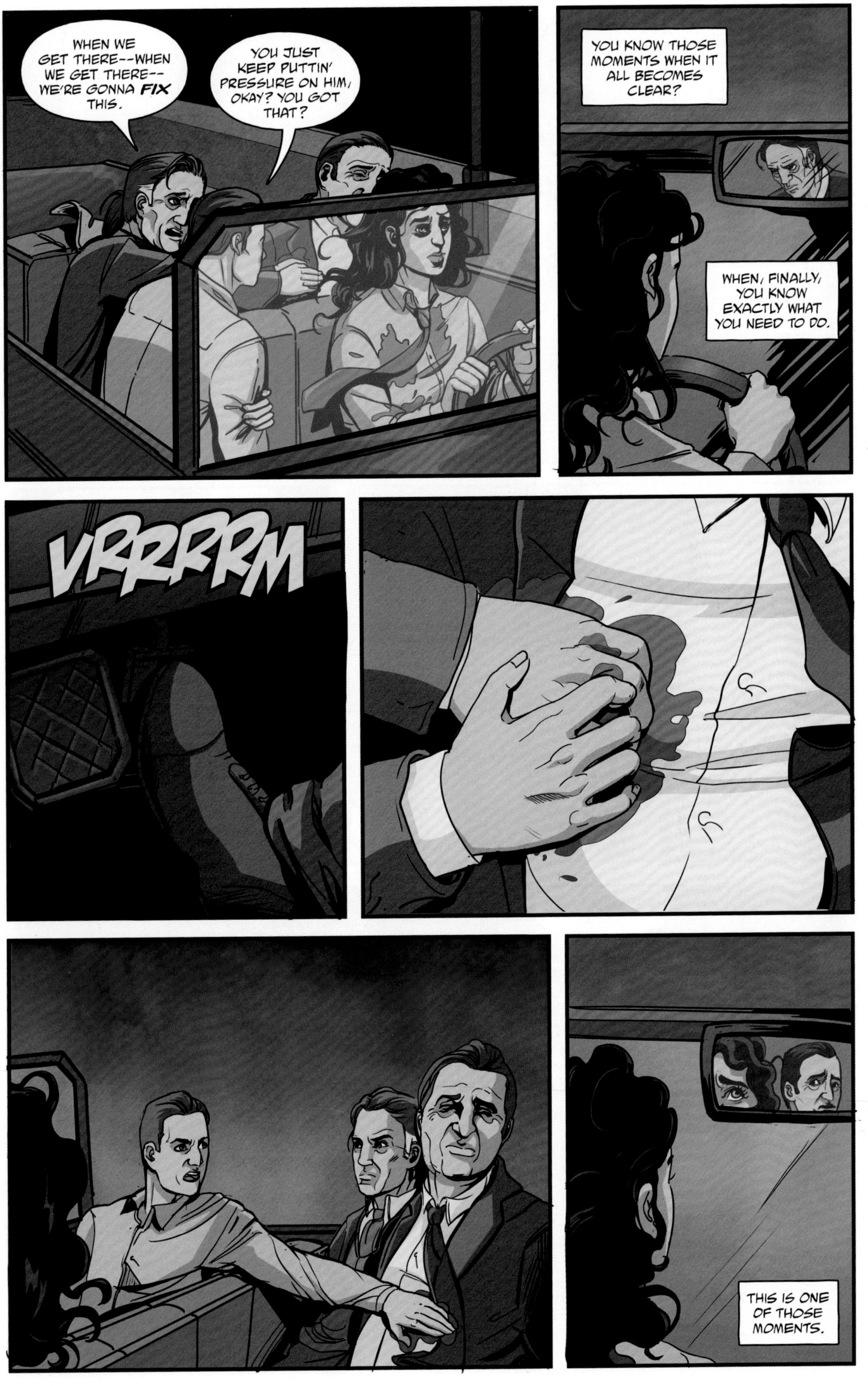
WHEN WE GET THERE--WHEN WE GET THERE--WE'RE GONNA FIX THIS.
YOU JUST KEEP PUTTIN' PRESSURE ON HIM, OKAY? YOU GOT THAT?
YOU KNOW THOSE MOMENTS WHEN IT ALL BECOMES CLEAR?
WHEN, FINALLY, YOU KNOW EXACTLY WHAT YOU NEED TO DO.
VRRRRM
THIS IS ONE OF THOSE MOMENTS.

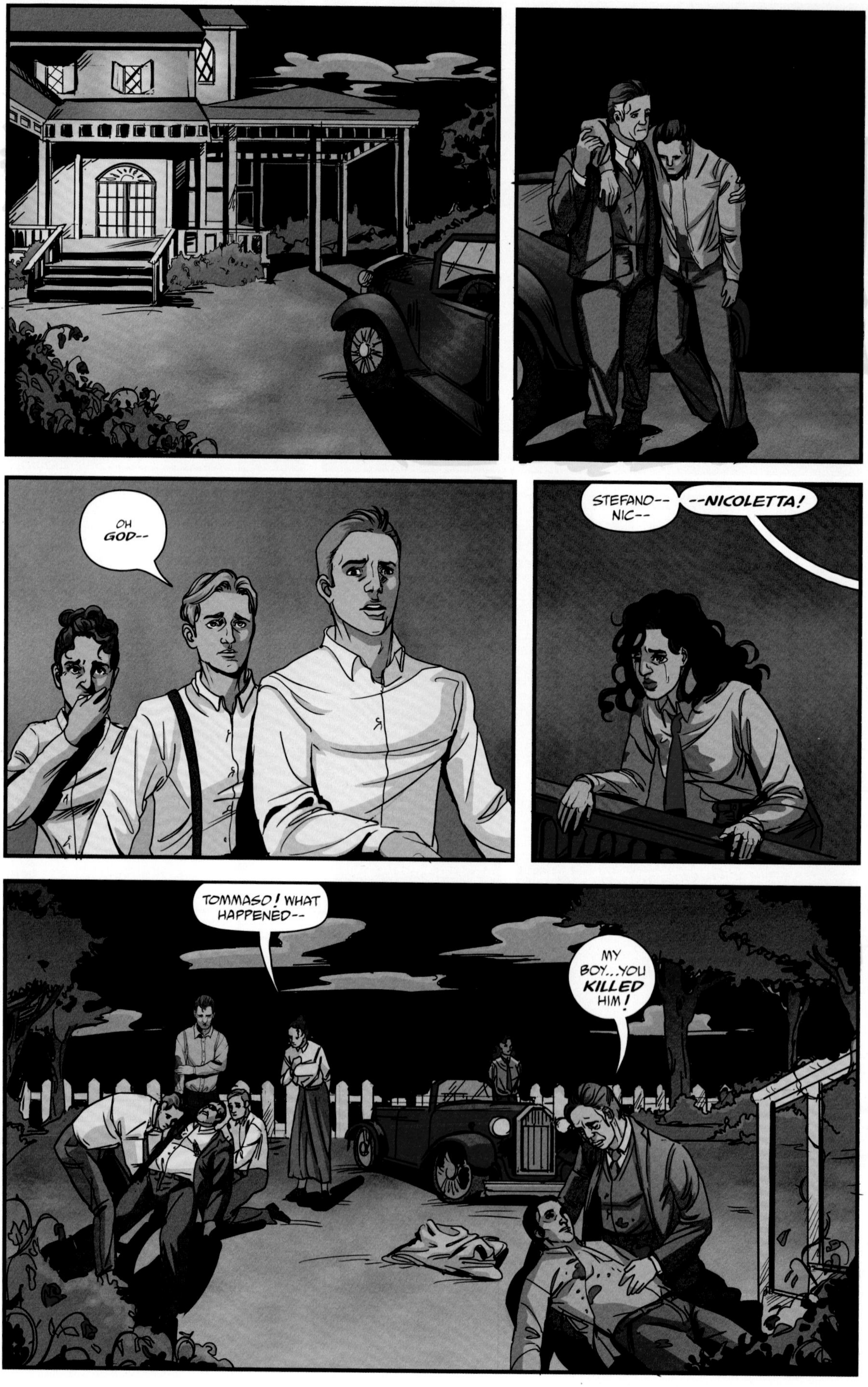
OH GOD--
STEFANO-- NIC--
--NICOLETTA!
TOMMASO! WHAT HAPPENED--
MY BOY...YOU KILLED HIM!

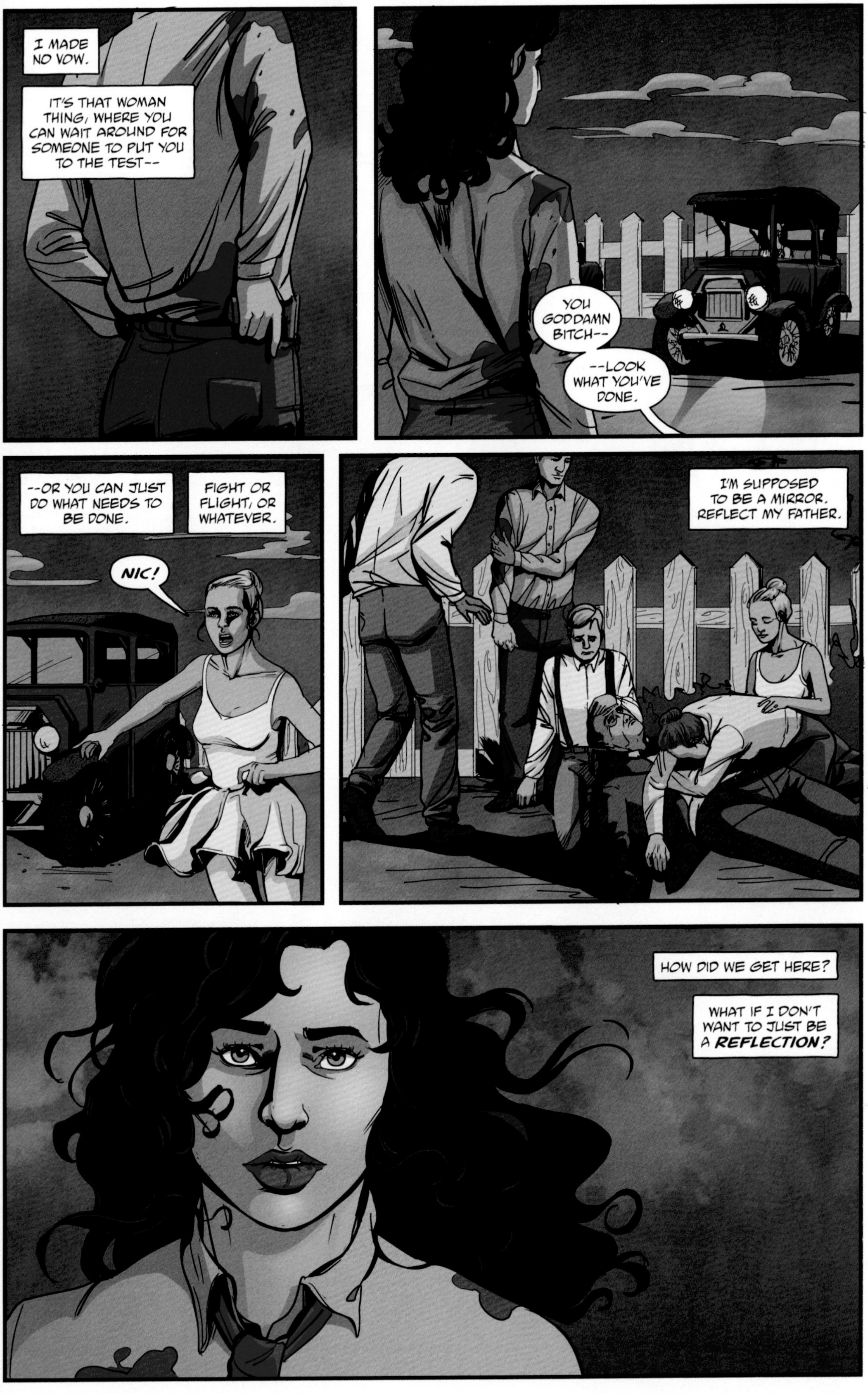

I MADE NO VOW.
IT'S THAT WOMAN THING, WHERE YOU CAN WAIT AROUND FOR SOMEONE TO PUT YOU TO THE TEST--
YOU GODDAMN BITCH--
--LOOK WHAT YOU'VE DONE.
--OR YOU CAN JUST DO WHAT NEEDS TO BE DONE.
FIGHT OR FLIGHT, OR WHATEVER.
NIC!
I'M SUPPOSED TO BE A MIRROR. REFLECT MY FATHER.
HOW DID WE GET HERE?
WHAT IF I DON'T WANT TO JUST BE A *REFLECTION?*

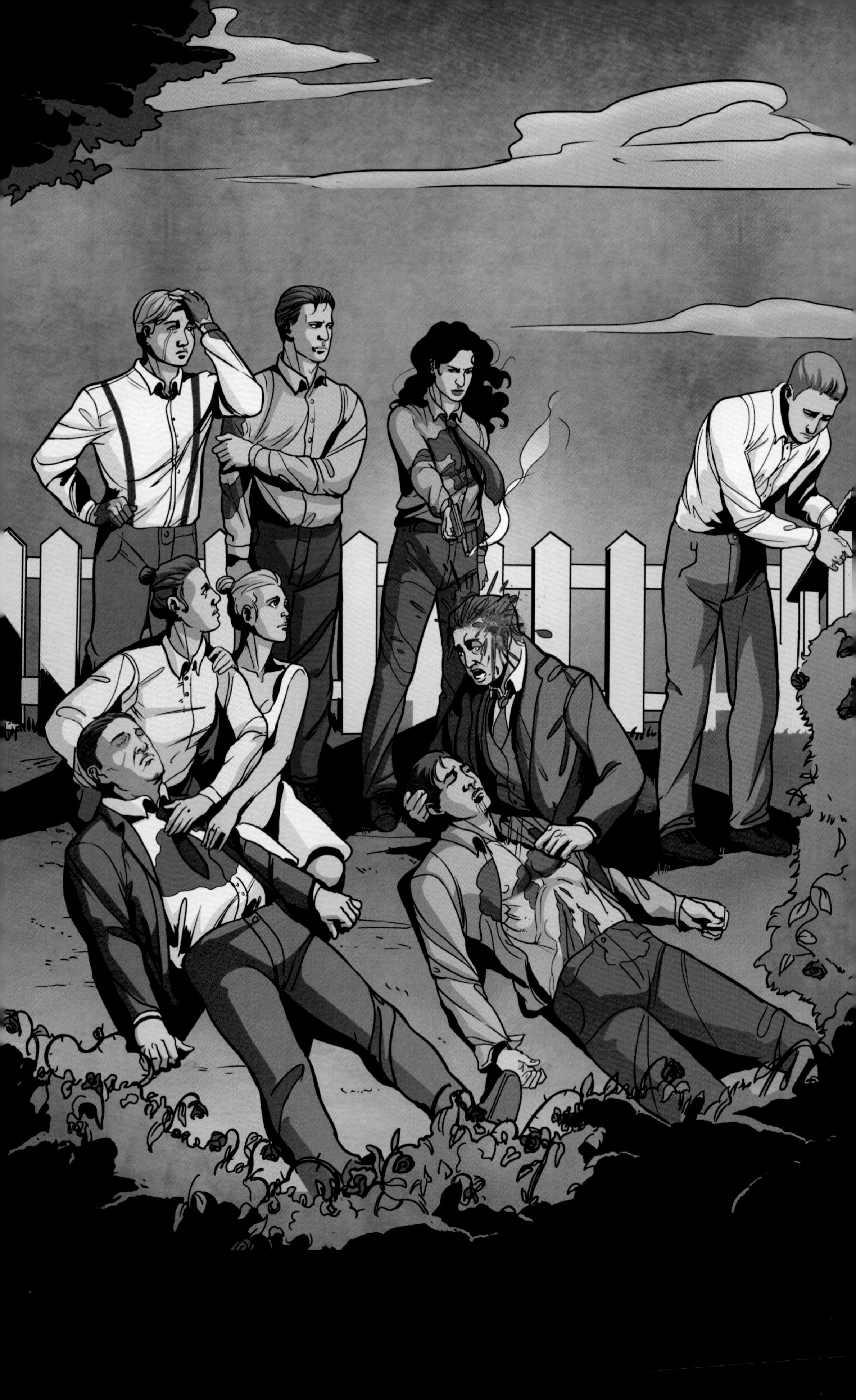

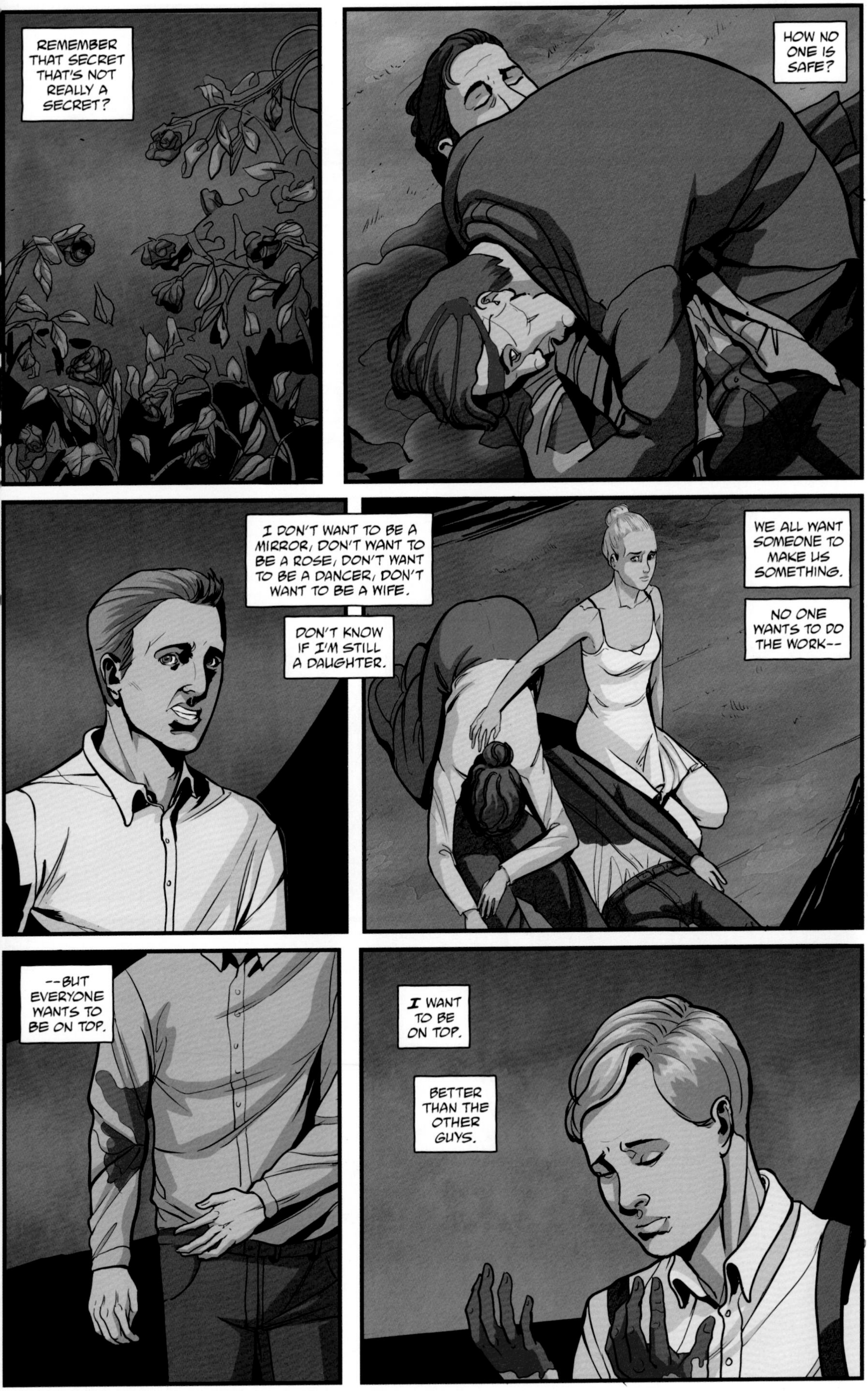
REMEMBER THAT SECRET THAT'S NOT REALLY A SECRET?
HOW NO ONE IS SAFE?
I DON'T WANT TO BE A MIRROR, DON'T WANT TO BE A ROSE, DON'T WANT TO BE A DANCER, DON'T WANT TO BE A WIFE.
DON'T KNOW IF I'M STILL A DAUGHTER.
WE ALL WANT SOMEONE TO MAKE US SOMETHING.
NO ONE WANTS TO DO THE WORK--
--BUT EVERYONE WANTS TO BE ON TOP.
I WANT TO BE ON TOP.
BETTER THAN THE OTHER GUYS.

OR ELSE, WHAT WAS THIS ALL FOR?

WELL, BELLA--

--HERE I AM.

CHIN UP.

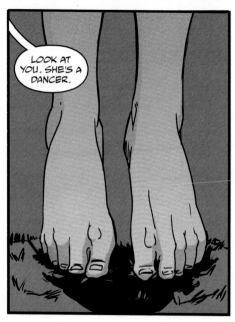

LOOK AT YOU. SHE'S A DANCER.

SHE'S HER FATHER'S DAUGHTER.

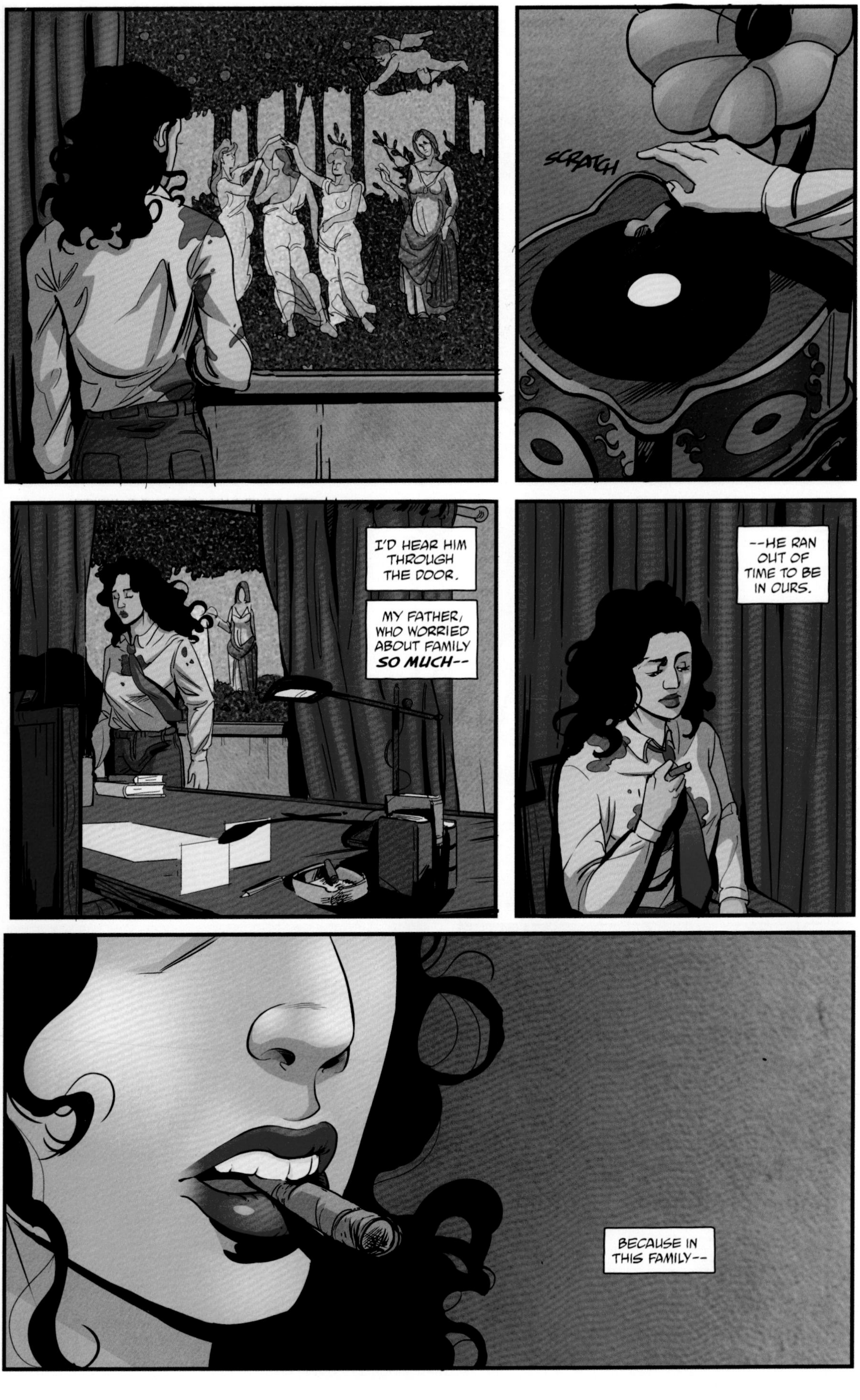
SCRATCH
I'D HEAR HIM THROUGH THE DOOR.
MY FATHER, WHO WORRIED ABOUT FAMILY SO MUCH--
--HE RAN OUT OF TIME TO BE IN OURS.
BECAUSE IN THIS FAMILY--

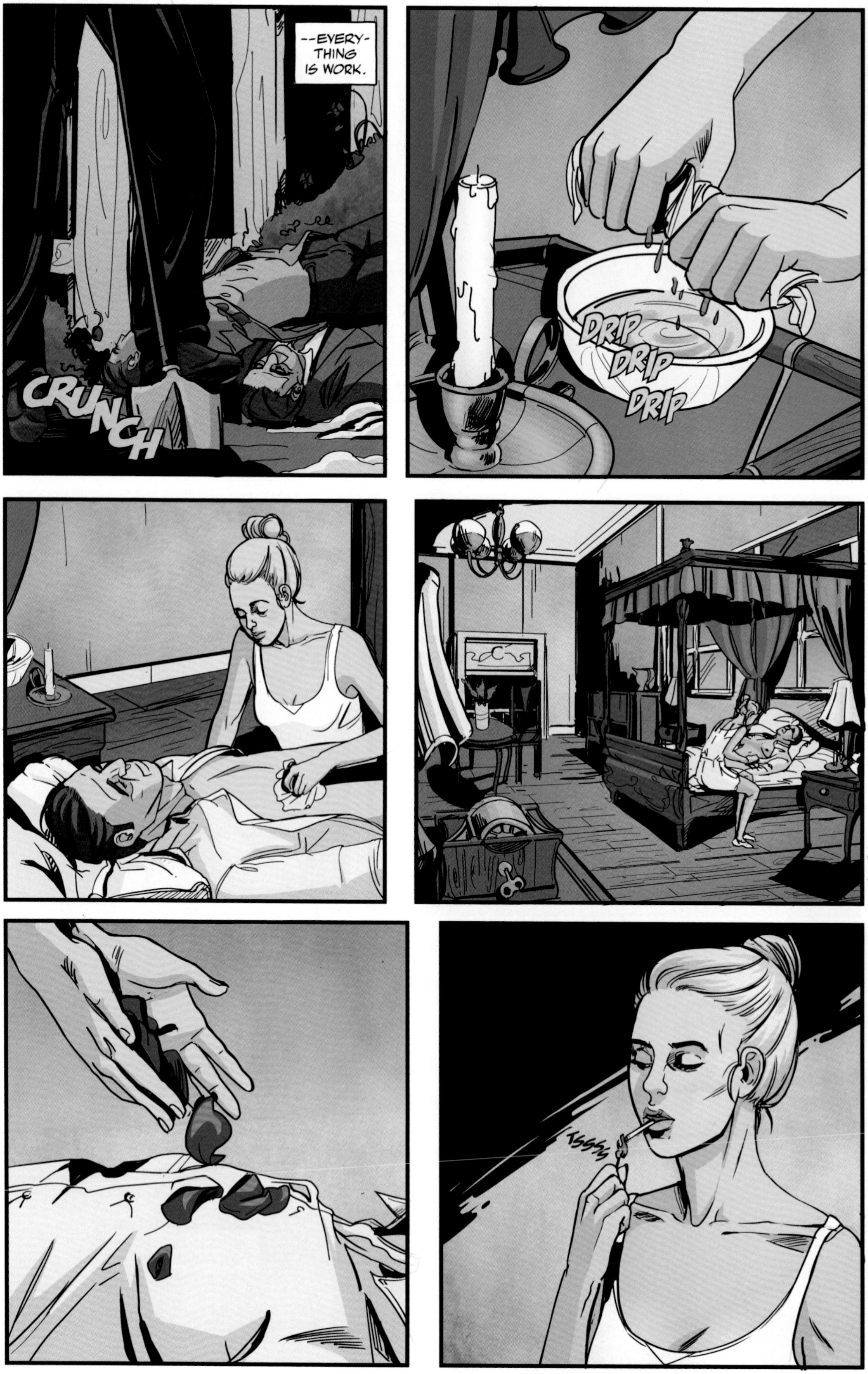
--EVERY-
THING
IS WORK.
CRUNCH
DRIP
DRIP
DRIP
TSSSS

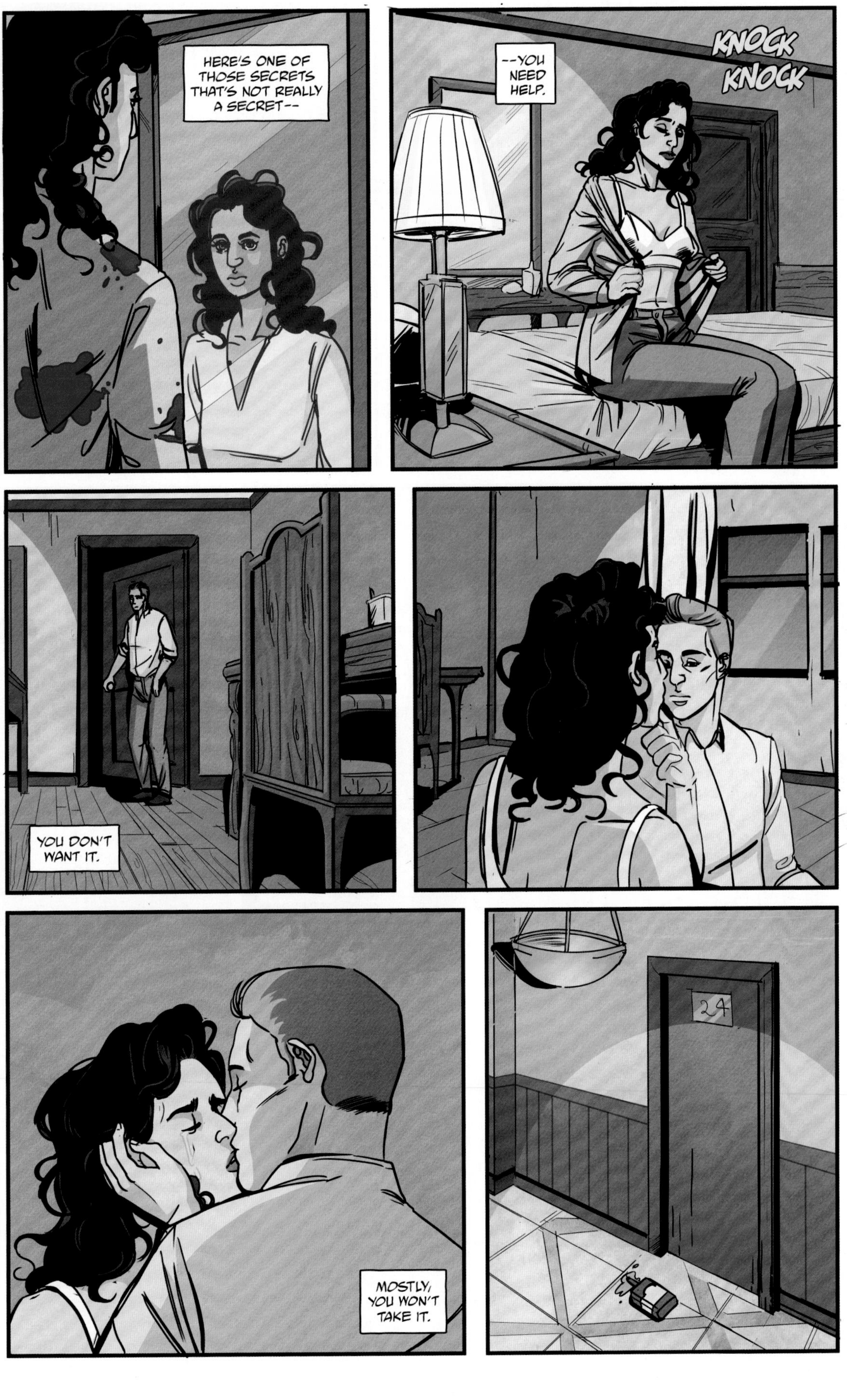
HERE'S ONE OF THOSE SECRETS THAT'S NOT REALLY A SECRET--
--YOU NEED HELP.
KNOCK KNOCK
YOU DON'T WANT IT.
24
MOSTLY, YOU WON'T TAKE IT.

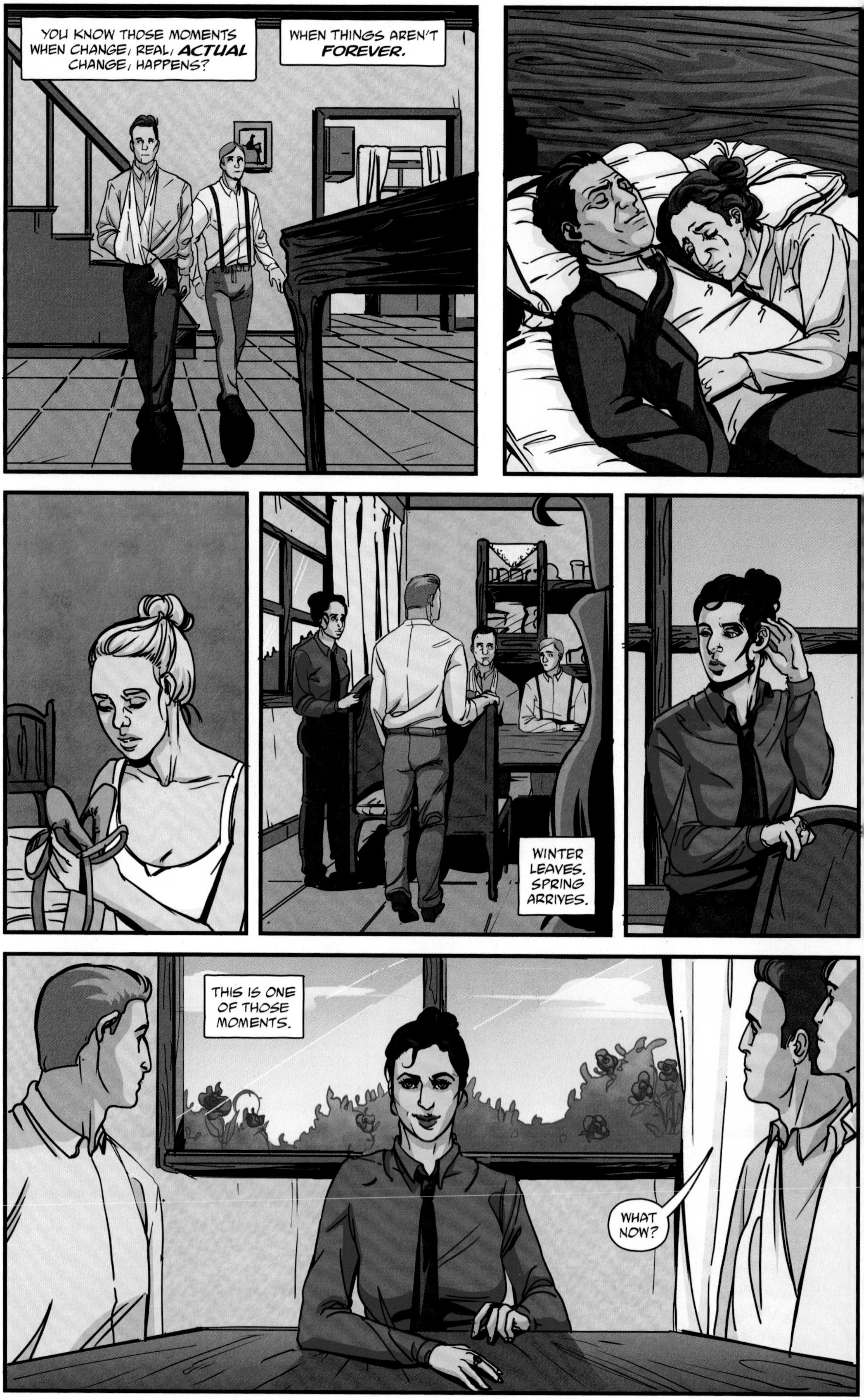
YOU KNOW THOSE MOMENTS WHEN CHANGE, REAL, ACTUAL CHANGE, HAPPENS?
WHEN THINGS AREN'T FOREVER.
WINTER LEAVES. SPRING ARRIVES.
THIS IS ONE OF THOSE MOMENTS.
WHAT NOW?

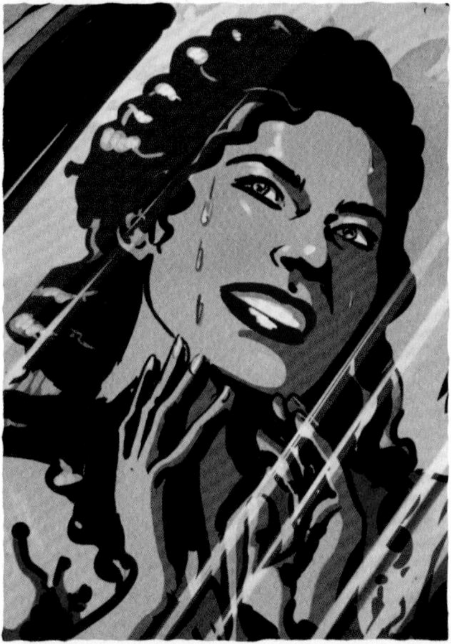

More great
NOIR AND ESPIONAGE
from Dark Horse Books

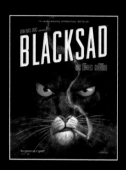

BLACKSAD
JUAN DÍAZ CANALES AND JUANJO GUARNIDO

The *Blacksad* books first took Europe by storm in 2000 and sold over 200,000 copies in France alone. Now Dark Horse presents the beautifully painted stories of private investigator John Blacksad, up to his feline ears in mystery, digging into the backstories behind murders, child abductions, and nuclear secrets.

ISBN 978-1-59582-393-9
$29.99

MIND MGMT VOLUME 1
MATT KINDT

A young journalist stumbles onto a big story — the top-secret Mind Management program. Her ensuing journey involves weaponized psychics, hypnotic advertising, talking dolphins, and seemingly immortal pursuers. But in a world where people can rewrite reality itself, can she trust anything she sees?

ISBN 978-1-59582-797-5
$19.99

THE BLACK BEETLE: KARA BOCEK
FRANCESCO FRANCAVILLA

The masked American hero ventures to the Middle East incognito (as Tom Sawyer) to fight Nazis in pursuit of a mysterious object of terrible power — an ancient weapon of unknown origin which could fuel the Thousand-Year Reich of Hitler's dreams.

ISBN 978-1-50670-537-8
$12.99

GREEN RIVER KILLER: A TRUE DETECTIVE STORY
2ND Edition
JEFF JENSEN AND JONATHAN CASE

The story of one of America's most notorious killers is revealed in this true-crime comic unlike any other! Written by case detective Tom Jensen's own son, acclaimed entertainment writer Jeff Jensen, this is the ultimate insider's account of America's most prolific serial killer

ISBN 978-1-50671-081-5
$24.99

AVAILABLE AT YOUR LOCAL COMICS SHOP OR BOOKSTORE • TO FIND A COMICS SHOP NEAR YOU, VISIT COMICSHOPLOCATOR.COM
For more information or to order direct: • On the web: DarkHorse.com • E-mail: mailorder@darkhorse.com

More great NOIR AND ESPIONAGE from Dark Horse Books

NOIR: A COLLECTION OF CRIME COMICS

Featuring stories by Brian Azzarello, Jeff Lemire, Ed Brubaker, Sean Phillips, and many more of crime comics' top talent! In these thirteen pitch-black noir stories, you'll find deadly conmen and embittered detectives converging on femme fatales and accidental murderers, all presented in sharp black and white by masters of the craft.

ISBN 978-1-50671-686-2
$24.99

POLAR: CAME FROM THE COLD
2ND EDITION

VICTOR SANTOS

Ripped out of retirement by an assassination attempt, the world's most deadly spy — Black Kaiser — is on a collision course with a stab-happy torture expert and a seductive but deadly redhead. His mission only ends if he dies or kills everyone out to get him, and he's not in the habit of dying. Now a major motion picture starring Mads Mikkelsen!

ISBN 978-1-50671-118-8
$19.99

THE WHITE SUITS VOLUME 1: DRESSED TO KILL

FRANK BARBIERE AND TOBY CYPRESS

They savaged the Cold War Russian underworld — then disappeared. When they resurface, leaving a trail of dead mobsters in their wake, an amnesiac and an FBI agent seek to answer a single question: Who are the White Suits?

ISBN 978-1-61655-493-4
$17.99

BANG!

MATT KINDT, WILFREDO TORRES

An elite secret agent with memories he couldn't possibly possess, a mystery writer in her eighties who spends her retirement solving crimes, a man of action with mysterious drugs that keep him ahead of a constant string of targeted disasters, a seemingly omnipotent terrorist organization that might be behind it all . . . They're all connected to a science-fiction author with more information than seems possible, whose books may hold the key to either saving reality or destroying it.

ISBN 978-1-50671-616-9
$19.99

AVAILABLE AT YOUR LOCAL COMICS SHOP OR BOOKSTORE • TO FIND A COMICS SHOP NEAR YOU, VISIT COMICSHOPLOCATOR.COM
For more information or to order direct: • On the web: DarkHorse.com • E-mail: mailorder@darkhorse.com

DarkHorse.com   All titles © their respective creators. Dark Horse Books® and the Dark Horse logo are registered trademarks of Dark Horse Comics, LLC. All rights reserved. (BL 6042 P2)

MORE TITLES FROM THE NEIL GAIMAN LIBRARY

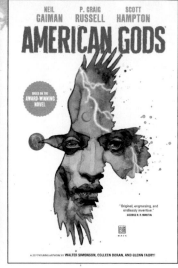

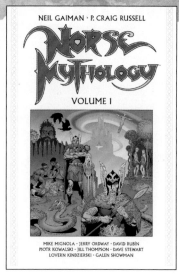

NEIL GAIMAN LIBRARY VOLUME 1
Collects *A Study in Emerald, Murder Mysteries, How to Talk to Girls at Parties,* and *Forbidden Bride*
Neil Gaiman and various artists
$49.99 | ISBN 978-1-50671-593-3

NEIL GAIMAN LIBRARY VOLUME 2
Collects *The Facts in the Departure of Miss Finch, Likely Stories, Harlequin Valentine,* and *Troll Bridge*
Neil Gaiman and various artists
$49.99 | ISBN 978-1-50671-594-0

NEIL GAIMAN LIBRARY VOLUME 3
Collects *Snow, Glass, Apples; The Problem of Susan; Only the End of the World Again;* and *Creatures of the Night*
Neil Gaiman and various artists
$49.99 | ISBN 978-1-50671-595-7

AMERICAN GODS: SHADOWS
Neil Gaiman, P. Craig Russell,
Scott Hampton, and others
$29.99 | ISBN 978-1-50670-386-2

AMERICAN GODS: MY AINSEL
Neil Gaiman, P. Craig Russell,
Scott Hampton, and others
$29.99 | ISBN 978-1-50670-730-3

**AMERICAN GODS:
THE MOMENT OF THE STORM**
Neil Gaiman, P. Craig Russell,
Scott Hampton, and others
$29.99 | ISBN 978-1-50670-731-0

THE COMPLETE AMERICAN GODS
$124.99 | ISBN 978-1-50672-076-0

LIKELY STORIES
Neil Gaiman and Mark Buckingham
$17.99 | ISBN 978-1-50670-530-9

ONLY THE END OF THE WORLD AGAIN
Neil Gaiman, P. Craig Russell,
and Troy Nixey
$19.99 | ISBN 978-1-50670-612-2

MURDER MYSTERIES 2nd Edition
Neil Gaiman, P. Craig Russell,
and Lovern Kinderski
$19.99 | ISBN 978-1-61655-330-2

**THE FACTS IN THE CASE OF
THE DEPARTURE OF MISS FINCH
2nd Edition**
Neil Gaiman and Michael Zulli
$13.99 | 978-1-61655-949-6

**NEIL GAIMAN'S HOW TO TALK
TO GIRLS AT PARTIES**
Neil Gaiman, Fábio Moon,
and Gabriel Bá
$17.99 | ISBN 978-1-61655-955-7

**THE PROBLEM OF SUSAN
AND OTHER STORIES**
Neil Gaiman, P. Craig Russell,
Paul Chadwick, and others
$17.99 | ISBN 978-1-50670-511-8

NEIL GAIMAN'S TROLL BRIDGE
Neil Gaiman and Colleen Doran
$14.99 | ISBN 978-1-50670-008-3

SIGNAL TO NOISE
Neil Gaiman and Dave McKean
$24.99 | ISBN 978-1-59307-752-5

**CREATURES OF THE NIGHT
2nd Edition**
Neil Gaiman and Michael Zulli
$12.99 | ISBN 978-1-50670-025-0

**FORBIDDEN BRIDES OF THE
FACELESS SLAVES IN THE
SECRET HOUSE OF THE NIGHT
OF DREAD DESIRE**
Neil Gaiman and Shane Oakley
$17.99 | ISBN 978-1-50670-140-0

**HARLEQUIN VALENTINE
2nd Edition**
Neil Gaiman and John Bolton
$12.99 | ISBN 978-1-50670-087-8

**NEIL GAIMAN'S A STUDY
IN EMERALD**
Neil Gaiman and Rafael Albuquerque
$17.99 | ISBN 978-1-50670-393-0

SNOW, GLASS, APPLES
Neil Gaiman and Colleen Doran
$17.99 | ISBN 978-1-50670-979-6

**NORSE MYTHOLOGY
VOLUME 1**
Neil Gaiman, P. Craig Russell,
Mike Mignola, and various artists
$29.99 | ISBN 978-1-50671-874-3

AVAILABLE AT YOUR LOCAL COMICS SHOP OR BOOKSTORE.
To find a comics shop in your area, visit comicshoplocator.com. For more information, visit DarkHorse.com

Likely Stories © Neil Gaiman. Text and illustrations of Only the End of the World Again™ © Neil Gaiman, P. Craig Russell, and Troy Nixey. Text of Murder Mysteries™ © Neil Gaiman. Adaptation and illustrations of Murder Mysteries™ © P. Craig Russell. Signal to Noise © Neil Gaiman & Dave McKean. Cover art © Dave McKean. Text of Harlequin Valentine™ © Neil Gaiman. Illustrations of Harlequin Valentine™ © John Bolton. The Facts in the Case of the Departure of Miss Finch™ text © Neil Gaiman, art © Michael Zulli. Miss Finch is a trademark of Neil Gaiman. How to Talk to Girls at Parties™ © Neil Gaiman. Artwork © Fábio Moon and Gabriel Bá. Neil Gaiman's Troll Bridge™ © Neil Gaiman, artwork © Colleen Doran. Forbidden Brides of the Faceless Slaves in the Nameless House of the Night of Dread Desire™ text © Neil Gaiman, art © Shane Ivan Oakley. The Price™ © Neil Gaiman. Daughter of Owls™ © Neil Gaiman. Artwork © Michael Zulli. Creatures of the Night is a trademark of Neil Gaiman. American Gods™ © Neil Gaiman. A Study In Emerald™ © Neil Gaiman. The Problem of Susan and Other Stories™ © Neil Gaiman. Snow, Glass, Apples™ © Neil Gaiman. Artwork © Colleen Doran. Norse Mythology™ © Neil Gaiman. Cover art of Norse Mythology © P. Craig Russell. Dark Horse Books® and the Dark Horse logo are registered trademarks of Dark Horse Comics LLC. All rights reserved. (BL 6043)

**DARK
HORSE
BOOKS**